D1383948

Rhetorical Philosophy and Theory
Series Editor, David Blakesley

Other Books in the Rhetorical Philosophy and Theory Series

Seduction, Sophistry, and the Woman with the Rhetorical Figure
Michelle Ballif

Kenneth Burke and the Conversation after Philosophy
Timothy W. Crusius

Breaking Up [at] Totality: A Rhetoric of Laughter
D. Diane Davis

Rhetoric as Philosophy: The Humanist Tradition
Ernesto Grassi

Unending Conversations: New Writings by and about Kenneth Burke
Edited by Greig Henderson and David Cratis Williams

Gorgias and the New Sophistic Rhetoric
Bruce McComiskey

Rhetoric on the Margins of Modernity

Rhetoric on the Margins of Modernity

Vico, Condillac, Monboddo

Catherine L. Hobbs

Southern Illinois University Press
Carbondale and Edwardsville

Library of Congress Cataloging-in-Publication Data

Hobbs, Catherine.
    Rhetoric on the margins of modernity : Vico, Condillac, Monboddo /
Catherine L. Hobbs.
      p. cm. — (Rhetorical philosophy and theory)
    Includes bibliographical references and index.
    1. Rhetoric—History—18th century. 2. Vico, Giambattista, 1668–
1744—Contributions in rhetoric. 3. Condillac, Étienne Bonnot de,
1714–1780—Contributions in rhetoric. 4. Monboddo, James Burnett,
Lord, 1714–1799—Contributions in rhetoric. I. Title. II. Series.

P301 .H63 2002
808'.009'033—dc21
ISBN 0-8093-2469-5 (alk. paper)   2002023013

Printed on recycled paper. ♻

The paper used in this publication meets the minimum requirements of
American National Standard for Information Sciences—Permanence of Paper
for Printed Library Materials, ANSI Z39.48-1992. ∞

For my parents,
Dan Stewart and Betty Jean Ray Hobbs

Contents

Acknowledgments

As with many historical monographs, this book has been many years in the making. It was conceived at Purdue University, where Janice M. Lauer was its first midwife. Others then at Purdue to whom I am grateful are the late James A. Berlin, Vincent B. Leitch, the late Virgil Lokke, and Patricia Sullivan. I have incurred many scholarly debts since these mentors and friends made their contributions to the project.

Two National Endowment for the Humanities summer fellowships proved invaluable: the first, for a seminar with Hans Aarsleff at Princeton University, where I focused on Locke and Condillac; and the second, at an NEH Institute directed by Donald Phillip Verene who along with Molly Verene and the Vico Institute at Emory University enriched my studies of Vico. I am indebted to Prof. Aarsleff for his translations of Condillac. My work on Condillac's pedagogical treatise on writing is partly based on Prof. Aarsleff's translation in manuscript; I was fortunate that his translation of Condillac's *Essay on the Origin of Human Knowledge* came out just as this book went into production. I am especially thankful to Prof. Verene and Molly Verene who provided additional support and advice at a crucial point in the project.

I also received institutional support from Illinois State University and from my current institution, the University of Oklahoma. Research grants from the University of Oklahoma College of Arts and Sciences, the Graduate School, and the Vice President for Research assisted, as did a sabbatical leave, for which I am grateful.

I am grateful to others who read parts of the manuscript or advised me, including Dan Cottom, Raymie E. McKerrow, Cecil L. Peaden, Craig Kallendorf, Patrick Hutton, Susan Kates, Cecilia Miller, Anne Rosenthal, John Schaeffer, Thomas Willard, David Paxman, Carey McIntosh, Tom Puckett, Eve Tavor Bannet, and Kathleen Welch. Vico scholar Andrea Battistini at the University of Bologna and Scottish studies professor Andrew Hook at the University of Glasgow were helpful during my sabbatical in 1999, as were J. P. Dedieu and Christian Lerat at the University of Bordeaux. My gratitude to Elizabeth A. Wallis, who helped with the final manuscript. A special thanks to Southern Illinois University Press acquisitions editor Karl Kageff for all his help, to copy editor Mary Lou Kowaleski for her good work in the final stage, and to Paula Durbin-Westby for the index.

I am grateful to all of these but a particular thank-you to my editor David Blakesley, formerly of SIU and now at my alma mater Purdue, and to SIU Press reader Thomas P. Miller of the University of Arizona. In nurturing this material and my sources over the years, I came to see that a book signifies more than the word denotes because it is a knot in a network of scholarship, scholars, and friends.

Early versions of chapters 4 and 5, here revised and expanded, appeared in journals: "Vico, Rhetorical Topics, and Historical Thinking," *Historical Reflections/Réflexions Historiques* 22.3 (1996): 559–85; and "Condillac and the History of Rhetoric," *Rhetorica: A Journal of the History of Rhetoric* 11.2 (1993): 135–56. I am grateful to the publishers for permission to reprint.

1
The Birth of Modernity
and the Death of Rhetoric

> The word "modern" in its Latin form "modernus" was used for the first time in the late 5th century in order to distinguish the present, which had become officially Christian, from the Roman and pagan past. With varying content, the term "modern" again and again expresses the consciousness of an epoch that relates itself to the past of antiquity, in order to view itself as the result of a transition from the old to the new.
>
> —Jürgen Habermas, "Modernity Versus Postmodernity"

> The impossible task [of modernity] is set by the *foci imaginarii* of absolute truth, pure art, humanity as such, order, certainty, harmony, the end of history. Like all horizons they can never be reached. Like all horizons, they make possible walking with a purpose. Like all horizons, they recede in the course of, and because of, walking.
>
> —Zygmunt Bauman, *Modernity and Ambivalence*

Despite its currency in literary theory and criticism and its popular usage as the language of political deception, *rhetoric* is a fossil word, silently impressing its premodern cast into our modern and postmodern discourses. The birth of the *modern* as a counterpoint to the rhetorical age of antiquity helped bring about this fossilized state of rhetoric. From its earliest uses, as Jürgen Habermas points out, the term *modern* has marked a distinct break of present from past, implying in its various meanings a sense of progress from past to present.[1] The progressive birth of the modern entailed the decline and ossification of rhetoric.

This book reexamines the relationship between rhetoric and the culture of modernity—modernity as we conceive it today as a historical period beginning at about mid-seventeenth century. From its earliest moments, the culture of modernity valued order and certainty, purity of concepts, and clean breaks—often expressed as "clear and distinct" ideas as in John Locke's *An Essay Concerning Human Understanding* (12). Nevertheless, it did not invent the concepts it foregrounded, most particularly clarity itself. Clarity is a sedimented term from the fossil rhetoric. That term and its diverse uses existed previously in the bonehouse of rhetoric; clarity of discourse stood ready to be appropriated and reactivated.

Yet from the standpoint of the modern, rhetoric and modernity appear as separate, even oppositional. Modernity foregrounded itself against a background of rhetoric and antiquity. Seen through the eyes of a modern, the very term *modern rhetoric* could seem to be an oxymoron—for was not rhetoric itself what modernity made obsolete and irrelevant? If at times classical rhetoric comes down to us from modern thinkers as an old coat in need of sprucing up, it can also appear as a heavy burden from the past, one that constrained progress and bound new generations into useless ways of thinking and valuing. Even today, while well-trained historians vigorously reject the stereotyped narrative of the triumph and rise of science, this narrative's corollary assumptions linger in the often-heard refrain of the dullness and sterility of rhetoric, long moribund, then finally, and, gratefully, dead.

Rhetoric was never more dead than in the era just following its revival in the late 1960s. Historians of English cultural studies such as Richard Ohmann and Gerald Graff have continued to enact the modernist rupture of present from past by paying no attention to the residual strand of rhetoric in English studies and by deliberately ignoring the history of writing instruction in their early histories. Yet not half a century earlier, Rene Wellek had not forgotten, nor had Cleanth Brooks and Robert Penn Warren in their *Modern Rhetoric*.

Having accepted the death of rhetoric with modernity, John Bender and David E. Wellbery write of the "modernist return of rhetoric" in "rhetoricality," the propensity to see all language as rhetorical in the sense that it is reality producing, not merely representational of an already-given (3). This poststructuralist position is modernist in that it centers on a break with an old rhetoric, a rhetoric portrayed as having an oversimplified representative theory of language and centering on persuasion and public civic discourse. Bender and Wellbery are modernist because they continue to measure the present against a past rhetoric that they portray as outmoded and antiquarian. They become progressivist and ahistorical when they celebrate the linguistic turn as something entirely new and better, the Whiggish modernist moment in poststructuralism (sometimes regretted by postmodernists). By making rhetoricality separate from rhetoric, they fail to see the interanimation of discourses, the hybridity that marks modern and postmodern discussions of language that they can clearly see and appreciate in the field of architecture, whose classical and modern styles they explore as an "analogous argument" in relation to rhetoric (4).

Postmodernist Bruno Latour carries the inquiry into modernity further by asking, "What if modernity never happened?" (at least in the ways we have heard the story thus far). The distinct separation of one concept from another, the rupture of one age from the next—or purification as he terms it—and the continuation and interbreeding of concept with concept, past with past, machine with human (hybridization) both continually occur. Looking at ruptures and continuities, at purifications and hybridizations, as do Raymond Williams and Timothy J. Reiss in their different fashions, can complicate our vision of histories of rhetoric. Viewing both rupture and continuity across time can change rhetoric and its history, making it possible to see a more nuanced view of classical and modern rhetorics of the eighteenth century by bringing into play conflicting voices. Theories that pay attention to impure conceptual intermingling can also help us see the intertwined relations of rhetoric to linguistics and literary studies as these fields take on the attitudes and values of modern science to produce new forms.

Here I offer three impure figures often considered marginal in rhetoric and philosophy as a way to develop a more complex account of eighteenth-century rhetorics and to suggest, in turn, how our better understanding of these histories might impact scholarship on contemporary rhetorical theory. These figures are the Neapolitan professor of rhetoric Giambattista Vico (1668–1744), the French philosopher and pedagogue Étienne de Bonnot, Abbé de Condillac (1714–1780), and the Scottish judge and intellectual James Burnet(t),[2] Lord Monboddo (1714–1799). These thinkers all write on rhetoric, and all three advance language study and linguistics as well. They span the century and allow me to weave strands of narrative from southern Italy, where Renaissance humanism lingered, to France, with its modern theories and practices of language and belles lettres, and to Scotland, the Scottish Enlightenment, and the formation of modern rhetoric and English study. Scottish rhetoric remains important in North America because, as Winifred Horner and Thomas Miller have shown, it directly shaped American curricula through exchange of scholars, textbooks, and pedagogies. Miller's book clearly shows how Scottish rhetoric formed the foundation of U.S. institutional English, centered primarily on literary studies, with the goal of developing taste.[3] This could only finally come about after aesthetics attained its own autonomous sphere—separate from science and politics—with the development of modernity.

Yet historians have lately arrived at a great insight: richly detailed studies of the marginal illuminate the mainstream as well. These three figures are marginal—even eccentric—in most fields today. Although marginal, the texts of these three figures contain complex thought in many ways representative of mainstream responses to modernity in their own times and places. They all build on classical sources entirely or in part—both Vico and Monboddo claim Plato as a key source; all three are infused with classical theories of the sublime. Yet they also constitute diverse, sometimes overlapping, reactions and responses to modern language and rhetoric that occur over the century and become available to future linguists and rhetoricians.

Vico's response to modernity is currently the most controversial and hotly argued. He has been called in turn antimodern (Mark Lilla), a precursor of countermodernity (Isaiah Berlin), and a modern (Andrea Battistini). Here I portray him as a critic of modernity, not a thoroughgoing antimodern. His rhetorical version of modernity centers on a transformation of tradition, namely the Latin vision of practical civic wisdom aiming to produce active citizens. He spent his life teaching Latin rhetoric, essentially second-language learning, to University of Naples law students.

In contrast, Condillac more matter-of-factly accepts the modern in philosophy and in rhetoric: as for imitating Latin rhetoric, he effectively asks, "Should we dress in the clothes of the ancients?"[4] He acknowledges the collapse of rhetoric into poetic; with a more modern conception of the individual, this constructs an expressivist, belletristic rhetoric.

Monboddo is the most reactionary of the three in his response to modernity: he returns not to the Romans but to the Greeks as his touchstone for rhetoric. To Monboddo, society in general has been declining since the Golden Age of Greece. Opposing the Latin of the Augustine humanists with Greek esoteric wisdom, he becomes paradoxically a countermodern precursor of Romantic thought, launching the future as he returns to the past. Weaving in the belletrism of French theory and his Scottish colleagues, he produces as his final work a volume of Milton criticism. Monboddo is best known today as a founder of modern comparative-historical linguistics.

The linguistic theories of these three figures, like mainstream eighteenth-century thought, are based on simple narratives explaining how language might have begun. Yet these language-origin theories have not been taken into account in histories of rhetoric until quite recently.[5] In positing their theories of language origins and development, eighteenth-century theorists attempt to reformulate accepted notions of what was natural to human life as opposed to what was cultural. Speculative histories of the origins of language, mind, and society served as evidence in the nature-culture debates. In narratives of origins, thinkers worked out their theories of the nature, purpose, and function of language, the development of mind and personality, and the relationship of the human subject to society. Explorations into language origins led to such fertile lines of inquiry as the processes of cognitive development, the role of human activity in constructing society, and constructions of proto-evolutionary, developmental histories. Each of the three figures I examine participates in speculation into language origins. This sort of speculation was later belittled, even overtly banned, in the more modernist, scientific, and positivistic century following. For this and other reasons, much Enlightenment thought based on speculation was all but forgotten in the nineteenth century, although it is being reconsidered in the early-twenty-first century.

Following the conventions of modern scholarship, I distinguish and attempt to classify their responses over the eighteenth century to modernity. Nonetheless, each figure is a hybrid of both ancient and modern language and rhetoric, containing both progressive and reactionary elements (as well as various outcomes). Perhaps this is merely commonplace, unavoidable, and perhaps unremarkable. It is difficult to compare them to any imaginably pure response to ancient or modern traditions, traditions that are legion and multiple in themselves. Yet, I believe there is a certain center of gravity in my conceptualization of each figure, an undiscovered center like a strange attractor around which the thoughts of each figure coalesce.

The relationship of the texts of each figure to the others is equally complex. I do not claim there is direct subsequential influence or that each read the texts of his predecessor (although each would have been exposed to texts and notions indirectly and might have read or even plagiarized the other.) Vico was influenced by the English, claiming Bacon as one of his four major figures. We know Shaftesbury visited Naples early in the century, forming a link or node between Scotland and Vico by cross-fertilizing Scottish and Neapolitan intellectual culture. Vico was also published in French philosophical journals. Condillac may have known of Vico, but what is certain is that thanks to the consolidation of print culture, Vico and he shared common sources in classical and contemporary texts. Monboddo read the same body of texts and at least a review of Condillac's major work on language theory, dedicated to Warburton, whom of course he also read. So the three shared not only a common cultural archive but a common exigency—a felt need to respond to issues occasioned by modernity in their historical moment—responses that challenged or consolidated contemporary thinking about language and rhetoric.

The conceptual grid with which I probe each figure grows out of the traditional elements of rhetoric: speaker, listeners or interlocutors, rhetorical and cultural situation, and language. Nonetheless, this grid remains only a flexible rule, such as Vico advocates, the "pliant Lesbic rule" (*Study Methods* 34) what we today might term a heuristic or contingent universal.[6] Although my examination is often based in the Aristotelian theory of the speaker, the speech, and the audience, in the context of the particular event and often national culture, these elements of rhetoric have their distinguishing characteristics as well as their lines of networking. Discussion of each figure's language theory includes attention to language origins and development because for each figure language provides the foundations for both collective social institutions and individual cognition.

In each figure's rhetorical theory, I examine the affiliation of his texts and his definitions of, claims regarding, and limits for rhetoric. I also use as an analytic the departments or offices of rhetoric, in particular those of invention, disposition, and style. With the consolidation of print culture, the arts of memory and delivery are less often addressed, so that we ignore the burst of elocutionary rhetoric in the late-eighteenth century's end emphasizing actio and gesture.[7] Vico, son of a bookseller, inquires into the profits and losses brought about by print technology and questions whether memory and delivery indeed should claim the status of arts and disdains to lecture on them in his rhetoric classes. Yet the role of natural memory in his theories looms large, as it does in the other two figures' texts.

In our own time, we are still assessing the transformation and consolidation of eighteenth-century print culture. Our interest no doubt stems from our own grappling with the effects of revolutionary change in our own communication technologies. The spread of eighteenth-century print culture, linked with the early development of capitalism and colonialism, produced an intense interest in the styles of writing and speaking, in the vernacular languages rather than the Latin that provided the universal language of education and other institutions. Each figure examined here writes his *major* works in the vernacular, so in this respect, the authors could be viewed as modern. The appreciation of each for the sounds of language, his interest in exploring the visual in relation to the verbal, the concern with the material effects of discourse on the body, and refusal to separate the body from discourse relate to themes of contemporary interest.

For example, the residual effects of Epicurean philosophy among the new sciences of optics led these three figures to theorize on the visual image and its relationship to words and text. Epicureanism offered in addition to its atomic theory a theory of vision explaining that vision was produced when tiny images thrown off from an object struck the eye. Heavily debated, this theory of vision spurred others, such as Newton's *Opticks,* offered as alternatives in the inquiry into light and visual perception. Along with theories of memory and imagination, these speculations on the mind and the senses formed early cognitive sciences.

An interest in vision and imagination lodged at the heart of the seventeenth-century belles lettres movement, which spread from France to the British isles. Belles lettres, heavily in debt to rhetorical theory of the sublime from translations of Longinus, included written forms such as history, essays, and poetry but also such visual arts as architecture and landscape gardening. In composition, as a result, textual description became an even more important mode, especially descriptions of landscapes. These were inevitably tied to moral values and were a continuation of epideictic rhetoric, the kind of oratory practiced at public ceremonials from classical times (Clark and Halloran 184–207). In a Platonic, Renaissance strain, Vico reflects the currents of both sublimity and Epicurean thought about the image: he writes in *New Science* that if one understands the *dipeintura* or pictorial frontispiece he had commissioned for his major work, one could even dispense with reading the book. Condillac, working in and furthering the pedagogy of the French belles lettres he had inherited, stresses the translation of visual to verbal, particularly in landscape descriptions. Meanwhile, to Monboddo, spiritual vision was as important as physical vision. He believed humans could access vision through spiritual as well as physical means.

This book tells an impure history, allowing discourses to interanimate and illuminating their resulting hybrids. Epicurean philosophy and Longinian sublimity hybridize, oscillate, and "interanimate," to use a term from M. M. Bakhtin (68). The effect calls into question the modernist belief in progress in rhetorical theory. Theories become occulted, overshadowed, and undiscursable as fields of vision shift. Historical shifts can also bring these texts back into play, re-illuminate them, and reanimate them. To transmute the analogy to the aural realm, many voices potentially exist at any moment when a historian intervenes. Which sounds are attended to and how depend in large measure upon the historian's position, for the story did not unfold with her in mind. How much will she try to harmonize the tones? How much cacophony will she tolerate? The register that rings true to the historian depends on where she stands and what problems she may be trying to solve.

Early in the twentieth century, New Critic and rhetorician I. A. Richards uses a term related to Baktinian interanimation—"interinanimation" (47)—to describe how a word or words illuminate and condition other words on the page. In the new millennium, we see the term applied more and more often to the interaction of words and graphics on a computer screen. Teachers today are living through a revolution in literacy brought about by the capability of computers to combine blocks of text with graphics, sounds, video, and other multimedia possibilities. We are forced—at times by our failures—to grapple with the potential relationships between the visual and the verbal. How to understand and teach language and literature in an age of transformation of communication technology is a significant issue that connects us to our Enlightenment predecessors. Bakhtin's insights into the mutual interillumination of the world's languages shift these issues to a global scale (68).

Such inquiries derive their significance in part from the political and ethical implications of our task of teaching of writing and literature. As James A. Berlin argues in a Foucauldian vein, pedagogical prescriptions of who can speak, when, and about what are ultimately economic and political. Debates arise about writing instruction because language is at the heart of the curriculum and helps shape ideas about the purposes of education, the kind of citizens we want to encourage, and the kind of society in which we want to live. Some of the social and political implications of later belletristic rhetorics became apparent in the 1960s when these prescriptive rhetorics hindered rather than advanced students' progress in open-admissions universities. Nonetheless, earlier rhetorics in this vein were a sincere attempt to be relatively more inclusive and helpful than the Latin rhetoric of the eighteenth century then taught in British and European universities.

This book attempts to contribute to a more complex account of the roots of English studies in their earliest moments. Chapter 1 addresses some aspects of theories of modernity and their relationship to the history of rhetoric and the relationship of rhetoric to the modern science of linguistics. Chapter 2 provides more of the intellectual and cultural background that helps constitute the scene of these crossings.

The chapters on Vico, Condillac, and Monboddo provide three stances on the modern. The three figures propose: first, to transform rhetoric by appropriating some past values and practices and grafting them to modernist advantages; second, to reject the past and to rethink a modern present; and third, to repudiate the modern and attempt to recapture the past in its linguistic golden age. Each of these positions carries a certain weight in each philosopher's texts. These alternatives are never pure nor are the outcomes under the authors' control. In rhetoric, the desire to build on flexible, heuristic traditions continues, as does the understandable impulse to break completely with the growing weight of the past. The hope of returning to a golden age of language persists, and this can be found at the heart of many of our textbooks and journals today. Attentive listening to the past may help us better to hear the harmonies and dissonances of our own age. To shift the metaphor, we will be treading upon the threshold of modernity: that threshold in rhetoric represents everything the stereotype of modernity is not—it is ambiguous, uncertain, self-contradictory, more than a bit chaotic, and slippery. It will be necessary to watch our step as we cross.

2
On the Threshold of Modernity

> If rhetoric is to have any future, or (better put) if rhetorics are to
> have any future-anterior histories, I am going to have to insist (or
> is it to incite)—they will have had to be nomadic.
> —Victor Vitanza, "Rhetorics of Histories"

> A definition of language is always, implicitly or explicitly, a defi-
> nition of human beings in the world.
> —Raymond Williams, *Marxism and Literature*

Hybrid notions and figures are more interesting today than they once
were. This is an index of how our culture has changed over the twentieth century and into the twenty-first. The clear-and-distinct ideas championed by modernity, the separate spheres—art, science, morality—and
modern disciplinary walls may have once been enabling and worked
toward greater inclusivity. However, today the unquestioned categories
of modernity seem commonplace, a bit dull, restrictive, and gatekeeping
in spirit even as they continue powerfully, if residually, to churn as the
engines of our institutional functioning. In contrast, grammar, logic, and
rhetoric—with literary studies interwoven—stood as the foundational
categories of the classical system of education, still residually in place
at the beginning of the eighteenth century. Traditional rhetoric was—in
theory, at any rate—on the decline, although in practice, it would remain
at the core of education as long as the culture of Latin learning held sway.

The three case studies examined here based on the texts of Vico,
Condillac, and Monboddo represent efforts to transform or infuse life
into the dying system or to create a new system of rhetoric for the modern world. A new science of language was midwife in this parturition,
and all three men were present at its birth. Linguistic science is pertinent to a history of rhetoric because the complex scene of language study
at the time closely overlaps that of rhetoric like a Venn diagram with

only a little crescent moon of territory each can truly call its own. These two intertwined realms also share complex relations with others, and this complexity makes any attempt to locate the modern in rhetoric a more difficult task. On the other hand, there is little hope of our understanding the problem of how modernity transformed rhetoric if we do not take an interdisciplinary approach. Roland Barthes writes that "rhetoric must always be read in the structural interplay with its neighbors (Grammar, Logic, Poetics, Philosophy): it is the play of the system, not each of its parts in itself, which is historically significant" (46). Considering language and rhetoric together makes for a richer history and allows us to see across the disciplinary walls that usually fragment the work of these hybrid figures.

Modernity, Language, and Rhetoric

As we have seen, the modern, modernity, and modernism are terms with long histories. Efforts to clarify their meanings intensified with twentieth-century postmodernist thought, even though that thought somewhat paradoxically rejected clear-and-distinct conceptualizations. The terms themselves carry different meanings and valences depending on the field of study, diverging primarily in the social sciences and the humanities. The use of *modern* here refers to a historical period arising in the mid-seventeenth century and consolidating its beliefs and practices throughout the next century in the West (as used by David Harvey, Raymond Williams, and Fredric Jameson, for example). Moving through the nineteenth century, these beliefs and practices extended themselves at the same moment they were being called into question, so that by the early-twentieth century, especially after the crisis of World War I, *aesthetic modernism* helped crystallize the discussion. The term *modernism* comes to stand for a critique of modernity in the aesthetic realm.[1] More than one writer on modernism or postmodernity has pinpointed the Holocaust as the end of the modern, as the nightmare in which the modernist goals of efficiency and rationality revealed their ultimate effects. On the other hand, although modernity was the author and scene of this horror, it can also be credited with constructing and extending democratic values of freedom and human liberty, inclusive forms of active citizenship, and associated notions of cultural relativity and individual difference. Attempting to account for the negative, Max Horkheimer and Theodor W. Adorno describe the double-edged sword of modernity in their *Dialectic of the Enlightenment*. Many poststructuralist and some postmodern thinkers remain wary of Enlightenment tenets because of this double edge and the evils such as fascism that were linked with rationality. However, along with philosophers such as Jürgen Habermas, I have not given up on the project of enlightenment and believe we need to rearticulate notions such as universal human rights and democracy as significant ideals, even if historians should treat them as limited, historical constructions enacted in particular times and places.[2]

The linking of rhetoric and its histories to discussions of modernity has only begun; meanwhile, it has become a commonplace that rhetoric begins to sicken if not to die with the birth of modernity.[3] The revival of rhetorical study in the 1960s produced the term *New Rhetoric* (the title of Chaim Perelman and Lucie Olbrechts-Tyteca's earlier groundbreaking work in 1958, published in English in 1969). That same sixties decade, the label of New Rhetoric was used by Wilbur Samuel Howell in his encyclopedic *Eighteenth-Century British Logic and Rhetoric* to name the two-centuries-earlier's shift from traditional or classical rhetoric to rhetorics based on empirical Lockean principles. To Howell, our exemplary modernist historian, these new rhetorics, including the now-canonical British rhetorical triumvirate of Hugh Blair, George Campbell, and Richard Whately, grew out of changing perspectives on language and knowledge produced primarily by Lockean theory. (Howell does not entertain the notion that they may have been produced in *reaction* to Lockean theory.) Modern in standpoint and a consummate scholar, Howell was one of the first to describe the rise of modern rhetoric; yet he did so without critical reflection on the concept of modernity itself, and he did not stray too far into philosophy of language, fencing rhetoric into its own autonomous, modernist field.

Nonetheless, in early modernity, no such disciplinary restrictions separated philosophers in their inquiries, leaving them free to range from natural philosophy to grammar to rhetoric and ethics. The lush growth of imaginative inquiry into language origins wandered through all four areas (and then some). Although these language-origin narratives are now dismissed as speculative philosophy, it must not be forgotten that they partook of the modern effort to be scientific. In the eighteenth-century, these theories became so popular in scientific circles that the debate was ultimately curtailed, because of their sheer abundance and impossibility of scientific proof. Language-origin papers were banned—by the Linguistic Society of Paris in 1866 and by the Philological Society of London in 1911.[4] The more positivistic nineteenth century required a different discourse, pushing the hybrid speculations that are our concern to the margins.

Historiographical Approaches to
Modernity and Modern Rhetoric

Modernity and a new science of language emerged entwined. Ulrich Ricken notes that linguistic theories of the eighteenth century were often constitutive elements in philosophical systems rather than just their expressions. Indeed eighteenth-century language-origin theory was essential to the working out of new, modern notions of human nature, culture, and society, as Hans Aarsleff has explained. This includes the subjects of primary interest here, rhetoric and what are essentially early theories of communication. Vico, Condillac, and Monboddo all propose theories of language origins, and these serve as foundations for their rhetorical theories. Themes common to their work (and the many others who wrote on language over the long eighteenth century) include epistemology, language origins and progress, language and social development, cognitive development, and language order and use. The very topicality and commonality of their themes and materials in their day, their very contemporaneity and centrality, paradoxically may be key factors in the marginalization of these three figures. Such received notions premised on language-origin theories have been the cultural ocean in which we swim when we submerge ourselves in texts of the Enlightenment. That we are now able to see these texts anew signals a late-twentieth-century and continuing shift in our historical position.

Historiography and the Modern Word

As Vico, Condillac, Thomas S. Kuhn, and other thinkers concerned with stasis and change have observed, what is revolutionary at one moment soon becomes the entrenched normal science or a rigid status quo. But how does a historian distinguish and mark out the period of normal science or stasis from the revolutionary moment? Theorist of modernity David Harvey explains:

> If there is any meaning to history, then that meaning has to be discovered and defined from within the maelstrom of change, a maelstrom that affects the terms of discussion as well as whatever it is that is being discussed. Modernity, therefore, not only entails a ruthless break with any and all preceding historical conditions, but is characterized by a never-ending process of internal ruptures. (11–12)

The modern project must seek the eternal and immutable while embroiled in discontinuity. Along with the task of judging the past and carving out distinct historical sequences from intertwining series, this problem becomes significant on the threshold of modernity. The confused swirling of historical lines seems at times to perplex Vico: his three historical ages—the ages of gods, heroes, and men—and the different signifying systems that make them a developmental sequence—were always already present, necessarily so, for each to function at all (Eco 108).

An associated historical problem becomes the refusal of once-institutionalized practices to die, their habit of lingering on, and the jealousy with which a later generation safeguards practices they have appropriated that were denied to their kind and their class in previous generations.[5] This is also why there can be no stark "death of rhetoric."

In *Marxism and Literature,* Raymond Williams contrasts the historically dominant with strands of emergent and residual cultural formations, the residual signifying that which was formed in the past but remains active in the present (122). Traditional rhetorics may exemplify the residual in the nineteenth century, but in the eighteenth they remain a dominant just beginning to lose ground to the emergent modern discourses. This point concurs in many ways with those of conservative historians like Jonathan Clark and Linda Colley who portray eighteen-century Britain as yet a traditional, hierarchical, religiously centered society. Daniel Cottom demonstrates that the time of aristocratic values such as good taste endured into the bourgeois era. He notes that social values are often resilient, having their own durations. Nonetheless, even small extensions and transformations over time cause traditional rhetorical systems to become something quite different because their values, strategies, and practices are encroached upon and reframed by dominant elements. That is why eighteenth-century Britain in particular can be at once the crucible of modern liberatory thought and a traditional, elite society—we must have it both ways if we aim for more accurate histories.

Working in a slightly earlier period, 1640–1720, and also in Britain, Richard W. Kroll's history of language, *The Material Word: Literate Culture in the Restoration and Early-Eighteenth Century,* approaches the changes taking place over these eight decades as a "multiple discursive orientation" rather than as a unitary shift or rupture (as both he and Robert Markley in *Fallen Languages: Crises of Representation in Newtonian England, 1660–1740* describe shifts in the periods they treat). Unlike others who discuss shifts or ruptures at the opening of the eigh-

teenth century, Kroll points to the mid-seventeenth century as the period of crucial debates. These debates represent shifts that later texts still
mull over, working out the implications. He argues against Michel Foucault, Stephen K. Land, Aarsleff, and others:

> I do not believe that we witness a sudden Foucaultian shift
> in linguistic attitudes in the 1670s or at the turn of the eigh-
> teenth century. Rather, I would argue that the changes hav-
> ing the greatest importance for literary representation had
> already occurred between 1640 and 1660, and, however
> strange we find Wilkin's *Essay*, it is by no means as secure
> about its ideal of linguistic reference as Jonathan Swift
> thought or as Wilkin's modern critics have often assumed.
> Nor am I persuaded by the view that we have a "seventeenth-
> century" tradition of Aristotelian taxonomic essentialism
> which is only revised late in the century by a nominalism
> represented best by Locke. (184)

Kroll reconfigures historical shifts primarily in response to a piece of the
puzzle he believes has been missing from previous language histories—
a serious description of neoclassical thought. He finds this project stunted
by earlier scholars like Richard Foster Jones who privilege Romanticism.
Kroll's key focus is on a "neo-Epicurean revival" centering on Lucretius's
De rerum natura as one of the "chief vehicles" of this "multiple discursive reorientation"[6] (3).

A primary element of neoclassical thought that Kroll emphasizes is
a classical epistemology stressing the uncertainty of knowledge due to
its mediated nature, often resulting in its rhetorical and linguistic ground-
ing. This mediated nature of knowledge primarily comes from the
Ciceronianism common to seventeenth-century schooling (notable in epi-
graphs in both Locke and Condillac). Kroll wields the probabilistic epistemologies of Ciceronianism and neo-Epicureanism as a probe to reread
texts previously interpreted as marking the beginnings of scientific certainty and naively representative theories of language. In particular, he,
along with Brian Vickers and Robert Markley, are highly critical of Richard Foster Jones's work on shifts in style featuring the progressivist
term the *rise of science*.

The Jones-Merton thesis directly connects this rise of science to a
"permeating realism and utilitarianism for literary expression," which
Kroll rejects in his New Historical view of multiple discursive reorientation (6). Neoclassical culture and its Ciceronianism already provided

for a plain style, Kroll notes, although the Jones-Merton thesis fails to describe what historical agents themselves intended, and it tends to over-emphasize style. Kroll's argument, which also cuts against that of Timothy J. Reiss in *The Discourse of Modernism,* is that the early scientific world view, because of the pervasive probabilism of neoclassical epistemology, does not produce an ideology that treats language as transparent and referential, an object to grasp objects in the world. Yet in Kroll's historiography, he does not concern himself with how that particular complex of beliefs that has become our common sense was constructed or the part the construction of early scientific discourses might have had in its rise to hegemony.

Nonetheless, in the long eighteenth century, to use a metaphor from the period, seeds were sown (and some germinated) of beliefs that lately we have described as modern: an obsession with order, a quantitative mentality with a greater interest in fact, a more individually based epistemology, an insistence on clear, linear discourse not only in history but in most genres—as well as a growing desire for relief from this complex of values, practices, and feelings. Williams notes that this relief was found more and more in the aesthetic experience and in the associated ideas of the private and domestic. However, this transforming structure of feeling loses the heat of glory contained in the heroic republican ideal of the virtuous citizen speaking and acting in the polis. When it moves toward the cooler feelings of "polite" gentlemen and ladies conversing sympathetically over print materials in the landscaped garden, one version of rhetoric waxes while the other wanes.[7] One imaginary gives way to another, and yet, the earlier does not disappear entirely. It may be thrown into shadow as a residual strand of theory and practice, making up part of the cultural unconscious. Like a receding wave, it may lap the shore again diminished.

In his controversial *The Discourse of Modernism,* Reiss reaches deep into classical texts for the term *occulted.* He charts the emergence, growth, and consolidation of an analytico-referential class of discourse that he describes as consolidating and rising to dominance in the eighteenth century and just now breaking down. Modifying Foucault, he sets up a model in which change manifests itself across various discourses, but in which one set of dominant values in discourse gives way through time to another. For him, the dominant class of discourse provides the conceptual tools that make the majority of human practices meaningful, although other strands of discourse continue to exist. These occulted discourses are marginalized practices that become a society's unthinkable or at least unthought, never gaining widespread meaningfulness within dominant culture. He describes dominant modernist discourse by its hypostatizations in various areas, including

THEORETICAL AREA	MANIFESTATION
Science	Truth and valid experiment
General	Referential language and representation
Politics and Economy	Possessive individualism
Sociopolitics and Law	Contractualism
Aesthetics	Taste
Philosophy	The concept and common sense

In addition to elaborating these manifestations, Reiss notes that modernist discourses generally assume that concepts are adequate to represent objects in an exterior world, that words are adequate to represent concepts, and that a properly organized sentence provides in its syntax a correct analysis of both the rational and material orders. The new discourses of modernism also build on a permanent and universal human reason and absolutely objective truth. Significantly, scientific discourse becomes the exemplar for all discourses claiming truth, along with its insistence on a linear narration of causality. Reiss's critics dispute his timetable as well as his descriptions of the changes taking place in eighteenth-century language theory, arguing that various changes are not monolithic but internally divided and complexly manifested. For example, emphasis on the sublime and the ambiguous or oblique undermines the emphasis on clear-and-distinct conceptualization.

Departing from the clear-and-distinct historical narrative of the homogeneous rise of science, Reiss attempted to make more complex the various effects of modern discursive practices. However, his work appeared at the same moment as historical deconstructions disproving any clear-and-distinct shifts in the seventeenth century. Yet again, it can be helpful to have it both ways. Reiss's presentation of dominant tendencies in modernist discourse will be used in these chapters as heuristic for general transformation and not as specific and verifiable historical moments of change. Notions of linearity and the valuing of rational order as Reiss describes them come directly from many eighteenth-century texts, in particular those of Condillac. Vico's critique of the modern echoes Reiss in many areas, and Vico's contrasting sense of baroque order and emphasis on interrelationship and the whole subverts modern disciplinary fragmentation. Like Vico, Monboddo critiques modern values, but he also helps found a modern antimodern discourse. The work of Condillac, spanning what is now six or seven disciplines, serves as a founding discourse of modern linearity and representation, although the French *philosophe* also vehemently constructs a base at times only to dismantle or subvert it with his expressive rhetoric.

Zygmunt Bauman's work identifies the "task of order" as one of the "multitude of impossible tasks that modernity set itself" (4), a task that produced the modernist dichotomy order-chaos:

> We can think of modernity as of a time when order—of the world, of the human habitat, of the human self, and of the connection between all three—is *reflected upon;* a matter of thought, of concern, of a practice that is aware of itself, conscious of being a conscious practice and wary of the void it would leave were it to halt or merely relent. (5)

To Bauman and other writers on modernity, modern consciousness *is* consciousness of order, manifesting itself in various ways. Since the Greeks, there had been concern for order and for order in connection with the search for truth. However, in science, this order was not that of a rational discipline in a purified and sterile way severed from every other. It refers to the harmonious and aesthetic order of the *cosmos*—in Greek *order* or *arrangement,* also the source for our modern term *cosmetic* (Hardison 11). The modern sense of order, however, appeals dominantly not to the aesthetic sense but to the intellect. Consequently, it begins a split that works to sever the aesthetic from science. In regard to language, this

> struggle for order [is] a fight of determination against ambiguity, of semantic precision against ambivalence, of transparency against obscurity, clarity against obfuscation. Modern existence, then, comprises an urge to order to avoid the fall into chaos, to order or design oneself to avoid the 'pure negativity' of chaos. (Bauman 7)

To Bauman, fragmentation, atomization, and reductionism become a primary "achievement of modernism: . . . The world that falls apart into a plethora of problems is a manageable world" (12). He adds that this may simply mean that the question of the manageability of the world never gets addressed, as it is not in question. The question begged reflects the anxieties of the age in the face of fear of a changing universe, but fragmentation or division has been a practice of problem-solving from the Sophists and Plato to cognitive science and modern engineering. This fragmentation manifests itself nowhere more clearly than in the fragmentation of the disciplines that motivates my inquiry here, which has necessitated transgressing the borders of history, linguistics, literary theory, communication theory, and rhetoric to name only the principal few. Vico stands on nonmodern ground in his insistence that "the true is the whole," in both a speech and a curriculum (*Study Methods* 77).

Rhetoric, for Vico and later critics of modernity, served as a pragmatic middle road between the modern and an antiquarianism that was nonproductive. It acted as an exchange-interchange translating between what is certain and what is random, thereby weaving together the Stoic fate and Epicurean chance. These rhetorics could give up on control, throwing the rhetor and his improvisational-rhapsodizing arts into a rhetorical situation, trusting an order that was at any particular moment a nonorder, an intuition based on an art and deeply internalized practice.

With modernity, the high value placed on control and order expresses itself through beliefs and practices emphasizing universal laws, fragmentation through orderly division, clear definition, self-conscious design, management, control, conquest, and certainty. These watchwords of a developing capitalist economy and its social structures are also keywords signalling the highly print-literate modernist rhetorics of the eighteenth century. Considering this complex of values and practices, it is no coincidence that the rhetoric of modernism has been classified as *managerial rhetoric*.[8] The opposite of this structure comprises residual values of traditional rhetoric centered on situatedness in time and place, orality, constructivism, ambiguity, free-flowing performance-in-practice, playfulness, openness to possibility—rhetorical *kairos*. These rhetorics have advanced once again as managerial rhetorics have receded.

Histories of Rhetoric

As in most histories, the tone of histories of rhetoric has generally been quite modernist (outside the notable poststructuralist variant by Vitanza celebrating an extremely kairotic, sophistic process). Histories of early modern rhetoric habitually use Locke's modern theories of language rhetoric as central touchstones (see Corbett, Covino, Crowley, Howell, or Ulman). For example, H. Lewis Ulman portrays Locke as the high ground one climbs onto in order to see the terrain[9] (10–11). The more positivistic thinkers of the nineteenth century were less admiring of Locke than are historians of linguistics and literature justifiably working to save his achievements from an often narrow and conservative nineteenth-century reading. This process of giving Locke his historical due, still going on in the twenty-first century, makes it tricky to critically analyze his part in modernity without seeming to regress to less rich prior readings. However, the eighteenth-century critics of modernity also criticize Locke. Even Condillac, for example, an admirer, presents his own work as essentially a celebration but more pertinently, a revision and enrichment of Locke and his theories of language. Vico rejects Locke outright; both he and Condillac view Locke in the context of the struggle between old and new, perhaps for Vico, the competition of French and Italian thought manifested most clearly in debates over Cartesianism and classicism. Politically, Locke stood for a kind of thought that was more and more threatening as the century wore on. Monboddo was part of the late-eighteenth-century conservative reaction to Locke that led into the nineteenth century. Locke's critics judge him through a lens tempered by classical works, such as those by Lucretius, as well as readings of their near contemporaries, Thomas Hobbes, G. W. Leibniz, and Pierre Gassendi, for example. Locke's conflicted language theory in *An Essay Concerning Human Understanding* especially becomes a kind of Rorschach test on which eighteenth-century thinkers (and later ones) project their own theories and fantasies. What interests me here is how historians of rhetoric have measured the advent of the modern in rhetoric with a Lockean rule.

Ulman in *Things, Thoughts, Words, and Actions: The Problem of Language in Later Eighteen-Century British Rhetorical Theory* places Lockean theory mostly in his category of "words as thoughts," along with Scottish philosopher of rhetoric George Campbell. In dialogue with Edward P. J. Corbett's suggestion that rhetoricians can learn from Locke, Ulman argues reasonably that we might want to both resist and learn from Locke, as did his eighteenth-century readers. Ulman sees eighteenth-century rhetoric as adjusting to Lockean rhetoric but notes that nineteenth-century rhetoric was doing something quite different altogether. By staying within the framework of Locke's semantic theories in the earlier period, Ulman emphasizes Locke's contributions to a modern epistemological rhetoric. Ulman's is the first major discussion of Locke in the history of rhetoric since Howell, who, in his 1971 *Eighteenth-Century British Logic and Rhetoric,* traces Locke's epistemological influence in both logic and rhetoric.

To date, the modernist Howell has been the primary interpreter of Locke in the field of rhetoric (although Corbett encouraged the study of Locke). Howell links Lockean philosophy with what amounts to a paradigm shift, noting developments in logic and six related advancements in modern rhetoric:

1. an expanded province of rhetorical theory
2. an emphasis on inartistic proofs or scientific facts
3. a decided preference for induction as the basic form of rhetorical proof
4. an emphasis on truth and scientific proof rather than probability
5. an altered approach to organization based on a "natural structure"
6. a preference for plain style (*Eighteenth-Century British Logic* 441–46)

This paradigm marks the coming of the modern to rhetoric for Howell, and unlike later theorists, he sees nothing to question or critique in the "rise of the modern."

Moreover, Howell confers the status of hero of an intellectual revolution on Locke, wholeheartedly welcoming these changes as progressive. Vincent M. Bevilacqua early on criticized "Howell's distinctly Lockean interpretation of eighteenth-century rhetorical theory" ("Nature and Scope" 345) for its emphasis on a Lockean relationship of rhetoric to logic. He writes in a 1972 review that, partly because of this approach,

> while Howell's 'six issues' do set in order the leading precepts of several diverse rhetorical works, the 'issues' characterise more the letter than the spirit of the eighteenth-century rhetorical theory. . . .
>
> Yet Howell's propensity to view eighteenth-century rhetoric narrowly as learned communication rather than broadly as stylistic embellishment . . . fails to account philosophically for the prevailing eighteenth-century connection of rhetoric with the various belles lettres. ("Nature and Scope" 345–46)

Although Howell protested Bevilacqua's review, especially its "twist-[ing]" the thesis of his book "until he has made it into nonsense" ("Relatives" 214), Bevilacqua zeroes in on the limitations of Howell's framework. For example, he notes Howell's failure to consider the connections of rhetoric with "mid-eighteenth-century psychology, aesthetics (the

Addisonian beautiful, novel, and grand), art theory (painterly *inventio, elocutio, actio*), and the belles lettres" (Howell, "Relatives" 345). He also argues that Adam Smith's Glasgow lectures owed as much to then-current ideas of sympathy, benevolence, and moral-aesthetic beauty as to the elements of Howell's Lockean framework of developments from "old logic" ("Nature and Scope" 216).

Despite this critique, Howell's historical analysis and encyclopedic work nonetheless remain valuable, a gateway through which all students of eighteenth-century rhetoric should pass and usually do so gratefully. However, Howell's work has remained a way of reading and valuing rhetorics that underlies the field today, if only in its unconscious. The paradigm shift he describes (the book was written in the heyday of Kuhn's *Structure of Scientific Revolution*) tells us as much about Howell and our field's own contemporary modernism as it does Locke. Howell's own structure and values closely match the patterns described by Reiss and other scholars of modernism, as he promotes values of fact, order, and representational clarity.

Howell first takes up the scope or province of rhetoric, arguing that Locke enlarged it to encompass all language use. However, it can also be argued that, on the contrary, Locke's texts do not enlarge the province of rhetoric but further diminish it in the wake of Ramus and the Cartesians. Classical rhetoric's canons of invention, arrangement, style, memory, and delivery had earlier been trimmed to style and sometimes delivery by those following Ramus. Ramus and his contemporaries essentially tidied up the curriculum, putting the departments of invention and arrangement into logic. This reduced structure has been well digested and incorporated into the Lockean-Cartesian corpus. As for the scope of preparatory studies needed by a rhetorician, Cicero's texts expanded those to encompass philosophy and other fields. If rhetoric is at heart concerned with invention, as in Aristotle's art, knowing something is important, but if rhetoric isn't concerned with knowledge, broad learning for the purposes of rhetoric is a moot issue. In the Lockean battle between rhetoric and philosophy, philosophy clearly wins the epistemological terrain, as it did in Plato. Locke divides language into philosophical and civil uses, and he shows little interest in civil—ordinary, everyday persuasive—uses of language such as form the heart of rhetorical logic and ethics. Locke's model for language use is philosophy, or science, although he incorporates some rhetorical constructivism and much moral philosophy into his program.

Second, happily for Howell (but not Vico), Locke turns away from the artistic proofs—arguments constructed by the orator based on memory and social knowledge—to favor nonartistic means of evidence and persuasion—external fact and testimony. Howell's explanation for this development in modern rhetoric is Lockean to the extreme. As he criticizes DeQuincey:

> Rhetoric in a culture permeated by the standards of scientific and scholarly proof must become scientific and scholarly itself, and must argue from the facts of the case, and not from suppositions that may represent mere popular misconceptions and prejudices.

Yet, understanding *doxa*, opinion, the common sense of one's interlocutors, stood at the heart of rhetorical invention. An orator forms a rhetorical syllogism—an enthymeme—by leaving out the logical step, the assumptions forming the middle term of argument, in part because they are already understood by the audience. The disappearance of a logic specific to rhetoric—enthymeme and example—marks a turn from a socially oriented rhetoric involving the interlocutors to a private text-and-fact-centered rhetoric. With such a strong progressivist and positivist stance, it is no wonder Howell rises to hyperbole in defending the moderns:

> I am not saying that the eighteenth-century British authors of the new rhetoric won a permanent victory on this point. But they resolutely tried for victory, and it is a calamity for twentieth-century rhetoric that they did not completely prevail. The theory that valuable arguments emerge from commonplaces unfortunately continues still to have currency, even in circles presumably dedicated to high rhetorical standards.[10] (*Eighteenth-Century British Logic* 443)

This notion that what is modern always represents progress has as its corollary that the nonmoderns, those who resist the new, those not "in the true" in the Foucauldian sense become, ultimately, more than unfortunate—they are premodern dinosaurs, irrational, and even immoral.

Associated with this disappearance of invention and emphasis on fact, the third development Howell sees in modern Lockean rhetoric is a shift from an enthymematic logic that sees induction as a variation on the enthymeme to a fundamentally inductive logic. In his *Essay*, like Bacon, Locke rejects the syllogism and favors an inferential approach from evidence. Again thoroughly Lockean in perspective, Howell writes, "Thus Locke's disparagement of the syllogistic process implies a necessary reappraisal of the value of the enthymeme in rhetoric" (*Eighteenth-Century British Logic* 288). Ramistic theory and previous logical handbooks had already collapsed Aristotle's two-fold rhetorical logic of the essentially deductive enthymeme and inductive example with the dialectical logic of syllogism and demonstration. Scholastic logic was not rhetorical logic. Modernist rhetorical theory was consistent in rejecting scholasticism and adopting a strictly inductive logic, but in doing so, it ignored the long traditions of rhetorical arts of everyday argument available to orators and audiences alike.

Closely linked with the key issue of syllogistic logic, Howell's fourth issue is "whether rhetoric should deal only in probabilities or whether it also has the responsibility to achieve as full a measure of truth as the situation allows" (*Eighteenth-Century British Logic* 444). This statement reveals Howell's failure to understand the probable reasoning of civic rhetoric based on prudence and phronesis as we will find it in Vico, for example. In this failure, it is likely that Howell also misreads Locke's theories of probable judgment. From the *Essay*'s beginning, Locke's epigraph from Cicero on probable knowledge and human limits helps us contextualize his knowledge claims. Both Kevin L. Cope and Hoyt Trowbridge agree that Locke's ethos of probablism is more rhetorical than it is mathematical. Yet at the same time, Howell picks up on a key difference in Locke's use of the concept of probability. Locke works just before the era in which probability becomes mathematicized, moving toward the statistical approach we find augured in George Campbell's *Philosophy of Rhetoric*, for example. The difference in Lockean thought from the old rhetoric is that it is not audience-centered and concerned about the truth or common sense of the hearers-interlocutors. Locke's sense of truth has as its goal to adequately—if probabilistically—represent a reality in the world external to human society. This represents a major shift from a rhetoric-centered to philosophical world, to a sense of the truth of things rather than rhetorical truth of practical wisdom in a common social life.[11]

Fifth, Howell asserts that the six-part Ciceronian organization of discourse was jettisoned by the moderns for a "simple and natural structure" such as Fénelon preferred for the sermon (*Eighteenth-Century British Logic* 446). Locke argues in favor of a logic ordered most often according to the linkage of ideas in a chain of demonstration. Generally, this order would run from elements closest to sense perceptions to those furthest away or from particular to general. This natural pattern was adopted by Condillac as the basis for his linear order, and he makes it axiomatic that material should be presented in teaching and discoursing in the same order in which it was discovered by the communicator. This egocentric, author–centered order is also a shift from the audience-and-purpose–centered rhetoric of Vico and the earlier rhetoricians.

Finally, the sixth development of modern rhetoric for Howell was that a "plain and unstudied" style came to be regarded with "special favor," although Howell finds "natural perversions" in style yet in favor today (*Eighteenth-Century British Logic* 447). Objections to the Jones-Merton thesis of the rise of science occurred before Howell, and he fell into many of the same traps as did Jones.

Not long afterward, what Howell found perverse in style—elaborate schemes and tropes—Vickers mourns as fading or lost and mounts a rousing campaign against their disappearance. Still, Vickers does not ally himself with and embrace those who seemingly value a rhetoric of style, such as Paul de Man and the poststructuralists. The style Vickers calls for represents a modernist expressivism as found in Condillac and other belletrists. Style, then, figures variously in accounts of rhetoric's modernity. There are calls for a plain style allied with modernity—often advocated for clearly representing a reality out there—as well as emphases on elaborate styles for expressing an individual's inner landscape. I will revisit Howell's six touchstones of modernism in rhetoric in the examination of Vico, Condillac, and Monboddo.

If Howell's criteria for modern rhetoric do not provide a satisfactory framework for elucidating eighteenth-century rhetoric, what other alternatives are there to evaluate rhetorics in light of modernity? Or perhaps rhetoric did die with modernity, and we can only explore its absence. Presenting the latter case, John Bender and David E. Wellbery offer a five-fold set of criteria comprising the *conditions of impossibility* of rhetoric sometime after the Enlightenment and the Romantics:

1. the rise of objective scientific discourse with the values of transparency and neutrality
2. the anchoring of imaginative discourse in subjectivity, with the attendant values of authorship and individual expression in the literary domain
3. the rise of liberal political discourse
4. the shift from oratorical to print culture—"Europe was alphabetized"
5. standardization of national languages with the rise of the nation-state (22)

These broad social and cultural considerations in many ways parallel Reiss's analysis of modernist discourse and serve to contextualize Howell. Yet again, in the general structure of modernity, a great chasm opens between the past and the modern. There is a revolutionary moment in which the modern, again a heroic if now suspect figure, triumphs. Historical time divides to produce a Great Divide between the past and the present, a touchstone of the rhetoric of modernity.

Plotting the History of Rhetoric

Setting out a historical timeline of rhetoric has always involved plotting a narrative. Histories of rhetoric have been criticized for being plotted unselfconsciously in one of two ways. Either the narrative is plotted as a tragedy, with a golden age of rhetoric in the past that we can never recapture or as a comedy, based on a perfection that we are perpetually nearing.[12] Such metanalyses of the plots of histories of rhetoric owe much to the rise of rhetoric, drawing on the rhetorical historiography of Barthes in the 1960s and subsequent historiographical work. Hayden White, in his books *Metahistory: The Historical Imagination in Nineteenth-Century Europe* and *Tropics of Discourse,* writes that histories are emplotted like fiction, arguing along with Barthes that historical writing cannot evade narrative forms and must be understood as such. Consequently, he adapts Northrop Frye's literary taxonomy as well as his own conceptions of tropic structures based on Vico's (and Burke's) four master tropes— metaphor, metonymy, synecdoche, and irony. His taxonomies have been enormously productive as hermeneutic tools both in the field of history and subsequent analyses of histories of rhetoric. Analyses of emplotment in history turn on these plots as well as considerations of continuity versus rupture in narrative lines.

In White's sense, Howell's history may be plotted as a comedy. Howell adopts many of the values of Locke, the admitted "hero" of his "history of an intellectual revolution," (*Eighteenth-Century British Logic* 7) but without Locke's central concern with language. Even though Howell cites Aarsleff's early work, he addresses neither the issues of shifts in language theories nor the significance of language theory in relation to rhetorical practice, accepting unquestionably the Jones-Merton rise-of-science theory locating a shift to plain style in the eighteenth century. Focusing on the shift from an old logic based on the syllogism to a new— and better—logic, Howell's work traces the progress of rhetoric as it discards the old, unscientific, language-based theories and practices and moves upward to more modern empirical theories and practices. He admires figures such as Smith and Campbell, who transform traditional rhetorical elements by transmuting them into more modern, empirically based rhetorics. Likewise, he often scorns or dismisses as sterile rhetoricians such as Whately who refuse to enter the realm of the new logic. In this comic plot, rhetoric necessarily must mature, progress, and move upward, toward the light of the present and future. In Howell's plot, a major rupture from the past at the beginning of the eighteenth century helped rhetoric to do this, ensuring our own progress.

Alternatively, writing in the tragic mode, Vickers in *Defence of Rhetoric* blames those with language-centered views such as Vico and de Man for rhetoric's demise. He furthermore rejects the view of a rupture, in this case, in seventeenth-century language and rhetoric, in favor of a view of continuity, which he also presents as revisionary theory.

> The history of the continuity of rhetoric in the eighteenth and nineteenth centuries has yet to be written. A true history might show the persistence of traditional rhetorical instruction in the schools, until the rise of modern subjects caused realignments in the curriculum which gave rhetoric an ever smaller and more specialised share. (*Defence of Rhetoric* 24–25)

In this plotting, rhetoric itself represents the premodern from which later rhetorics broke or ruptured. However, Vickers sees a much-diminished rhetoric continuing.

Foucault emphasizes the notion of rupture in history, maintaining a suspicious attitude toward traditional histories tracing continuity. In an early work, *The Order of Things: An Archaeology of the Human Sciences,* he sets his point of rupture between the sixteenth and seventeenth centuries describing a shift in discourse from the Renaissance age of resemblance to the Classical age of representation, based on theories of language and epistemology. He labels these formations of enabling or constraining conditions epistemes and discusses three—the Renaissance, the Classical, and the modern (beginning with the nineteenth century). Foucault emphasizes institutional history and "history from below," both of which resist simple emplotment, so that his work seems to oscillate between tragedy and comedy. If there is the Nietzschean-postmodern openness to difference and change, there are also moments of near nostalgia, such as the *Order's* lamentation over the reduction of the triadic notion of the Renaissance sign—the marks, the signified, and the connections between the two—lost with the signified-signifier reduc-

tion of the eighteenth century. If the opposition of signified and signifier enabled the rise of a true science of language, it also constrained the
production and circulation of interpretive commentary and associated
word magic that characterized the Foucault's Renaissance patterning.
Although Foucault doesn't point to rhetoric here, he might have done
so, for the Classical era of language was the period that Nietzsche notes
was deadly to rhetoric.[13]

Critiquing Foucault and working from a more progressive plot,
Aarsleff rejects much of Foucault's work as relativistic and overly Franco-
centric (although Aarsleff is admittedly a Francophile himself). He de-
lays the break in what might parallel Foucault's Classical episteme to
the beginning of the eighteenth century, and again we see the advent of
Locke's texts treated as signifying a rupture and as progressive and
modern. Yet Aarsleff's efforts to establish the historical unity and continuity of the main traditions of language study are posited in direct
opposition to Foucault's skepticism over the historical search for continuity (Aarsleff, *From Locke to Saussure* 22–23; Foucault, *Archaeology
of Knowledge* 25). Aarsleff's primary antagonists are Chomskyan Cartesian linguistics and the once-powerful European historians of philology who plotted main features of the historical linguistic landscape to
found their own discipline, in their own way, through Franz Bopp and
Rasmus Rask, for example. In their place, Aarsleff sets others, especially
Locke, Condillac, and Alexander von Humboldt, paying especially attention to figures such as Horne Tooke, a central British figure who became
marginal when disciplinary progress in a narrowed institutional philology became the sole criterion of inclusion. My own narrative line owes
much to Aarsleff's because I am convinced by his demonstration of the
widespread availability and centrality of Condillac's work. Both ruptures
and continuities exist, but Aarsleff's arguments persuade me that he has
the more accurate genealogy concerning the line of continuity.

Linguistics historian Land works in the comic mode presenting a
rupture in language theory at the beginning of the seventeenth century
paralleling many theories of modernity. In *From Signs to Propositions:
The Concept of Form in Eighteenth-Century Semantic Theory,* he focuses
on evolution *during* the eighteenth century away from atomism or attention to individual signs to formalism or signs conceived as parts of
systems, tying this movement to a breakdown of representational theories. Discussing Vico's conception of language, Land calls attention to
the diversity of eighteenth-century linguistic theory. His work highlights
what can be seen as the seeds of the current breakdown of analytico-

referential discourse in the weaknesses of referential theories of language. However, because his linguistics narrative begins with referential theories and follows a line progressing toward a systems approach to language, his texts have been faulted for overgeneralizing and ignoring evidence that does not fit his model.

Ruptures and continuities, transformations and stabilities are traced, plotted, and charted according to the texts these historians discuss as well as the fields they address—philology, linguistics, literature, history of science, and history of rhetoric. However, the historical relationship of rhetoric or of rhetoric to modernism is not the task or inquiry to which most set themselves. The concepts of transformation and threshold allow for both continuity and rupture. Marking one edge of the threshold in events occurring before the eighteenth century, Vico, Condillac, and Monboddo step out, Condillac quite confidently, Vico more hesitantly, and Monboddo reluctantly, even inadvertently onto the threshold of modernity.

Scholars attempt in later analyses to work with alternative models of emplotment, time, or different metaphors, such as the concept of threshold. The most striking example may be Bruno Latour, working with metaphors of hybridity, questioning the great divides of modernity in his book *We Have Never Been Modern*. He sees modernity's founding as based on a constitution of paradoxes, such as, his first paradox: "Nature is not our construction; it is transcendent and surpasses us infinitely;" countered at once by "Society is our free construction; it is immanent to our action." Likewise, the second paradox: "Nature is our artificial construction in the laboratory; it is immanent;" opposed by, "Society is not our construction; it is transcendent and surpasses us infinitely." This is followed by various guarantees, especially that "Nature and Society must remain absolutely distinct," much as "the work of purification must remain absolutely distinct from the work of mediation." Latour proposes and claims to believe in nonmodernity—he attempts to weave a history in which there is no great divide between the premodern and modern, the postmodern and modern (32).

He does this, he writes, by paying as much attention to the networkings and interweavings of history as he does the purifications or analytical moves to separate phenomena, moves that were emphasized by modernity. Nonetheless, both the purifications and the interweavings were always taking place. When we write from within modernity, we emphasize the analysis and ignore the interweavings, he believes. Timothy Reiss refers to the processes Latour refers to as networkings, interweavings, or translations as strands or processes that were occulted in modernity. He means occulted both in the sense of being overshadowed and the magical sense of being rendered invisible. Both Latour and Reiss attempt to understand the interweavings and continuities of history as well as ruptures, and both concern themselves with understanding the simultaneous rise of modernity and science. In Latour's nonmodern formulation:

> As soon as we direct our attention simultaneously to the work of purification and the work of hybridization, we immediately stop being wholly modern, and our future begins to change. At the same time, we stop having been modern, because we become retrospectively aware that the two sets of practices have always already been at work in the historical period that is ending. Our past begins to change. (11)

Perhaps challenging the easier frameworks of modernity as rupture, or indeed of uncritical continuity, may help us better understand the history of rhetoric. In Bender and Wellbery's formulation, the demise of rhetoric coincides with the rise of modernity. The return of rhetoric coincides with the advent of postmodernity. Yet such narratives do not help us understand the complications and imbrication of these divisions—premodern-modern-postmodern—as used in rhetoric. Historians of rhetoric face such complex issues every day as they write of such things as sophistic rhetoric, rhetorical notions of the sublime, rhetorical probability, identification, the aleatory, discovery heuristics, social epistemologies, the complex subject of rhetoric, and the heroic self of the rhetor. Great-divide theories cannot help us understand how, despite the putative death of rhetoric, we can never find a time in history when a form of rhetoric is not being studied or promoted as rhetoric or under another name—even those traditional or classical Greco-Latinate rhetorics that always somehow and somewhere remain on the stage.

What would an inquiry into modernity and rhetoric look like from a nonmodern perspective taking both continuity and change into account? It is time for comparative history of Western rhetoric to highlight occulted strands that have been woven into the background of the historical record of modern rhetorics. Comparative studies such as these could help us see change occurring in rhetoric over time, change that sometimes appears as a rupture but may manifest itself in other ways. Attention to processes of change as well as to processes of dominance and marginalization might help us construct more inclusive and more effective histories.

As a modernist rhetorician who prefigures postmodernity, Kenneth

Burke speaks of history in terms not of ruptures and continuities, but in terms of transformations.[14] He describes transformation as a process in which the situation at the end is qualitatively different from that at the beginning, although those who experience the changes detect nothing abruptly shifting, indeed, nothing occurring outside the normal course of events. An insider might even say that nothing has changed.[15] The concept is useful here because it is found in the archives: sixteenth-century French writers speak of devouring the ancients, digesting and transforming rather than repeating them. Transformation, in the sense of growth and development, is an important topos of eighteenth-century language theorists—most pertinently Condillac—as they chart the rise and progress of language and culture.

Just what transformations are being spoken of here? What has been consumed, altered, *détourned*, from the past? Some subtle repositioning takes place around:

- new uses of texts on language from classical archives to Renaissance humanism cross-fertilizing in various ways texts past and present
- an intensification of the already ongoing shift from traditional preparatory grammar of Latin and Greek to the national vernaculars—Italian, French, and English (but note, not to Basque, not to Gaelic)
- a more generalist and philosophical language study moving toward a more atomized science of language for specialists at the eighteenth-century's end
- diffusion of speculations on language origins and development, accessible as popular knowledge (for example, the well-known Mandevillian bees and Monboddoan monkeys) before they suddenly end and are replaced by the science of comparative-historical linguistics

These new developments occur alongside continuation of traditional and hybridized transitional forms of grammar and rhetorical study:

- The expansion of belletristic rhetorical traditions begins to shift rhetoric from a system of arts with five traditional departments (containing also literary study) aimed at teaching public persuasive discourse to a collapse of rhetoric into poetic and an emphasis on reception and polite taste in France and in Britain, moving toward a science of aesthetics at the long-eighteenth-century's end.

- Associated, a movement begins away from the priority of persuasive language to an intensified interest in both informational and aesthetic texts.
- There is a growing acceptance of written communication in pedagogy as equal to speaking or even the norm.
- Paradoxically at the same time, an emphasis on sound and gesture, as natural-language theory is appropriated to help the colonized persons on the peripheries learn to speak like centrists.
- A transformation from the traditional Horacean aims to teach, to delight, and to move *(docere* or *probare, delactare,* and *movere),* to the imagistic trio in Fénelon, to prove, to paint, and to touch or move *(prouver, peindre,* and *toucher,* with the "painting" to address the faculty of the imagination) (Ricken 53).
- Verbal arts of analysis formerly based on legal and legislative disputation and syllogism begin to shift to the model of the controlled experiment, observation of empirical facts, and the report of mental observations in the reflective essay.

Along the route of these transformations, a "network of variants" is produced (Veyne 287), linked to what Kroll terms the "multiple discursive reorientation" produced by modernity (94).

One of the most important shifts for rhetoric is the emphasis on vernacular language that begins in the mid-sixteenth century and finally—some would say not completely until the twentieth century—vanquishes the culture(s) of Latin learning. More widespread changes in how people viewed language and the cultural context of rhetoric were beginning the process of transformation over the long eighteenth century so that new and modern rhetorics eventually replace classical rhetorics in most modern institutions. Rhetoric begins its existence as an "art of positionality" in discourse (Bender and Wellbery 7) and it ends somewhat the way it began. However, now the rhetors-interlocutors have changed; they are no longer citizens or courtiers but chiefly the rising middle class seeking to advance or consolidate their social positions or their self-images as rising gentry with a transformed rhetoric.

These transformations in discourse have only recently become recognizable to us. Perhaps this is because we are witnessing the breakdown of old discursive practices that had become naturalized and that seem to have no history at all, much less a history imbricated in eighteenth-century language and rhetoric. The next chapter explores some of the intellectual and cultural context of these transformations to hybrid rhetorics of modernity.

3
Transformations in Western Rhetoric and Language

> The Revolution cited ancient Rome, just as fashion cites an anti-
> quated dress. Fashion has a scent for what is current, whenever this
> moves within the thicket of what was once.
> —Walter Benjamin, cited by Jürgen Habermas
> in "Modernity and Postmodernity"

> The increase in the status of language does not endow the arts of
> verbal language with the same primacy and power of motivation
> enjoyed by music in the pre-romantic and romantic periods, with
> their great theory of harmony. It is not the arts of language which
> are foregrounded but language *per se,* with the result that it becomes
> the paradigm for all the other arts.
> —Henri Lefebvre, *Introduction to Modernity*

One can find no more clear or charming emblem of the transformation
to modernity than John Locke's herbarium. This botanical collection
comprises two large volumes from his library, manuscripts created in the
years he taught at Oxford, two large, bound folios containing pressed
flowers, *Herbarium Vivum,*

> objects which gave such a shock of excitement when they first
> came to light, daffodils and larkspur, deadnettle, and bettony,
> still yellow, purple, white, and green . . . some of the oldest
> flowers of the English countryside to survive from the time
> when the countryside was the universal background to En-
> glish life. (Harrison and Laslett 26)[1]

Locke finally collected almost a thousand specimens between 1661 and
1665 when he studied and taught at Oxford. They were gleaned from
the Oxford Botanic Garden, which was also called the Physick Garden

because botany was a medical study. However, as Locke had no heavy book paper upon which to mount the flowers, he substituted the exercises delivered by his undergraduate pupils of Christ Church—their Latin themes and verses, along with one exercise in Greek. Thus, Locke's specimens are "meticulously set out and annotated on pages which bear the boyish hand of his pupils," so that the volumes "comprise not only a great collection of early English flowers and plants but also by far the largest number of undergraduate exercises, not many of them corrected it may be said, to survive from seventeenth century universities" (26). These pages, their classical writings overlaid by the inscriptions of what had become for Locke a new, more absorbing course of studies, parallel the seventeenth-century's reinscription of scholastic and humanistic study by natural philosophy, of *verba* by *res*—the flowers of rhetoric literally overlaid with flowers of nature. Not surprisingly, Locke, whose philosophical texts would similarly preserve and offer up the modern thought he found all around him, wrote not in Latin but in English. One of the touchstones of modernity is this turn from the culture of classical Latin to literature and literary studies in the mother tongue, the vernacular. In France—the country in the middle, between Italy and England, the country in which Locke began his turn to modernity—advocates had argued the case for the vernacular for more than two centuries. French was to be the international language of the Enlightenment, not English. Thus the year 1549, the date of Joachim DuBellay's *La Déffence et Illustration de la langue françoyse,* provides as likely a spot as any to step onto the threshold of modernity. However, the emergence of this text is not *the* beginning but is *a* beginning, a middling step onto the threshold.[2]

The defense of the French language as opposed to Latin was part of a larger effort by humanists to free letters from the Church and also from the grasp of Scholastic educators. However, DuBellay's work also serves to mark the intensification of the struggle of French intellectuals against the domination of Italian humanists. DuBellay comes in the middle of forces pushing for use of the vernacular: he follows and responds to earlier Italian promoters of the mother tongue who dominated European letters—the Tuscan poets Dante (1265–1321), Petrarch (1304–1371), and Boccaccio (1313–1375). These poets wielded great power over the early European intellectual community, gaining dominance and devotees over centuries with the beauty of their language and force of their arguments.

The ongoing promotion of the vulgar tongue was bound up with a revival of Greek and Latin literature by humanists who, notably, were adherents of Ciceronian rhetoric. Early humanism signified an effort to laicize and free letters from Church domination and from scholastic Latin. The return of Greek and also Hebrew with humanism made possible the Reformation and the reading of the Bible in vulgate. The Reformation was perhaps the greatest cause of the undermining of Latin culture, and the counter-Reformation marshalled not only Inquisitorial force but the beauty of art and an emotional rhetoric in its defense.

As the decades passed, vernacularization was identified more and more with nationalism. In France, as the monarchy strengthened with Louis XIV, the struggle was transformed into advocacy of the language of the king. The *bon usage* of the courts became the standard for elegance in spoken, then written French. Humanism over time came to be seen as associated with Italy, the church, and their dominance. However, before this time, DuBellay had declared war against Tuscan literary hegemony as well as the sacred language of Rome. René Descartes joined him in the early-seventeenth century, disparaging the arts of Latin rhetoric in favor of everyday argument in the vernacular. By the second half of the seventeenth century, the moderns were winning the Querrelle des Anciens and Modernes in France. The prestige of French philosophy and letters was growing, the French waxing while Italian waned.

However, the Quarrel was not as clear as its polarized name suggests, even seen from the middle distance. For, in their own terminology, the moderns practiced devouring and transforming the ancients. So, the quarrel was not a question of choosing a return to the past, nor was it simply a call for imitation of the ancients. As the Romans devoured the Greeks and turned them into nourishment and blood, many in the Quarrel sought to transpose and adapt the ancients for new times. Pascale Casanova calls this a "*détournement* of capital" of the literary economy, an economy that early on was held mainly in ancient literary stock (80). We should also take note of Andrew E. Benjamin's point about citation and fashion in the epigraph. It became fashionable to cite the ancients even—or often especially—in the act of declaring difference from the past and thus modernity.

Like Descartes and Cartesians such as the Port Royalists, whom Locke read early in his career on a sojourn in France, he was an early adopter and promoter of modernism and the use of the vernacular. In his educational writings, he advocated doing away with student themes in Latin—clearly, whatever their number, he had read far too many as a tutor at Oxford. Yet, though he recommends vernacular writers, he does not go so far as to do away with Latin—in his educational advice, he particularly encouraged the reading of Cicero to form a gentlemanly style and acquaintance. Locke's *An Essay Concerning Human Understanding* and letter on education spread throughout Europe and fed back into England as it was devoured and transformed, in particular by the French. Four decades after Locke's death in 1704, his follower Condillac would begin to revise and operationalize Locke's theories in both philosophical and pedagogical programs. Condillac would, however, return language, the social, and the body to the center of his inquiries into knowledge. Lockean language theory is a common cord knotting up the narrative of modernity running through these three figures in their various locations.

In his 1708 address *On Method in Contemporary Fields of Study,* Vico treated Locke purely as a Cartesian in reacting against Cartesian thought. As seen clearly from our middle standpoint, his oration constitutes an important Italian response to the growing dominance of French thought. However, Vico cannot be dismissed simply as an anti-modern—he approved of English science.[3] He named Francis Bacon as one of his four great influences; the others were Plato, Tacitus, and Grotius. By Vico's day, Isaac Newton had written his *Principia Mathematica* (1687) and his *Opticks* as well (1704). Newton had also dabbled in Hebrew linguistics and Biblical chronology as did Vico, who recognized their intellectual kinship. Vico sent Newton a copy of his masterwork *New Science* several years before Newton died.[4] Despite the constraints of the Inquisition and Spanish, followed by Austrian, rule, Neapolitan intellectual culture was lively, international, and scientific. In the seventeenth century, Lord Shaftesbury had visited Naples and cross-pollinated British language theory, stressing the notion that human language and culture developed in tandem. In the first half of the century in Naples, Vico stood at the confluence of the major modern philosophical streams and the waning Renaissance humanism emphasizing classical thought.

If Naples was not the intellectual backwater it has often been presumed, it is still clear that for France the end of the seventeenth century and the first half of the eighteenth were a golden age of belles lettres. The French genius for rationalism, however, became hybridized with a practical English empiricism and residual neoclassicism. After writing *Lettres Philosophiques* (1733), Voltaire spread Newtonian thought in his translation *Elements of the Philosophy of Newton* (1738). Language theory by English thinkers spread throughout Europe, especially Warburton's *Divine Legation of Moses* (1737–1741). Condillac, one of the few true philosophers of the French Enlightenment, was one of many who read this work and built his own theories of language origins in his *Essay on the Origin of Human Knowledge* of 1746 that treated language and knowledge in a Lockean vein. Rousseau (a friend and once tutor to Condillac's nephews) and other French *philosophes* learned of Condillac's language theories through conversation or his influence on Denis Diderot and Jean le Rond d'Alembert's new *Encyclopédie*. However, Condillac was not only a philosopher but a teacher. His pedagogical theories and course of study were adopted as revolutionary in France after his death in 1780.

Whether read in French or in English—Condillac's *Essay* was translated into English in 1756—Condillac was devoured in turn by the Scots. Figures including Adam Smith, David Hume, Hugh Blair, and Lord Kames used Condillac and similar contemporary language theorists in their modern literary and philosophical treatises. Lord Monboddo read at least a review of Condillac; they shared many sources, especially Mandeville and Warburton. Language theory was a foundational element in the Scottish Enlightenment in the second half of the eighteenth century, and French language theory nourished it. The newly united Protestant Great Britain grew in economic and military power throughout the century, primarily fostered by wars with Catholic France. In part because of trade (notably Bordeaux wines) and in part because of the Jacobite cause, Scotland early in the century remained closer to France and French theory.

Despite the attacks by Locke and many others, British universities remained rigidly classical throughout the century. Much of the intellectual vigor of French modernity flowed from France to Scotland and to Scottish and other dissenters' colleges (see Miller). However, Scottish linguistics in turn would feed back into European thought—most immediately and pertinently diffused from Vico and Condillac but also directly from Monboddo to Herder, informing German Romanticism, and to von Humboldt and the beginning of modern linguistics. All the conflicts of the earlier eighteenth century, all the paradoxes and tensions were carried in these theories of language and rhetoric: debates about language and knowledge, about different ways of knowing, and whether to value the passions, the intuition or the reason, the importance of the history of human culture, the status of the imagination, questions about the relations of cognition and the senses, implications of various theories of mind for human social organization—all are worked out in language theory by the last quarter of the century. Most thinkers on language at the end of the eighteenth century—as with these three figures from across the period—had feasted on Locke's work of a century earlier, and it was still providing fodder for active rumination.

To shift the metaphor, some of the important intellectual and cultural capital invested in modern language and rhetoric can thus be found in three major deposits: first, theories invested in revising or extending Cartesian thought and later Lockean philosophy; second, transformations of language theories based on classical or neoclassical thought; and third, interwoven theories and practices of belles lettres. The next section will elucidate these three because they directly affect the modern and countermodern tendencies in the texts of our three figures.

The interest on these intellectual deposits was often paid in sharp conflicts inherent in language study and rhetoric: debates over sensualism and rational thought (see Ricken, for example), the neoclassical turn to neo-Epicurean schemes (discussed by Kroll), and the conflict between country and court in England that Pocock discusses in political terms and McIntosh has described in terms of common and courtly language. The growing power of the middle class in England particularly focused attention on the power of general human reason. In France, *raison* had perhaps broader associations and networks with discourses on the senses, imagination, and passion. By century's end, in both England and France, values and practices from aristocratic or courtly language were transformed into politeness or cultivated language and claimed also by the bourgeoisie (see Miller). However, politeness became more than just a private social ritual, it became political—a civic virtue and a type of desired citizen for education to reproduce.

My discussion of these matters reveals how language was often theorized at the crossroads of mind and body, occurring at the site of articulation of the mind-body split of rationalism and empiricism. The abstraction of mind from body, however, is only possible with the overshadowing—the occultation—of the social body from the modern individual mind and body. At the inception of this theory and infused into its being was Descartes's dualistic system of spirit and matter, soul and body, as well as his severance of metaphysics and physics.

Cartesian Linguistics and Rhetoric

Descartes's system cleaved into a metaphysics that did not threaten established religion and into a physics that was able to be perceived as materialist. His physiology, for example, was based on minuscule atoms or corpuscles striking the body and carrying ideas such as color, weight, and sound to the mind to be distributed by animal spirits to the muscles mechanically, as in an automaton. Animals—mechanized beasts—were seen as nothing more than automatons (see the detailed discussion by Hanafi for examples). Shocked by Galileo's conviction in 1633 for advocating Copernican theory, Descartes emphasized the dualism in his system, maintaining an orthodox spirituality.

Significantly, human language stood at the intersection of body and soul as the distinguishing mark of human beings. Descartes's suturing of physics and metaphysics worked mysteriously or, some would say, impossibly—like the soap that Peter Pan hoped would stick his shadow to his figure. Human language was also dualistic, both material and spiritual; nonetheless, its spiritual essence was given by God and was noncorporeal but intellectual, belonging to the soul. The proof of this to Descartes was the arbitrary character of the sign, the mark of the separation of thought and language. For if a word could be expressed otherwise—in, for example, another language—the concept itself must be innate and ideal. Sound and the physical mechanism of mouth and tongue were physical, but the idea itself was intellectual, spiritual, from God. As Hans Aarsleff notes, in the Cartesian view, knowledge is also private, "For in the Augustinian sense, we do not truly learn anything from anybody. God alone is the teacher. Communication is key." Thus the social contract was needed to "ensure social bonding"[5] (*From Locke to Saussure* xii).

Cartesian rationalist language theory was but one of many positions on language theory at the time, and it was by no means immediately accepted. Ulrich Ricken's history of French language theory follows the antagonism of opposing camps of rationalists and sensualists that he makes a mainspring of change over the century.

The opposition to Descartes spoke out loudly and claimed its adherents. Responses to Descartes's *Méditations métaphysiques* (1641) came from Thomas Hobbes and Pierre Gassendi, emphasizing the sensual nature of humans. Rationalists were religiously scrupulous, careful not to contradict the spiritual realm; sometimes sensualism was seen as a threat to established religion, but not always. The Aristotelian axiom that there is nothing in the mind that is not first in the senses was a common Scholastic dictum *(Nihil est in intellectu quod non prius fuerit in sensu)*. However, this old saw, when repeated in combination with something new—the emerging emphasis on the centrality of the imagination— would produce something new.

A return to St. Augustine, Bishop of Hippo, was one factor in the new emphasis on the imagination; Augustinian theory converged with notions of the Epicurean image. According to an Augustinian Biblical view, humans once were spiritual creatures, but since the Fall, they must live a predominantly physical existence. The imagination, the faculty of storing and reviving images, was often described as the intermediary between human's physical and spiritual natures, between the senses and pure thought. It was, significantly, the faculty of representation. The centrality of the imagination as intermediary is held by many throughout the century. Therefore, it will be helpful to keep tabs on the relation of the passions and the imagination and language in Descartes, but also later, in Vico, Condillac, and Monboddo.

To Descartes, who is not always consistent in the matter, the imagination is linked with a purely mechanical revival of sense impressions. Animals have only this low-level recall of sense impressions. However, for humans, representation functions in two realms—on the spiritual level in pure thought without images and on the physical level in the sensuous representations of the imagination.

For Descartes, language functions in the realm of the physical, involving both imagination and memory, which work together in the faculty of the imagination. Descartes's rejection of rhetorical teachings, in part a reaction against the Scholastic method, also grows out of a Platonic denigration of the physical and the dependence of persuasion (at least, of those lower on the social scale) upon pathos and appeals to physical appetites. Because persuasion depends on lower appetites or instincts, it is not surprising that Descartes ranks the vernacular rhetorical capabilities of the peasant woman of Brittany as equal to classically trained rhetoricians. Natural eloquence of this type is not, however, valued as much as a pure, nonmaterialized, and imagistic idea[6] (Ricken 11).

In contrast, for Hobbes, all knowledge of the world comes from the senses: our world is all body and motion, and the soul is only the physical movement of the organic body. Words and reason together depend on the imagination, which Hobbes agrees is a physical cognitive faculty. Thought *itself* depends on language, he believed; thus it may be physical. He refuses Descartes's dualistic system of cognition, in which thought occurs in parallel processes in the physical brain and in the spiritual center, linked only by the arbitrary sign, and he makes a key distinction between the "meanings expressed by phonetic forms and the things to which they referred" (Ricken 21). Hobbes's mental conceptions follow each other in associative ways in the imagination, constituting private, internal discourse. Private marks or a public system of signs (language) become necessary to guarantee our memories of the train of these conceptions. It is the fallibility of memory that causes thought to depend upon a public system of signs.[7] Although these notions seem radical, Hobbes actually accepts more traditional ways of thought than does Locke, remaining closer to Scholasticism and producing a neoclassical rhetoric.[8]

Whereas rationalists focused on the nonlinguistic nature of ideas, sensualists such as Hobbes and Gassendi tended to give more weight to language. Locke studied in France and, outside of rejecting innate ideas, reiterates much of Descartes's rationalism. In Locke's *Essay,* he combines rationalism and a sensualism close to Gassendi's with British empiricism. A sensualist, Gassendi opposed Descartes. (Nonetheless, they both sought new conceptions of science to overturn the entrenched Scholasticism of the universities.) Gassendi's work proposes that the key to understanding is the imagination, the faculty of representation, and, like Hobbes, he believed in the physicality of the brain and its cognitive capacities. Unlike Descartes, whose dualism led to the view that animals were automatons, Gassendi believed animals and humans had much in common and that animals do have communicative capabilities. Gassendi points to the eighteenth-century shift away from theories that separate humans from animals and toward theories of natural sociability upon which communication rested.

Yet the opposition between rationalists and sensualists can be traced to an older conflict of Epicurus and Lucretius and to Platonic and Augustinian notions of language and thought, which led to different outcomes in inquiry into what it was to be human:

> But the antagonism between the basic rationalistic position of the one and the sensualistic position of the other could not be so easily resolved. Whereas Gassendi combined a new ideal of the natural sciences with the conception of humanity as a primarily physical and sensual being by linking this ideal to the assumption that all human knowledge stems from sense experience, Descartes's conception of humanity originated in the a priori notion of an intellectual substance that was opposed to a material one. (Ricken 23)

Language was the bridge linking the two, once more at the center of an effort to define what it means to be human.

Cartesian thought is often linked with the Port Royalists and their followers who produced influential rhetoric and logic texts (although they are more than just transpositions of Cartesian thought into rhetoric). Descartes and the Jansenists were associated with Pascal and the Port Royalists, Antoine Arnauld, and Claude Lancelot. Like Descartes, these rationalists generally hold to innate ideas and the divine origins of language, believing in an inner spiritual nature of language itself.

The Port Royal school had opened in Port Royal, France, in 1643 and moved to Paris in 1646. The Port Royal *Grammar* (*Grammaire générale et raisonnée, contenant . . . Les raisons de ce qui est commun à toutes les langues, et des principales différences qui s'y rencontrent*, 1660) is now seen as a hybrid of earlier conceptions of language and Cartesian philosophy rather than a transposition of Descartes into grammatical theory (see Ricken). It was written by Arnauld and Lancelot, with Lancelot as primary author. The Port Royal *Logic* (*La Logique ou l'art de penser*, 1662), however, by Arnauld and Pierre Nicole, was primarily written by Arnauld and combines Cartesianism with Jansenism,[9] Augustinianism, and philosophy of language. The authors believed that Gassendi the sensualist was in conflict with religion. They echo catchphrases from Descartes, especially his notions of clear-and-distinct ideas, and agree that the bedrock of evidence is his credo "I think, therefore, I am." They espouse a return to the vernacular but also a return to oral speech over written dead languages.

They also propounded the arbitrary nature of signs, for Augustine believed the sounds of language had no connection with the ideas they expressed. It is only through habit that the soul learns to combine mental representations of ideas with mental representations of sounds. Thus imagination coupled with habit—both important in modernist rhetorics—early takes on a major role in language learning, with the Port Royal rhetoric and logic popularizing the concepts.

In Port Royalist rhetorical theory, although rhetoric is linked with a debased physical existence, it is yet necessary. Since the Fall, humans prefer sense to intellect. Therefore, on earth we must use persuasion based on the nonintellectual pathos and ethos, for humans accept truth more easily when they are in the right emotional state. Thus, figures of speech are important expressions of passion, needed for persuasion, as are intonation, gesture, and facial expression. Logos remains, of course, on a higher plane because intellect is associated with universal rules.[10] In contrast, the passions cannot have rules, because they are too changeable. The volatility and variability of passions determine the nature of rhetoric. Curiously, rhetoric represents a cultural phenomenon outside natural laws because of its basis in nature; but because of its contingent nature, no absolute rules are possible. Language itself remains somewhat debased, linked as it is with the physical. It is often described as a tool or instrument to convey preexisting and spiritual ideas. This tendency becomes at once neoclassical and belletristic.

Locke's Cartesian and Newtonian Language and Rhetoric

Locke's *Essay* paid enormous dividends in language theory, especially for Condillac and Monboddo. Locke and his role in rhetoric have become a central feature, a benchmark, in H. Lewis Ulman's terms, in our present histories. Significant to this inquiry, Locke has been used as a touchstone for the modern in rhetoric, particularly by Howell. In somewhat earlier scholarship, because of his arguments against innate ideas, Locke was seen in opposition to Descartes. More recently, the many parallels between Locke's work and Cartesian theory have been foregrounded, and Lockean philosophy has been seen as both empiricist and rationalist. Although Locke displaces notions of innate ideas, he does allow for innate cognitive faculties, something Condillac faults him for. Locke emphasizes the importance of the senses and experience from the senses yet repeats and develops Cartesian and Port Royalist beliefs about ideas, language, and rhetoric. He symbolizes the reinscription and transformation of Cartesian philosophy after Newtonianism swept Britain early in the eighteenth century and crept stealthily into Continental philosophy by midcentury.

Locke and his *Essay* represent a complex and controversial phenomenon in eighteenth-century cultural history of language and rhetoric. As Aarsleff puts it:

> The *Essay* was literally epoch-making, and such works never fail to efface their own past; in fact, one can almost say that the *Essay* has no other history than that which was its own future, as if Locke merely wrote to give Berkeley and Hume something to write about. (*From Locke to Saussure* 43)

However, Aarsleff goes on to point out that Locke, unlike Gottfried Wilhelm Leibniz, did not name his sources or leave voluminous citations or letters discussing the evolution of his *Essay*. As a result, and because of peculiar and narrow nineteenth-century readings of Locke, we are only now discovering how much Locke stands as a synthesis and key to divergent seventeenth-century theories of language and thought. Like Vico, he is an owl of Minerva, signifying the close of one era as well as the dawning of the new, or one could just as well say Newtonian.

Locke's attention to language and rhetoric was informed by his reading of Descartes, the Port Royal *Logic* and *Grammar,* and Lancelot's grammars during the four years he spent in France (Aarsleff, *From Locke to Saussure* 45).[11] He also read and absorbed much of the associated French belletrism. His epistemology was drawn from the Ciceronianism of both Continental and British seventeenth-century culture as well from the associated Epicureanism, which, harmonizing with Newtonianism, also influenced Robert Boyle and other Royal Society members. Locke also studied and later taught classics, including Latin composition, at Oxford. In Britain, the popularity of Locke's work helped bring about the transformation of rhetoric from scholastic and classical models toward the modern theories of knowledge, aesthetics, and psychology in eighteenth-century rhetoric, especially in Scotland. Notably through Condillac, French language and rhetorical theory appropriated Locke, and by the eighteenth century's end, the Scots had received both the Anglo and the French interpretations and popularizations of Locke, which they immediately recombined into wonderfully fertile rhetorics.

Socially, Locke's family belonged to the smaller landowning gentry of the Puritan trading class (Cranston 5). As a reward for his father's battles on the side of Parliament in the Civil War, Locke received a true gentleman's education and rose in social standing. Early in his career he was an Oxford don, and like many interested in signs and signifying, he was a physician. As is well known, the *Essay* was begun shortly after Locke officially became a Royal Society member in 1668, although it was not published until after twenty years of constant revision. His other texts that can be found weaving in and out of rhetorics of the period are his logic, *The Conduct of the Understanding,* published posthumously in 1706, and *Some Thoughts Concerning Education,* a model compilation of advice on child rearing written as a letter to a distant relative and appearing in 1693. Like other texts coming out of a period of national disruption (most notable Monboddo's), he values order, stability, civility, and tolerance, and especially in light of his political involvement, his epistemology and language theory should be read as inquiries prompted by the national political context. His arguments against an emotional rhetoric can then be seen as symbolizing his political and social alignments as much as a literal statement of his rhetorical theory.[12]

Locke's *Essay* takes as its approach the "historical, plain method" of Boyle and Newton, with his language theory concentrated in book 3, "Of Words" (*Essay* 1.1.2: 44). This chapter is sandwiched between the first and second chapters, which deny innate ideas and discussing experience as a basis for knowledge and the fourth, which discusses knowledge as a set of mental operations performed upon ideas. Through all, Locke maintains that words are signs for ideas, and that all humans can ever know is their own idea of things, not the real essences of things themselves. Michael Ayers calls this ideational theory *concept-empiricism*, in which all our ideas derived from experience, as opposed to *knowledge-empiricism*, in which propositional knowledge is ultimately based on sensory knowledge (1: 14). However finely we may read Locke's intent, eighteenth-century (and later) commentators clearly take him both ways, as well as interpreting language theory in Locke's essay in multiple other senses. His self-reflexive method, part of his rejection of innate ideas, was revised and extended by Condillac. It is harmonious with other historical methods, including tracing of etymologies at the end of the seventeenth century. It also led to developmentalism, especially in regard to language origins. Paradoxically, and although his *Essay* intensified the genealogical thrust in philosophy of language, Locke was the least interested in speculating about language origins, his interest in language being but a means to explore his primary concern of the extent and certainty of the understanding.

In his *Essay,* Locke calls words "signs of internal conceptions," "marks for the *Ideas* within [Man's] own Mind, whereby they might be made known to each other, and the Thoughts of Man's Minds be conveyed from one to another" (3.1: 402). Such a mentalistic linguistic theory has been termed *semantic idealism* because statements have no meaning unless they correspond to ideas present in the speaker's mind. The privacy and individuality Locke's language theory rests on leads to communicational skepticism because no two individuals will have precisely the same ideas in mind at the same time (although the ideas may be qualitatively the same). The lack of faith in clear communication poses a problem for scientific discourse and knowledge that Locke attempts to solve in *Essay* by laying down rules for language use. Yet at moments in Locke's text, language represents the very social contract itself, moving out from its individualist foundations. Language in use provides the central switchboard for connecting individuals' private visions.

Aarsleff contrasts Adamic theories, or theories of natural language where words bear essential qualities of things, to theories of intentional or arbitrary nature of words. Locke argues against Adamic theories in this sense, arguing against the double conformity of signs—their conformity both to the essences of things they represent and intersubjectively to others' ideas of things. Not only are signs and signifieds arbitrarily linked in Locke, but words do not reveal essence and knowledge. Instead, they are "perfect cheat[s]" (*Essay* 3.10: 508), problematizing the very possibility of our knowledge. Locke, then, follows Descartes in the arbitrariness of the sign if he disproves his principle of innateness. However, Locke's language theory remains undeveloped and rationalist, something Condillac will critique him for in *Essay on the Origin of Human Understanding*.

In addition to new revisions of Ciceronian and Epicurean texts in Locke's synthetic text, late Aristotelian and Scholastic texts are very much still present in Lockean epistemology. Locke describes the process of coming to know as a two-step operation: first the senses perceive, then the mind reflects on these perceptions. Sense perception itself is involuntary and passive, but reflection is an active process under human control. Along with this perception-reflection duality, Locke offers another pair, primarily from Epicurean theory—that of primary and secondary qualities of things. Primary or original qualities are essential to physical things, while secondary qualities are colors, sounds, smells, and tastes produced in us by the primary qualities in things. Locke further classifies ideas into simple or complex—singular ideas or ideas compounded of simples and combinations of simple ideas. The first cannot be learned from language through a process like definition but must be objected directly from experience in a passive manner. Complex ideas come more under human control and can generally be transmitted by language, if with difficulty. To understand and communicate clearly, complex ideas must be analytically divided into their component simples and words applied to the simple ideas that make up the complex idea, a process similar to Platonic collection and division in *Phaedrus*. Using Scholastic terminology, Locke also breaks down complex ideas into *modes, substances,* and *relations.* Modes are further divided into simple and mixed, and it is these mixed modes and relations that are always adequate to the human-created mental reality of the mental patterns they represent. Through mixed modes in particular—abstract ideas such as beauty, gratitude, glory, and theft—a social and constructivist strain enters Locke's text. Language, the ground of the social contract, is nonetheless always in tension with individual mental experience.

Despite Locke's frequent emphasis on words, he is not a nominalist because of the priority of these mental ideas. He does see knowledge and words as with "so near a connexion" as to be "scarce separable," even if they are not the same (*Essay* 3.9: 488). However, because language is imperfect, the closeness of language to knowledge creates difficulties that he attempts to resolve in his discussion of the abuse of language, where he cites six imperfections and their remedies (*Essay* 3.10: 490–508). These abuses include first, using words with no clear ideas; second, using words inconsistently; third, using jargon or "affected obscurity," taking words for things instead of ideas (*Essay* 3.10: 493); fourth, making words stand for the real essences of things; fifth, using words whose meaning is unclear to others, a difficulty at a time when English had to borrow from Latin because of lack of words; and finally, using figurative speech in discourse intended to instruct. The last abuse led to Locke's often cited denunciation of a figural rhetoric in which he portrays rhetoric as a seductress attempting to deceitfully draw men away from truth (*Essay* 3.10: 508, par. 34).

The *Essay* also includes an Epicurean theory of attraction and repulsion of ideas similar to the Port Royal *Logic* but that is more often linked with Newtonian axioms. Knowledge or truth to Locke is the perception of the agreement or disagreement of ideas, "as Things signified by them do agree or disagree on with another" (4.5: 574, par. 2). In his hierarchy of certainty, Locke writes that knowledge can come directly and immediately through intuition, the highest level of certainty in knowledge; mediately by reason or demonstration involving chains of inference; or directly by the senses. The bringing of ideas together to compare or judge their agreement or disagreement is at best a rational, conscious, controlled mental operation. Involuntary association of ideas is suspect, its connections quickly rejected by Locke as eccentric, even linked with madness. Somewhat contradictorily, overquickness in making connections between ideas is disparaged as "wit," placed into opposition with the more valued "judgment," as in Hobbes.

Theories of associationism shaping eighteenth-century philosophy and rhetoric are often attributed to Locke. Nonetheless, Locke's own theory of association is part of his attempt to control associations and enforce greater rationality. Both Condillac and Vico also theorize on mental operations involving associations, Vico approving of instantaneous leaps to connect diverse matters, crediting them as demonstrating ingenuity, and Condillac basing his theory on conscious ordering and linearity in connections. Monboddo, late in the century in Scotland, draws from the rich discussions of associationism of his compatriots.

Translating Boyle's and Newton's natural philosophies into language theory, Locke's texts transmit some of the same values of moderation, tolerance, and hopes for peace and political stability, primarily through a stable oligarchical rule in England. This political balance, which Locke himself helped to bring about in the Glorious Revolution of 1688, was based on parliamentarianism and a limited monarchy. As well, it relied upon harmonious economic, religious, and scientific world views that have been identified as modern. A growing gentry capitalism, secularism, and mathematico-technological progressivism have been hallmarks of this movement to modernity. However, the objective correlatives for the modern in rhetoric are not yet well understood.

The Classical Tradition

The continuing pervasiveness of the classical canon meant that most educated persons had studied rhetorical texts, as well as the standards in language theory, such as Aristotle's *Rhetoric* and *Poetics* and much of Plato, especially *Phaedrus* and *The Cratylus,* the latter his dialogue on natural versus conventional language, in which the debate in the book over whether language is natural or conventional essentially comes to a standoff. Also key are Lucretius's *De rerum natura* and Cicero's *Orator,* as well as other works less familiar to us today. How these and other texts were creatively read and appropriated in mid-seventeenth century is only now being appreciated. Twentieth-century elevation of Romantic literature and its major figures has left us with many histories (in both literature and rhetoric) that plot neoclassical thought as the dull foil for a keener Romantic thrust.

Our contemporary return of rhetoric is in part responsible for the replotting and revival of Enlightenment studies; in addition, the rebirth of rhetoric also renewed interest in classical and neoclassical texts. New work on neoclassicism has enriched and added intellectual excitement to what had previously been considered dull.[13]

Classical rhetoric was centrally organized by place as well as time— the public forum, where ceremonial rhetoric celebrated the present; the legislature, where deliberative rhetoric projected the future; and, finally, the courts, where judicial rhetoric weighed the past, although Plato and others also integrated personal settings such as in the *Phaedrus* dialogue. The tradition of classical rhetoric fed various streams, from a more informal and privatized tradition of sermons to the better-known channel institutionalized by the Scholastics and a primarily Latin language culture, centered in the seventeenth century on Aristotle. By the late-seventeenth century, many, especially in England, were openly hostile to the latter logic-based tradition. Nevertheless, the culture was so steeped in the contradictions of Aristotelian thought that it became necessary to use Aristotelian argument even in arguing against it. At the same time as a Baconian spirit of inquiry fueled the millenarianism of the time, the expanding middle classes more and more declined to attend the classics-based public schools. Respect for the vernacular was everywhere on the rise, although concurrently, Latin terminologies were being translated, if at first awkwardly, into vernacular languages. Yet the culture of Latin learning held firm, leaning to the civic ideals of the Roman republic and Ciceronianism in England, France, and Naples.

Ciceronian civic rhetoric celebrated debate in the law courts and public assemblies, appropriate in Britain, France, and especially the kingdom of Naples in the eighteenth century. Ciceronian and Epicurean philosophies informed polite literature and conversations in private settings. Ciceronian rhetorical canons were appropriable by those in various rhetorical traditions: those holding to the full range of rhetorical arts and sciences could rely on Cicero's presentation of the five canons or offices of rhetoric: invention, arrangement, style, memory, and delivery. Others in the traditions of Renaissance stylistic rhetorics found Cicero's principles of appropriate and effective style useful and repeated his advice on the three levels of high or elaborate, middle, and low or plain style. Both stylists and those building their rhetorics around models of texts, whom Howell terms the *formulists,* also turned to the late-Greek rhetorician pseudo-Longinus, whose *On the Sublime* was translated by Nicolas Boileau-Despréaux in the seventeenth century as well as variously into English in the following century. These Ciceronian and Longinian stylistic rhetorics also formed the backbone of the Continental belles lettres movement transformed by the Scots over the century.[14]

Concerning Britain, Adam Potkay believes there was a tension in the eighteenth century between this classical or neoclassical strain of eloquence and the values of belletristic rhetoric:

> Tensions between a nostalgia for ancient eloquence and an emerging ideology of polite style defines both the literary and political discourses of mid-eighteenth-century Britain. . . . Politeness, a social ideology in formation, gains ascendance over, but never manages to silence, the renascent republican ideal of eloquence and its masculinized political assumptions. (1)

He describes this scene of eloquence as often set in Athens, with Demosthenes the orator-hero. However, it moves to Rome in the republican era, with the Roman Senate representing the British Parliament, the public sphere of print in part replacing the public forum.[15]

Civic virtue among free men holding public debate is foremost in this republican value system, which Potkay and others have linked to masculinist ideals (Potkay 3). As the eighteenth century progresses, "the clamor of feminizing sentiment" waxes (Potkay 2). The belletristic theme of politeness Potkay identifies with feminine values and a shift to greater inclusion of women in public discourse.

Politeness is both a literary and social ideal, contrasting with eloquence as a style that "seeks to placate or stabilize rather than to make things happen; and as an ethos of concealment, entailing an aesthetic of invisibility—an ethos thought suitable to a sexually integrated public sphere and family circle" (Potkay 5). Potkay identifies the key factor in the shift in discursive models to shifting configurations of political power over the century in Britain.[16] So in addition to operating in the literary and social realms, politeness is shown to be political.

Richard W. Kroll's history of language, *The Material Word: Literate Culture in the Restoration and Early-Eighteenth Century,* not only reconceives the historiography of the period as one of a "multiple discursive reorientations" (94), but he reemphasizes the seventeenth-century appropriation of notions of the Epicurean image. During the Restoration, this interest in and attention to the secular, nonidolatrous image come to provide a theory of how the passions are moved and the will stimulated to action, a theory that gets transferred to rhetoric. Blended with the later faculty psychology, Epicurean theory suggests the efficacy of exhibiting (textualized) images to the intellect through the imagination *(phantasia)* to arouse the passions and motivate the will. In Epicurus's philosophy, especially as interpreted through Lucretius's first-century-BCE *De rerum natura,*

> the atomic and dynamic constitution of bodies causes them continually to throw off microscopically thin representations of themselves *(eidola),* which almost instantaneously strike the eye or another sense organ, producing a presentation *(phantasia).* The mind can then take hold of the image by an act *(epibole).* Thus the entire basis of Epicurus's mental economy presumes the mediating function of the *phantasia.* (Kroll 101)

Although such images are true in that they exist, because of this chain of mediation, primarily involving the image-making faculty, they are not presumed to match the actual nature of things. Epistemologically, this means that judgments of truth are in the realm of the probable, weighed through contingent judgments ultimately concerning language. Similar to Vico's rhetorical epistemology, this methodologically should aim to produce the many possible causes of a matter rather than the one true cause of modernist science. Although neither Vico nor Condillac nor Monboddo uncritically links himself with Epicureanism, this Roman systematizing of a classical Greek philosophy was part of the common archive that is appropriated in their texts.

In the Lucretian version of Epicurean philosophy, mental images are to cognition the equivalent in physics of the atom or minima. They result from the things of the world's continual throwing off of images that strike our minds whether we are asleep or awake; the mind cannot think without images. Lucretius's analogy between atoms and letters of the alphabet finds its way into nearly every major consideration of natural science at the turn of the seventeenth century, both in Bacon and Boyle, and extended to rhetorical topics in Vico's scientific inquiries. This image is a familiar one in Gassendi, whose language theory is itself Epicurean.

For Gassendi, words are *ostensive* (Kroll 128), analogically pointing to things. Utterances partake of symbolic action, pointing to the cognitive image. As Kroll points out, the mind is then free to choose whether or not to assent to the image. This "ethical voluntarism" arises from the free movement of atoms in the void in Epicurean physics—where indivisible physical bodies have freedom of movement (131). The existence of the world itself is attributed to the originary swerve of atoms in the void (the *klinamen*), causing them to collide with each other and bind. Language then becomes a site for freedom of intellect, a tool for inquiry, suppressing superstition and fear (130):

> Gassendi's conceptualist metaphor assumes the activity of individual acts of judgment, which willingly select and bind the atoms of cognition into some larger construct. Hence the perceiver's assent to the cognitive image is inherently voluntary, a determinate act of bridging the cognitive differential between the originary particles of cognition and the perceiver. (Kroll 131)

Finally, the ethical orientation of Epicureanism is symbolized in the mythologized garden and intimate, polite circle of private friends—which could include women and slaves. This image of the quiet, harmonious garden—removed from the violence of the political realm—originally produced during political upheaval, was reactivated by Lucretius during the breakdown of the Roman republic and became again compelling during the rough and tumble of politics and religious furor in both England and the Continent. The ideal of friendship it represents and the avoidance of politics parallel the respect for natural law and the passion for order that became understandably valued in dangerous political climates.[17]

Locke's language theory, in touch with Boyle, resonates with the spirit if not the letter of Epicurean thought. Key Epicurean concepts include the dualism of primary and secondary qualities found in both Locke and Boyle. Vico, Condillac, and Monboddo stand in different relationships to Epicurean as well as other classical lines of thought. In addition, they place different emphasis on and combine differently the textual strands enumerated here. Nonetheless, their discourses share common themes and elements, themes so commonplace over the century as to fade into the eighteenth-century wallpaper. Some would be overshadowed and forgotten as the transformation to modernity proceeded while others would be foregrounded and become so commonplace as to seem natural. Only in early Romantic theory and later with postmodernity would they be called into question. For example, the suppression of the social from language in modernity would intensify a mind-body rift that later thinkers would once more bridge with social theories of language.

Belletrism and Rhetoric

Modern belletristic rhetorics, a phenomenon emerging in the Scottish Enlightenment, do not develop until late in the eighteenth century, but they have their roots in the seventeenth-century rhetorics of René Rapin *(Réflexions sur l'éloquence)*, Bernard Lamy *(La Rhétorique ou, l'art de parler)*, reformist bishop François de Salignac de La Mothe-Fénelon *(Dialogues sur l'éloquence)*, and Charles Rollin *(De la manière d'enseigner et d'étudier les Belles Lettres)*. Eighteenth-century French contributors to belletrism include Dominique Bouhours, Boileau, Abbé Jean-Baptiste DuBos, and the pedagogical systematizer Condillac. Belletristic rhetorics most often maintain language-origin theories as foundational; a driving engine of these rhetorics is a theory of language as originally expressive of human emotion and as poetic at its origins. As language develops, over time it moves away from the emotional force of this origin and becomes more analytical and philosophical than poetic.[18] A correlative theory of the mind holds that because of these emotive and aesthetic origins, the mind remains naturally open and recep-

tive to sensory re-presentations of experience in aesthetic modes of poetry, painting, landscape, and music or in oral or textualized versions
of them. Thus, the visualism and sensualism of Epicurean theory find their
expression in these rhetorics. Developing the receptive and affective competence suggested by Epicureanism and other philosophies becomes a
central aim of later belletristic theories of rhetoric. The linguistic side
of these theories is best articulated and consolidated early in the century
in Condillac's *Essay on the Origin of Human Knowledge,* repeated in
Smith's lectures,[19] and directly cited in Blair's *Lectures on Rhetoric and
Belles Lettres.* Most eighteenth-century Scottish belletrists could read
French and often cite French texts in the original, as do Smith, Blair, and
Campbell. For example, Campbell cites in the original Boileau, DuBos,
Fénelon, and Rollin, along with more than a dozen French authors.

A view of language compatible with these earlier French belletrists
is transmitted in Locke's *Essay Concerning Human Understanding* because Locke portrays the language of children and women as qualitatively different from that of philosophers. The children's and women's
unphilosophical language is not, however, valued as being closer to the
origins of truth, as good belletristic theory would suggest. Instead the
language of primitives is farther from the truth because of the high value
Locke places on philosophical language, at the other end of the developmental spectrum, a language conscious of the clear-and-distinct mental
ideas associated with its words. Locke and his focus on mental contents
is the middle term linking any discussion of relationships between Scottish and French rhetorics. Influenced by Cartesian theorists such as Lamy
and the Port Royalists during his time in France, Locke's language theory
contains the binary between an emotive and aesthetic language and an
analytical philosophical language that we see in later belletristic rhetorics. In Locke's later works on education, we also see training in speaking and writing used in the service of demonstrating class and social rank
through exhibiting a standard of taste, another tie with belletristic rhetorics especially in Scotland.

Eric William Skopec, in the wake of Douglas Ehninger's systems
theory of rhetoric, identifies a system he calls expressive rhetoric that
includes some of the same texts, features, and defining elements as
belletristic rhetoric. Barbara Warnick's book on belles lettres and rhetoric, the *Sixth Canon: Belletristic Rhetorical Theory and Its French Antecedents,* later examines the traits in more detail. Others such as Vincent
Bevilacqua and Dennis R. Bormann have also linked French and Scottish belletrism. However, Warnick's work is the most intensive, making

it possible to begin to assess how French belles lettres contributed to a general transformation in rhetorical theory and the teaching of speaking and writing that continues with us in some measure up to the present.

Warnick focuses on aesthetic receptive competence as well as on three themes or dimensions of belletristic rhetorics and shows how French and Scottish texts relate. Her themes are those of propriety, sublimity, and taste, which she explicates within an Aristotelian framework of logos or intellect, pathos, and ethos. Propriety, the rational component of aesthetic influence, closely tied to experience refers to textual dimensions of a discourse such as style or arrangement. These formalisms create experience in the reader or hearer, experiences that are favorably "proportionate or suitable," and thereby "plausible and satisfying." Sublimity, the second theme, represents the pathetic component of belletristic rhetorics, producing the effect of awe and transport that Boileau reflects in his 1674 translation into French of Longinus's *On the Sublime*. (*On the Sublime* was first translated into English by William Smith in 1737.) However, "[t]he belletrists took care to dissociate this [concept of the] Sublime from strategic use of style and to invest it as a touchstone of creativity, grandeur, and uniqueness." The third theme is that of taste and standards of taste; Warnick notes that propriety and sublimity are textual—qualities of the discourse itself—whereas belletrists locate taste in the recipient. Standards of taste are generally tacitly agreed to be held by an (actual) elite, highly polished group somewhere (5).

Smith, Blair, and Campbell theorized propriety, sublimity, and taste and other dimensions of reception, defining and conceptualizing them into what Warnick terms a Sixth Canon that focuses on receptive competence. This Sixth Canon can also be interpreted as a rewriting of the traditional canon of invention, writing over as it does the emphasis on production of text and language to focus on reception. Several factors were converging in the eighteenth century to transform the traditional canons of rhetoric. As in evolutionary theory, differences in historical and cultural contexts producing different views of the human mind or human nature can produce convergent tendencies in rhetorics. For example, Cartesian psychology is based on a physiology of animal spirits, spirits that run from the pineal gland to the muscles, causing movement. Empiricist psychologies are based on a theory of corpuscles, but both emphasize sensory stimulus in generating emotional response. Moreover, both Cartesian and empiricist rhetorics share a common, familiar metaphor for speaking and writing, that of painting—painting one's emotions and one's internal landscape to produce a sensory effect on the audience.

Skillful writing *will* produce this effect with certainty because of commonalities in human minds that make their responses nearly automatic. These commonalities were more and more frequently through the century referred to by the term *sympathy.*

Rhetorically, one element all belletrists share is a disparaging of and a transformation of—or dispensing with—the classical canon of invention. Invention is not needed because beginning with Lamy's Cartesian rhetoric, belletristic theory rests on a different epistemology from classical rhetoric. Belletrists concern themselves with truths in the external world and how these truths are mirrored or correspond to an internal truth. Therefore, belletristic rhetoric has both a subjective and an objective side. To most theorists this means that the central problem is not one of constructing arguments and truths for and with a social group but of being sensitive to an internal perception of truth and re-presenting it faithfully in language to recreate the experience for the reader or hearer. As we see in Locke, language then becomes a central problem, a problem solved in rhetoric and writing instruction by emphasis on clarity and propriety in discourse. Again, the emphasis is on receptivity over constructivity of discourse.

Yet in the French precursors to belletrism, understanding the audience's receptivity so that it could be manipulated emotionally by insinuative rhetoric became part of the art, an art closely associated with courtly rhetorics. Courtly rhetorics were necessary in cultures without the possibilities of free and open expression: the courtier could thus persuade in a civil, flattering fashion and not be perceived as either threatening or manipulative. Perhaps his time in France left Locke wary of such civic uses of discourse and eager to promote a clear and open dialogue, but in Britain, the motive for rejecting excessively emotional rhetorics was more obviously the turn away from enthusiasm after the political and religious upheavals of the seventeenth century.

At any rate, a courtly rhetoric of insinuation, coupled with a theory of automatic responses by the mind, presents many dangers. It can become deterministic and mechanistic, easily sliding into manipulation by an expert who knows how to play his audience like an instrument—hardly a model for democratic life. (Admittedly, our tendency to condemn it as such, in the wake of twentieth-century fascist rhetorics, may be anachronistic.)

In France at the time, vernacular belletristic rhetorics arose both out of and in reaction to rigidified classicism and the scholastic status quo and became a factor in regulating social letters and social conversation in the salons. If a formalist belletristic rhetoric can be accused of depoliticizing and universalizing human response, making rhetorical and cultural contexts less important, it is no less quietist than the Epicurean conversational garden. However, again, belletrism must be contextualized, for in France, the withdrawals to the private salon were often neither private nor nonpolitical (although many were quietist). The *philosophes* and other salon frequenters were mixed in class, although they tended to be solidly center and rarely marginal figures.

Later Scottish belletristic rhetoric is somewhat different, with conditions in the striving British outpost at once conformist and revolutionary. Thomas P. Miller's account of Scottish rhetoric and English studies is highly critical of this Scottish belletrism. This belletristic rhetoric, along with centralization of education and general assimilation into Great Britain had its costs for the Scots, as Miller points out. Although more study is needed, literacy may actually have been restricted as traditional egalitarian access to education was eclipsed by the more elitist English educational system (Miller 147–48).

In France, after Napoleon, more vigorous belletristic rhetorics lose their standing, resulting in the return of classical approaches in higher education. Thus, Ricken in his language history describes these French belletristic, sensualist approaches as more politically free, but this freedom shuts down with the advent of the Empire.

Whether Scottish belletristic rhetorics can be linked with political freedom is questionable. Early in the nineteenth century when depoliticized Scottish belletristic rhetorics replaced classical rhetorics in the United States, training in public political debate in English classrooms diminished. By century's end, literary study aiming to increase receptive competence and form the taste had replaced a previous focus on production of public discourse. French belletrism did lend itself to standards of wit and conversation carried from court into the freer air of the salons. Because both French and Scottish belletristic rhetorics were written in the vernacular, they also provided greater access for learning by marginalized women and men. By century's end, Condillac's and Blair's similar aesthetic belletristic rhetorics had monopolized the Western world, easily accessible in popular textbooks in Europe in French and across the English-speaking world.[20] We are still assessing the data on the results of this monopoly. Nonetheless, in the U.S., many large public universities have recently returned their first-year composition programs to a theoretical base of civic literacy and argumentation.

The belletrism of Renaissance humanists in the revived texts of

Cicero and literary classicism was the revolutionary starting point for these late theories and practices of belles lettres that fed into early English studies. In previous centuries, it had been the wedge that opened a space for letters closed off by domination of scholasticism and the church. If humanism itself came to be identified with domination by Italian hegemony in religion and letters, it could be devoured and *détourned* to nourish new life. However, Vico prophesied that the new Cartesian-based diet would result in generations of malnourishment for citizens. What appeared to some contemporaries as an art of language more refined, cultivated, and polished *(poli)* to Vico signalled the return of the barbarous. He denounced the growing individualism as the core of the "barbarism of reflection," leading to "deep solitude of spirit and will," so that "no matter how great the throng and press of their bodies, they live like wild beasts" (*New Science* 424). To Vico, only a rhetoric and poetic that worked together to develop a society's common sense and practical wisdom might provide nurturance.

This overview of three major intellectual formations that overlap and interact to form new rhetorics has exposed various strata of older discourses. Mixing religious, political, rhetorical, and literary texts—and particularly mindful of the discourses of emerging science—these crumbling formations provide a rich ground for nurturing our three authors' emerging theories of language and rhetoric. Paying particular attention to the varied strata of discourse in our texts keeps us alert to the polyvocality of our histories. It prevents us from reifying or naturalizing concepts such as the mind-body split, so that we become more acute and critical readers, productive readers with agency. As English studies theorist Robert Scholes writes:

> It is a tenet of semiotic studies—and one to which I fully subscribe—that much of what we take to be natural is in fact cultural. Part of the critical enterprise of this discipline is a continual process of defamiliarization: the exposing of conventions, the discovering of codes that have become so ingrained we do not notice them but believe ourselves to behold through their transparency the real itself. (127)

Some present-day consequences of modern rhetoric might include an uninspiring pedagogy of rhetoric that has broken with the political and lost its role of producing an active citizenry, literary study ruptured from rhetoric and public discourse, disciplines that produce knowledge only an expert can comprehend, rational experts who are minds without bodies; a society fragmented into individuals who must pull themselves up by their own bootstraps and polite but prejudiced citizens who feel passive and alienated from their cities. These are cultural productions, not natural phenomena, nor are they clearly products of a process of modernity, but of a modernity gone awry. This is the present as it might be viewed from the perspective of that critic of the modern Giambattista Vico, a figure on the threshold of modernity.

4
Vico on the Threshold:
Modern Language and Rhetoric

For the first indubitable principle . . . is that this world of nations has certainly been made by men, and its guise must therefore be found within the modifications of our own human mind. And history cannot be more certain than when he who creates the things also narrates them.

—Giambattista Vico, *New Science*

So far as I have been able to discover, Vico is the prototypical modern thinker who, as we shall presently see, perceives beginning as an activity requiring the writer to maintain an unstraying obligation to practical reality and sympathetic imagination in equally strong parts.

—Edward Said, *Beginnings: Intention and Method*

Giambattista Vico's modernity and his ambivalence toward the modern have become increasingly a point of contention in Vico scholarship. Although his title *The New Science* sweeps in Galileo, Francis Bacon, and Isaac Newton, it is disputable in what manner Vico wished to count himself among the moderns of his own time. Nonetheless, reflection upon and critiques of modernity were at the center of his life's work. This is so even though he comes in midlife to reject Cartesian thought (including Locke, whom he saw as Cartesian) and even though he ultimately fails to be recognized as a modern by his contemporaries, who by some accounts suspected that he was neither ancient nor modern but mad.

Today he is variously labeled modern, countermodern, and even antimodern. However, in his day the pertinent tension was between the ancients and the moderns, who were primarily French and Cartesian. Vico's texts work to redefine the paradigm of the ancients and argue for his own proposed version of a modern paradigm as well. Yet his eccentricities and his rethinking of such binary arguments with alternatives such as both-and thinking have helped both doom and redeem Vico for us in the postmodern age. His bricolage and his syncretic thought make him a sublime figure of baroque complexity; his tendency to offer us a third way leads me to view him as one who lingers on the threshold of modernity.

This chapter considers the crossroads joining ancient and modern in Vico's theory, the intersection of his speculative theory of language origins and his rhetorical theory and pedagogy. At the point of merger, Vico offers us a sublime rhetoric of the active and creative mind; yet his rhetoric begins with the body, alternatively and analogically, the social body. For Vico, rhetoric remains necessary for our social existence because in our origin, humans began to speak as rude poets, bound to their bodily passions. This moment in our history can never be effaced; therefore, a rhetoric that can speak to our bodies and passions remains necessary for civilized life. In Vico's social hierarchy, rhetors who are also philosophers represent the head, able to persuade by transporting and transforming the more stomach-oriented social body through the use of sublime and fiery rhetoric.

This sublime rhetoric, made over time by humans, necessarily will change; for Vico, Cartesian thought is bad because it does not allow for historical change. Yet human culture will suffer if it fails to conserve a form of sublime rhetoric, if it promulgates a rhetoric that does not take into account more than reason and intellect. A healthy civilization requires a rhetoric that can address the whole wellspring of human motivation and emotion, a body of eloquence capable of embracing the *sensus communis*.

Vico at the Crossroads

Writing early in the eighteenth century and having only slight knowledge of Locke, Vico preceded both Condillac and his English source Warburton in his anthropological concern for the origins and development of language. Vico serves as the crossroads of texts from post-Renaissance humanism, early English empiricism, and Cartesian rationalism, in many ways signifying the "middle or medium term"—one of his key concepts—between the old discursive paradigms and the new (*Art of Rhetoric* 126). His texts bear the marks of a passage from older discursive practices to the new, but they also show his continuing effort to integrate newer scientific practices with older values, an effort ripe for marginalization by the growing dominance of the new Lockean and Cartesian discourses.

Although rejecting Locke, Vico did embrace the British, both politically and scientifically—but through Bacon and Newton, even through some acquaintance with Robert Boyle. In this and Vico's early Cartesian thought lie some of his modern and progressivist tendencies, yet in his later rejection of Descartes, his continuing Latin classicism, and his situation in inquisitorial Naples lie the seeds of what has been seen as reactionism. Perhaps most crucially, what kept Vico from seeming to be in the true of eighteenth-century thought was his placing of ancient rhetoric at the cornerstone of his philosophizing. Although he concerns himself intensely with contemporary issues in natural philosophy, his philosophical core is mined from more traditional Renaissance humanisms, particularly the arts of rhetoric. Because his thought is based on an idiosyncratic appropriation—and, in a real sense, performance—of ancient texts on language and rhetoric, his texts were no doubt even more difficult for his contemporaries to understand and appreciate. Certainly they or most commentators over the next two centuries never take or mistake Vico for a modern or think of Vico's rhetoric as modern. Yet he is classified today as modern or as a point of origin of many modern-era developments, especially the disciplines of the social sciences. He has also been seen as a precursor of counter-Enlightenment and of Romanticism, a movement at the center of the modern era and modern(ist) aesthetics. Edward Said's analysis of Vico's concern with beginnings ignores the archaic nature and form of his thought and places Vico squarely within the modern camp. Isaiah Berlin identifies Vico as a leading edge of the counter-Enlightenment and Romanticism. Mark Lilla, who titles his book *The Making of an Anti-Modern,* emphasizes and deplores the Roman sources of Vico's texts and their authoritarian politics and ignores the modern resonances of Vico's insights. Donald Phillip Verene's Vico is the heroic antimodern who divined from afar the barbarities that would afflict our own age. Marcel Danesi argues that Vico's account of language origins is today more modern and scientific than current rationalist accounts. Guiseppe Mazzotta and Andrea Battistini both insist on Vico's modernity. My argument is more double- (or triple-) edged: Vico was more completely a man of his time than we have acknowledged, and our relatively slender knowledge of his time and place has made him seem more marginal; separated from their cultural contexts, his texts may be more easily appropriated as modern. The more we learn about the Enlightenment in Naples, the clearer we see how and why Vico remains hesitating on the threshold.

Until the 1970s, work on a rediscovered Vico was carried out primarily in the fields of historiography, literary theory, philosophy, and sociology, although Vico was for forty years a professor of rhetoric or Latin eloquence at the University of Naples. Perhaps it is because little work on Vico's actual rhetoric course has been done that Brian Vickers in his defense of rhetoric is able to, too easily, blame him for a progressive "atrophy" of rhetoric, "brought down finally to a handful of tropes" (*In Defence* 439). Vickers condemns Vico's condensation of tropes to four categories—metaphor, metonymy, synecdoche, and irony—used both in his rhetoric course and in structuring and presenting the history of human institutions in his major work, *New Science.* It is true that this dimension of Vico's theory of historiography has received much attention in recent decades, but it is ironic that Vico should be charged with reducing the scope of rhetoric when he wished to do just the opposite— to elevate the humanities in his reconfiguration of the sciences at a time science—especially the move to mathematicize—was becoming the exemplar for all knowledge.

Vickers senses and rejects what postmoderns celebrate and Henri Lefebvre suggests: the modern shifts the terms of the debate from rhetoric as a system of arts to rhetoric as language. Vico's tropes and his *New Science* do participate in this shift, and in this sense, Vico is modern. Yet Vico's thought is wholly based on rhetoric as a system of *arts,* and it is through the making of arts that humans make themselves and become fully human. Vico's philosophy initiates the turn to a language-centered world while describing a historical-cultural process that necessitates a social conception of language arts.

Vickers assesses Vico correctly in one aspect: Vico does not give sole pride of place to the arts of style in his rhetoric. Invention and elocution work together to form a sublime rhetoric. Rhetoric for Vico includes, but is more than, lists of schemes and tropes, as is clear from various texts prior to 1725, the first edition of *New Science,* including his rhetoric lectures *The Art of Rhetoric (Institutiones Oratoriae, 1711–1741).* Vico also emphasizes the arts of invention, to him the processual logic of social and political discourse, the kind of everyday thought people use to make decisions in the face of life's contingencies. For the field of law, paradigmatic for Vico, rhetoric is the art of adjusting law to the facts, of thought and language together establishing reality in matters of human action (Mooney 198). Yet despite its juridical perspective, Vico's rhetoric remains sublimely expressive, including elements similar to those of Condillac's expressivism, yet it is not what we today think of as a mod-

ern individualist or Romantic expressive rhetoric. Aesthetic considerations are never absent, but they, too, figure differently as a hybrid of
functional and significatory. Tropes are treated as forms of thought, and
expressions of passion are always in the service of persuading social
humans to act as citizens for the sake of a well-functioning society.[1]

That this society for Vico has been read alternatively as authoritarian and as liberating is no different from readings of other rhetoricians,
most notably Aristotle and Plato. It is part of the dialectic of the Enlightenment that Max Horkheimer and Theodor W. Adorno describe and
that deserves to be warily observed and critiqued. Reading Vico's rhetoric
in its historical cultural and intellectual context gives us a different
view from the one held by previous Romantic interpreters, especially
Benedetto Croce, who scarcely pardons Vico's connection with rhetoric. Studying Vico without sublime rhetoric excises the heart and passion of his work.

Yet Vico's humanistic rhetoric reflects Renaissance-filtered republican values and practices more so than the later neoclassical values that
are ultimately transformed into belletristic rhetoric. Although Vico's
rhetoric contains elements of belletristic rhetoric, it is not a modern
belletristic rhetoric, because it is turned not toward the development of
individual aesthetic taste but toward the development of the individual
in the context of the *polis*. The primary aim of rhetoric is to produce a
certain kind of citizen functioning in the civic realm through speaking
and writing. Rather than producing the man of taste who can appreciate and produce belles lettres, Vico's rhetoric aims to produce the citizen who creates the good life for his community through combining
creative rhetorical and critical thought. Taking into account the common origins and intermingling of these old and new ideals obfuscates,
even deconstructs, the opposition of belletristic and civic rhetoric. After all, Vico was early in his career a poet, he celebrated poets, he educated his daughter Luisa to be a poet, and he continued as a public poet
and scribe until his final decrepitude. He spent his life as professor of
rhetoric, teaching rhetoric in part as a critical hermeneutic, and his son
Gennaro followed him in his post, repeating Vico's rhetoric lectures
throughout his own career.

In an address to open the school year at the University of Naples,
Vico most clearly speaks of his own relation to the modern in *Study
Methods,* which Leon Pompa in his translation called "On Method in
Contemporary Fields of Study." In the spirit of the wars between the
ancients and the moderns, Vico comes out as much on the cusp as

Socrates in the *Cratylus* in the debate over language as conventional or natural—while Vico leans to the side of the ancients, he does not reject the moderns. Rather than choosing one side of the binary or the other, he descends through the opposition, declaring that both ancient and modern methods are needed, but each has a different function to perform. As both Verene and James Robert Goetsch Jr. note, Vico seeks in a sophistic manner to "surmount" oppositions, balancing them in an heroic manner to arrive at (self) knowledge (Goetsch 50). For the Sophists, reality was dualistic. For Vico, multiple causes usually claim a share of right in any dispute. From his early work on, Vico recommended rhetorical, topical thought as a method to recognize and judge between multiple causes in an uncertain world. Consideration of multiple causes on the part of rhetor and audience might best approach the reality of a civic life through judgments made on the basis of (nonmathematical) probabilities.

The Setting of Vichian Rhetoric

Vico's Naples, where he spent his life, was anything but a stable society, resembling more "a perpetually stormy sea, which becomes monotonous by the changeless uniformity of its motion" (Villari qtd. in Flint 6). In this, his motivations become very much like Locke's, who came out of a similarly stormy era and sought political stability throughout his life. During the first thirty-two years of Vico's life, Charles II of Spain was sovereign, ruling through viceroys until his death, whereafter Naples suffered from turmoil and misrule for more than a decade. The city was then ruled by Austrian viceroys until 1734 when Charles of Bourbon (later Charles III of Spain) became ruler, again ruling through agents, but more fairly and calmly. Under the remnants of the feudal system, law was the only secular profession that could lead to affluence and power. Many young men of Naples sought to become highly paid civil servants; thus the study of law was important, and Vico was but one of many consumed with the study of jurisprudence, although it never brought him wealth or power. Afraid democracy would lead to mob rule, Vico found monarchical government attractive, in part because of the successes of Charles of Bourbon and in part because of his admiration for the British system.

Despite the turmoil, during Vico's life the city was undergoing a revival of literary activity following that which produced Lorenzo Valla and other scholars. Naples became the center of Cartesianism in Italy, and academies were active, although the Catholic Church grew inquisitorial and would not tolerate heretical writing so that many were persecuted, including the historian Giannone and two of Vico's friends.

The son of a bookseller, Vico boasts in his autobiography of being largely self-educated; he lived "under the shadow of the Investigators" (Fisch, "Academy" 552) and was influenced by Naples's scientific and intellectual academies, although he always preferred the human to the natural sciences. He was associated with Cartesian influences until his forties, and throughout his life he associated with those who promoted modern ideas and were in touch with French and English philosophy. His friend Doria was well read in Locke and English philosophy, and Vico also admired English philosophy. Bacon was among his four revered models, along with Plato, Tacitus, and Grotius.

However, alongside the working out of a new theory of science, the Roman ideal of *civitas* was Vico's passion, and he spent his life teaching and writing in an effort to combine wisdom and eloquence in such a way as to serve human civilization. Michael Mooney calls *civitas* the "well-functioning republic in which men act as citizens" (196). Jeffrey Barnouw argues:

> It is not the prudentia of the classical republic that Vico claims as a model for modern civil life, but the jurisprudentia of the popular monarchy of later Rome, an orientation that places Vico in the line of political thinkers that leads from Hobbes to Montesquieu and Hume. (612)

Like the Romans, Vico always saw rhetoric, or eloquence, as the power that leads the social body to wisdom.

His rhetorical perspective and his historical studies in language origins and development led him to Enlightenment views in many ways parallel to those of Condillac. Like Condillac, Vico believed that it was necessary to understand the origins and development of a thing—its construction—in order to know it. Vico encountered this Epicurean idea in Lucretius, whose primary mode of thought is to return to origins and trace development and decay. Lucretius, especially among the ancients, rejected superstitions and saw human creative activity as formative of what new generations of humans found in the world. However, Vico, living in Naples, the center of classical Epicureanism, may have been reminded of his earlier knowledge of Lucretius in reading Bacon. Although he rejected the notion of chance in Epicureanism, Vico's knower was neither the contemplator of unchanging Platonic ideas nor the passive receiver of empirical mental sensations, but the creator of truth.[2] As emphasized in Longinus, who provides a familiar contemporary framework Vico uses for understanding historical change, these truths are best communicated in a language of "surprising force . . . with the rapid force of lightening," of wonder and the marvelous, and of heightened rhetorical effects—Vico's sublime rhetoric (Longinus 3).

Vichian Language Theory

Vico's insights into language origins in his *New Science* led him to the belief that the first humans spoke in poetic language, and from this principle, he realized that primitive humans were different from modern humans because human nature gradually produced itself by its social institutions, at the origins and heart of which stands language. As Max Harold Fisch notes in the introduction to a translated *New Science,* "Humanity is not a presupposition, but a consequence, an effect, a product of institution building" (Introduction xliv). Thomas Hobbes and other philosophers of the social contract imagined primitive humans as earlier versions of moderns, whereas Vico saw them as the children of the human race, imaginative, violently emotive, and full of awe and wonder at the world. These insights into the different nature of early humans, based on his reflections on language origins, spurred Vico's new science of the history of human jurisprudence and society, a science that ruptures the foundations of his early Cartesianism, creating a space for an alternative vision, not only of rhetoric but of history and also various efforts in natural philosophy.

Because of the sensory and expressive origins of language and mind, language is fundamentally metaphorical and is the foundation of a society's common sense *(sensus communis),* the sense that creates the social body. Along with the faculties of *ingenium,* memory, and imagination, common sense forms the basis for "topical thought," in Grassi's terms, Vico's alternative to Cartesian critical thinking and the highly collectivist art undergirding his rhetorical theory. Notions of *poesis* ground his epistemology, which remains neither purely objective nor subjective, neither purely social nor purely individual, holding neither rhetoric nor science as its sole exemplar for knowledge production—in short, it deconstructs and intermingles these modern purities producing a hybridity—sometimes a syncretism of medieval quality.

Vico's great anthropological insight that language change can provide insight into social change grew out of a lifetime of linguistic study.

However, as Naomi S. Baron notes, few current linguists have written about Vico, although linguistic analysis was his key to the reconstruction of human social history. She links his interests with the recent re-emergence of social issues among contemporary sociolinguists such as Labov, Hymes, and Halliday.[3] The phenomenon of Vico's disappearance from linguistic history results no doubt from some of the same practical forces that kept him marginal outside Italy in philosophical circles. One reason was that his masterwork, *New Science,* was written in a difficult Italian dialect, dense and full of obscure allusions and perplexing etymologies. Translations first into French and now into English have greatly increased Vico's readership. Moreover, Vico's treatment of even the commonest contemporary questions and issues, such as setting the chronology of universal history, deciding the merits of the ancients or moderns in the face of new scientific theories and practices of inquiry, or deciphering the role of providence in the world have no doubt perplexed many. Yet his speculation into the origin of language proved to be a mainstream rather than marginal inquiry over the next century.

Language Origin and Development

Vico's explanation of the origin of language links language development to the development of mind, the common sense of a community, and the production of human institutions and humanity itself. As with Condillac's later narrative of origins, the first language for Vico is mute, which is based on gesture and natural signs, followed by natural speech, which is monosyllabic and onomatopoeic. According to Vico's theory of origins, gentile language arose primordially with the human mind and social institutions when early humans were giant beasts in the fields, having been dispersed and degraded from their natural social organizations by the Flood.[4] One day in the fields, 200 years after the Flood, as Earth was drying out, the first thunder boomed, startling some of the *giganti.* They identified the thunder with a booming voice, Jove, and the sky with the body of Jove. As Vico explains:

> When men are ignorant of the natural causes producing things, and cannot even explain them by analogy with similar things, they attribute their own nature to them. . . . [T]he human mind, because of its indefinite nature, wherever it is lost in ignorance, makes itself the rule of the universe in respect of everything it does not know. (*New Science* 70, pars. 180–81)

Fear of the thundering voice causes that sublime sense of wonder, and the beasts look up at the sky, which helps them distinguish their place on earth from the sky, which they imagine as the body of Jove, trembling with anger. Beginning with that first instance—which Verene insightfully terms the first *universale fantastico* (*Vico's Science* 66), the first *topos* from which to think—language arose, as did religion, marriage, burial, and the idea of law. Quaking with that first crash of thunder, the first fathers caught the "wild, indocile, and shy" women with whom they were procreating in the fields and out of shame and guilt dragged them into caves, founding the institutions of marriage, family, and ultimately the state (Vico, *New Science* 2: 113, par. 369). Thus language, mind, and institutions began and developed together. For Vico, religious belief occasioned by fear is the initial constraining force necessary to hold humankind in society when their vicious instincts would lead them to destroy it. The frightful thought of the thundering voice also leads men to restrain the motion of their bodies *(conatus)*, and this control paradoxically and dialectically gives rise to free will.

Importantly, from that first instance of the construction of Jove, language was based on the mind's propensity to make analogies and connections and was thus metaphoric, poetic, and musical (for, as with Condillac, the first language would be a kind of song or rhythmic chant). Grammatically, language develops through interjections, pronouns, particles, and only later nouns and verbs. From speculations on this origin, Vico derives the principle he calls the master key to his new science: that the first men spoke in poetry. This key represents his critique of contemporary rationalist accounts of humans who were fully reasonable creatures at the origins. The important corollary becomes that primitive minds, immersed in the senses, differ from rational, prosaic contemporary minds, for "[m]en first feel without perceiving, then they perceive with a troubled and agitated spirit, finally they reflect with a clear mind" (*New Science* 75, par. 218). A forerunner of Sigmund Freud, Vico conceives of rational consciousness as a smaller outcropping from a massive historical base that is physical, passionate, imagistic, and symbolic.

Humans began to form themselves with their first common institutions—religion, marriage, and burial of the dead—and especially with their language, based on metaphor, myth, and fable, forming what Vico calls a "poetic wisdom" with a "poetic logic." Poetic logic, bound up with the development of society and mind, was tied to images, myths, and religion, all dependent on analogical thought and language, so that language, mind, and social institutions arose together. In Vichian linguistic history prefiguring Jacques Derrida, a broadly conceived writing precedes speech, as all nations, at first mute, begin to speak by "writing," which is both gestural and graphic. This mythical "scene of language origins" presents a speculative narrative, the type of thought rejected by the more positivistic nineteenth-century linguists and scientists. Yet Danesi argues that Vico's hypotheses are more plausible and scientific than rationalist accounts of language development such as those of Noam Chomsky.

Beginning with visual and gestural iconicity, Danesi analyzes Vico's narrative of origins and development into separate hypotheses, continuing through hand signs captured in cuneiform writing, the audio-oral stage when the first articulation appeared, to the metaphorical, the chief event in the development of language linking the systems. Providing modern scientific evidence from anthropology, linguistics, psychology, and paleoneurology to argue for Vichian origins, Danesi seems to place Vico squarely in the moderns because of the acuteness of his linguistic insights.

Metaphor and Language Development

Vico identifies analogical thinking based in the senses as a formative principle of language, so that the universal principle of etymology for all languages is that "words are carried over from bodies and from the properties of bodies to signify the institutions of the mind and spirit" (*New Science* 78, par. 237). Metaphoric thinking is thus the basis for the three types of language characterized by Vico's *New Science,* corresponding to the ages of gods, heroes, and humans: the hieroglyphic or sacred language with signs based on natural objects, the symbolic or figurative heroic language of Homer's age, and the vulgar language with instituted signs belonging to humans (69, par. 173). Vico shows preference for the second age growing out of heroic emblems, a kind of middle terrain, clearly sublime, containing some elements of the first and third. He writes that the best language is heroic, and heroic verse "the grandest of all" (155, par. 463). This language was the language of symbol, composed of divine and heroic characters with vivid representations, images, similes, comparisons, metaphors, circumlocutions, and digressive patterns of a mind as yet unable to stay on a linear track, which Vico says can be seen naturally in his day with the feeble-minded and "above all with women" (153, par. 457). Seals, shields, family coats of arms, and symbolic signatures have also been linked with oral cultures by our contemporary anthropologists of literacy.

Stephen K. Land credits Vico's metaphor-based linguistics as being
one of the first to conceive of language as a sign system, while Umberto
Eco's *Semiotics and the Philosophy of Language* finds fault with readings of Vico's theory of metaphor and offers a radical new reading. Land
associates Vico with the turn to modern language theory, pointing out
that a metaphoric model of language such as Vico's is incompatible
with a representational model, for if language is fundamentally metaphoric, "the relation of words to ideas must be more complex than
the [one-to-one relationship] the representational model allows" (*From
Signs to Propositions* 187). Because Vichian language grows not by ac-
cretion of signs, but by modifying itself structurally, it is not a collection of words but a system of signs, and meaning is at least in part a
function of form. Moreover, metaphor for Vico is linked with the expression of emotion, a rhetorical surplus in language not addressed by
a representational theory.

However, just how meaning emerges from metaphor culturally has
been explored by Eco, who notes that interlocutors must undertake a
complex sort of "hermeneutic circle" to understand metaphors. For this
reason, Eco emphasizes metaphors as cultural constructions, selections
of pertinent aspects of a material reality, a "subtle network of propor-
tions between cultural units" (102). The process of decoding them assumes a cultural code against which the simile is verified. For example,
Eco supplies the comparison "Thy teeth are as a flock of sheep which
go up from the washing" (*Song of Songs* 4.2). In the poetic tradition in
which the poet worked, the properties of sheep selected were obviously
not their smell, bleating, or dripping shagginess but their whiteness and
uniformity. However, Eco sees in Vico's *New Science* a contradiction.
In stressing the primary nature of metaphor in the development of language, he says, Vico seems to deny the preexistence of cultural networks,
the preestablished process of semiosis necessary to the creation of metaphor (107). At the same time, he admits to the cultural difference in the
diversity of language, born of the response of communities to their
material environments, seen by different communities from different
viewpoints. Eco argues: If metaphors require an underlying cultural
framework, then the hieroglyphic language of the gods cannot be a
merely primitive stage of human consciousness; it needs the presence of
both the symbolic language of heroes and the epistolary language of men
as its starting point. Thus, Vico is not speaking of a linear development
from a metaphoric language to a more conventional language, but of a
continual, cyclical activity (108). Therefore, Eco suggests, Vico's ages

existed at the same time, a theory for which he finds support in one of Vico's statements about the origins of language and letters:

> To enter now upon the extremely difficult [question of the] way in which these three kinds of languages and letters were formed, we must establish this principle: that as gods, heroes, and men began at the same time (for they were, after all, men who imagined the gods and believed their own heroic nature to be a mixture of the divine and human natures), so these three languages began at the same time, each having its letters, which developed along with it. (*New Science* 149, par. 446)

Eco notes in support of this theory of continuous development that the language of the gods is a heap of unrelated synecdoches and metonymies, with no fewer than 30,000 gods counted by Varro. The language of heroes created metaphors; metaphor or catachresis invents new terms using two terms already known presupposing another unexpressed. Thus, symbolic language could not express itself without epistolary language, Eco argues (108).

As with the many other contradictions in Vico, the proper response is not a forced choice of either-or but an inclusive both-and, at times a juxtaposition of contradictory theories. Vico discusses the ages as following linearly, and that remains important to his narrative of development; however, his statement in paragraph 446 shows that he recognizes the difficulties. The importance of Eco's complication of Vico's scheme is that Vico's semiotic is read as emphasizing less an "aesthetics of ineffable creativity" than a "cultural anthropology" based on language, one that "recognizes the categorical indices on which metaphors are based, indices whose historical conditions, birth, and variety it researches even as it explores the variety of brave deeds, of medallions, and of fables" (108). This reading is important because Vico's *New Science* is a theory of history, an effort to produce cultural anthropology, a modern moment. The potential for metaphor exists because of cultural networks and cultural production. Yet human (aesthetic) creativity is a significant theme in Vico, and the creation of metaphor is for Vico a sign of creativity, a natural propensity of the mind to make connections between disparate things. In Vico as in Aristotle, metaphor is a cognitive instrument more than an ornament, productive of new knowledge for the individual and the culture. Cultural anthropology and theory of creativity and constructivity are imbricated and inseparable.

Although Vico privileges the heroic age, the potential for metaphor exists during all ages, both in the culture and in the individual who participates in that culture. For Vico sees the individual as a microcosm of the culture, repeating cultural development in the process of moving from childhood to adulthood. Old age is powerful in reason, just as it is during the human age; adolescence excels in imagination, as it does in the heroic age. Because humans live in communities, they are able to observe others in the process of development and reflect on this process. Therefore, humans contain in themselves the potential both to create and understand their language and to know their history, based on imaginarily entering into their continuous cycles of development.

Vico's modernity is in his understanding that systems of metaphor stand as the foundation of language and culture and are socially and historically conditioned and conditioning. Metaphor is not an element separable from language, for we are born into metaphor, the source of both our culture and our creativity. Thus for Vico metaphor is an important intellectual development that must be nurtured. Although early humans immersed in sense could only express their knowledge in a poetic language, this language, in a concrete, metaphoric, imaginative fashion, contains the seeds of reason, later expressed in heroic symbolism and then reasoned discourse. Because Vico believes that the development of an individual mirrors the development of the race, invention and poetic imagination will unfold before judgment and the critical faculty both in individuals and in society; moreover, the full development of the critical faculty depends upon traversing the earlier stages. Successful persuasion comes about through a sublime address to the passionate child of a citizen mired in the senses and desires.

Vichian Language and Mind

Vico's developmentalism has a rhetorical base explained in *On the Most Ancient Wisdom of the Italians: Unearthed from the Origins of the Latin Language* in which he discusses the mind in terms of ancient dialectic and its division into the arts of invention and judgment. Invention, or topics, was the art of finding elements or middle terms for argument; rhetorical judgment, or criticism, was the art of selecting loci and judging arguments to choose the best and avoid defective arguments.[5] Vico names three mental operations—perception, judgment, and reasoning—regulated by the arts of topics, criticism, and method respectively (*Most Ancient Wisdom* 97–98). With the exception of geometry, he writes, the ancients handed down no art for method, believing it should be left to prudence or practical wisdom.

The distinction between topics and criticism is part of the very structure of *New Science:*

> Providence gave good guidance to human affairs when it aroused human minds first to topics rather than to criticism, for acquaintance with things must come before judgment of them. Topics has the function of making minds inventive, as criticism has that of making them exact. . . . Thus the first peoples, who were the children of the human race, founded first the world of the arts; then the philosophers, who came a long time afterward and so may be regarded as the old men of the nations, founded the world of the sciences, thereby making humanity complete. (166–67, par. 498)

However, Vico does not set up a true polarity between invention and judgment, with invention the privileged member, as some have read his texts. Indeed, at times he even seems to prefer science and reason, which complete humanity, to the creative arts. Vico never treats the invention-judgment duo as an either-or pair but always as both-and, as he explains in *Study Methods* as well as in this passage from *Most Ancient Wisdom:* "[T]he Academics were concerned only with [discovery] and the Stoics only with [judgment]. Both were wrong because there is no invention without judgment and no judgment without invention" (98). Going head to head with Cartesian theory, he terms his *New Science* a new "critical art," able to assist even in the judgment of historical narratives. With this, Vico deconstructs the opposition critical-creative. Again, as with the three ages of language, what may seem to be a mechanistic, linear division becomes more complex. Because of the conflation of topic and critic, the sublime art of metaphor making becomes a faculty for making truths, a "philosophic faculty" that educators should take pains to nurture in their students (*Study Methods* 24). Vico complains that the "severe," "limited" style of Cartesian exposition

> is apt to smother the student's specifically philosophic faculty, i.e., his capacity to perceive the analogies existing between matters lying far apart, and apparently most dissimilar. It is this capacity which constitutes the source and principle of all ingenious, acute, and brilliant forms of expression. (*Study Methods* 24)

He warns that a critical Cartesian education constricts students' minds like Terence's young virgins, "whom their mothers compel to bend their shoulders, to stoop, to bind their bosom in order to achieve slimness." Metaphoric ability and the ability to make philosophic truth will only develop as they are cultivated by the arts and not stifled by "such as method as to dry up every fount of convincing expression, of copious, penetrating, embellished, lucid, developed, psychologically effective, and impassioned utterance" (*Study Methods* 37). This fountain-like sentence illustrates Vico's copious (and gendered) ideal of a rhetoric that would be both expression and persuasion, tied to practical wisdom drawn from the common sense of a society. In his rhetoric course, he argues that "dry" arts such as mathematics stifle the fount of sublime rhetoric (*Art of Rhetoric* 21).

In *Most Ancient Wisdom*, the mental operations of invention and judgment are discussed in connection with mental faculties, based on the theory of "maker's knowledge" because linked with the Latin term *facilitas*, "an unhindered and ready disposition for making *(facere)*," a definition Vico takes from Cicero and Quintilian (93). The ability to spontaneously and fluidly produce persuasive discourse, about truth, is at the heart of sublimity and linked with passionate, sensuous rhetoric.

Senses for Vico are faculties, faculties by which we "make the color of things by seeing, flavor by tasting, sound by hearing, and heat and cold by touching" (93). Yet the body is never completely materialistic or mechanistic because of the soul, which is power, sight, and activity; in contrast, a sense such as sight is a faculty. True intellect is described as the "faculty by which we make something true when we understand it" (94). Like Locke and Condillac, Vico sees faculties not as mental entities but as actualization of powers, the powers linked with the soul. Vico's faculties here include the traditional will and intellect but also human makings such as arithmetic, geometry, and mechanics. Physics itself, however, is excluded as a human faculty in *Most Ancient Wisdom*, because unlike geometry it is not made by humans but exists as a faculty of God.

Mental Powers: Imagination, Memory, *Ingenium*

Vico's mind has three significant operations: imagination, memory, and *ingenium*. He defines the imagination as the faculty used to "feign images of things" (94), but he does not insist on distinguishing it from memory, instead deliberately entwining the two. Vico's etymological method in *Most Ancient Wisdom* showed him that the Latins used "memory" as faculty of storing sense perceptions, with "reminiscence" as the faculty of recalling them. However, memory is also *phantasia* in Greek, the faculty that fashions images, and *immaginare* in Italian (95–96). In *New Science,* Vico explains that in Greek myths, Memory was the mother of the Muses, which were forms of imagination (314, par. 819).

Vico consistently keeps memory and imagination closely linked and relates them to the most sublime concept of *ingenium,* "the faculty that connects disparate and diverse things." L. M. Palmer translates this central theme in Vico as "ingenuity," "inventiveness," and "mother wit," tied to the "wit" disparaged by Hobbes and Locke yet celebrated by Vico as a key to invention and the intellect (*Most Ancient Wisdom* 96). Pompa defines it as:

> [a] capacity, peculiar to man, for perceptive or insightful creation or construction. Although it requires imagination, it is not identical with it, since imagination can work blindly whereas ingenuity has a cognitive element in it. (*Vico* xv)

In *New Science,* Vico gives memory three aspects: remembering, imitation, and ingenuity; "memory when it remembers things, imagination when it alters or imitates them, and invention *[ingegno]* when it gives them a new turn or puts them into proper arrangement and relationship" (313–14, par. 819). This is stated as an ascending scale, putting at the top invention, twinned with ingenuity here and described as a combinative and ordering operation. However, memory later plays a central role in cognitive development and the activity of reflection in *New Science,* particularly in constructing a science and social history. Metaphor and language, memory and imagination converge in Vico's concept of *ingenium,* the human capacity par excellence, not as in Condillac in a theory of individual geniuses affecting humanity, but, as has been noted in Vico studies, a theory of the genius of humanity.

Language and Society: *Sensus Communis*

Vico's course manual stresses inventional faculties but includes the faculty of will as closely linked with intellect as well as spirit. Will and free will become important inquiries for the philosopher if their discussion is often integrated with other issues. What Vico often seeks is a medium point between extremes, as in his discussions of determinism and free will. His axiom on the natural social state proves to him that man has "free choice, however weak" (*New Science* 62, par. 136), choice that is aided by an immanent providence. Thus, he criticizes both Stoic (or Spinozan) and Epicurean theories of causation (*New Science* 61, par. 130). The Stoics erred by introducing the concept of fate or metaphysical determinism into society, the Epicureans by introducing the concept of pure chance or contingency. Social history for Vico is conditioned but not determined; it is contingent but not purely contingent as evidenced by common systems of institutions arising in different nations throughout history. As commonality of structure exists across cultures, each culture develops a common sense that despite individual differences and contingency allows it to respond as a social body.

Like Valla, Vico, as noted by humanist Nancy S. Struever, held to the Renaissance commonplace of a social human nature. One central insight also characteristic of Renaissance humanist inquiry is the "social nature of innovation, that society invents. Note that a [set of] topics consists of commonplaces, a shared inventory of shared consciousness." She also points to Vico's pervasive social orientation in *New Science,* in which there are few proper names, "language is hero," and "socially determined words mold our consciousness" (182). Tradition and individual talent are not "locked in some agon" in Vico, but "tradition nourishes the individual." Unlike Condillac's classical view in which the individual's potential is limited by the community's language, with Vico, language, a social invention, offers "infinite riches of expression" (183).

This recurrent emphasis on the social nature of language and rhetorical thought is central to the understanding of Vico's rhetoric and his central concept of common sense, or *sensus communis.* This common sense has been linked with ideology and the Gramscian concept of hegemony.[6] It is bound up with language, although it has a prelinguistic, prerational base. In an oft-cited passage in *New Science,* Vico calls common sense "judgment without reflection, shared by an entire class, an entire nation or the entire human race" (63, par. 142). In the paragraph just before, he has clarified this: "Human choice, by its nature most uncertain, is made certain and determined by the common sense of men with respect to human needs or utilities, which are the two sources of the natural law of the gentes" (63, par. 141). Common sense is the accumulated wisdom of societies that comes from a shared way of life and language, helping to narrow the ill-defined world of human choice. It is the standard for practical judgment and for eloquence: thus, "learning to indwell this world and to incorporate it in his fantasy is the young orator's primary task" (Schaeffer, *Sensus Communis* 155).

Hans-Georg Gadamer calls common sense "a moral sense which founds the community," and there is a broader aspect to common sense that includes a natural predisposition for religion and law[7] (qtd. in Schaeffer, "Vico's Rhetorical Model" 152–53). Vico disputes Pierre Bayle's view that a society of atheists is possible. Vico writes that man "fallen into despair of all the succors of nature desires something superior to save him. But something superior to nature is God, and this is the light that God has shed on all men" (*New Science* 100–101, par. 339). This broader common need and desire result in the creation of the common institutions of marriage, civil religion, and burial, which, Vico says, are universal, eternal, and established by divine providence (*New Science* 102, par. 342) but an immanent providence working through human free choice. This immanent providence, as Pompa points out, is a "fundamental category" of the *New Science* whose "workings are largely to be identified with those of common sense" (*Vico* 58). This common sense represents in turn the communal decisions of humans in their historical, social, and institutional contexts, resting ultimately upon language. Always important to Vico, common sense produces the desire for law and guides its construction across the world of nations.

Common sense forms the core of Vico's important conception of a "mental dictionary" from which he draws his anthropological theory: "Uniform ideas originating among entire peoples unknown to each other must have a common ground of truth" (*New Science* 63, par. 144).

> There must in the nature of human institutions be a mental language common to all nations, which uniformly grasps the substance of things feasible in human social life and expresses it with as many diverse modifications as these same things may have diverse aspects. A proof of this is afforded by proverbs or maxims of vulgar wisdom, in which substantially the same meanings find as many diverse expressions as there are nations ancient and modern.
>
> This common mental language is proper to our Science, by whose light linguistic scholars will be enabled to construct a mental vocabulary common to all the various articulate languages living and dead. (*New Science* 67, pars. 161–62)

This common mental dictionary is the theoretical basis for *New Science*'s three ages or natures of man, historical and sociological laws Vico draws from the "tangle of associational thinking that is the root of community," the nourisher of the common sense. At the historical root of common sense lie the *universale fantastici,* the imaginative universals "formed naturally in the imagination . . . on certain occasions of human need and utility," such as ideal portraits of the character of Ulysses found across cultures[8] (Covino 46). These nonrational poetic characters were the first common moral ideals.

Language and its processes of production from imaginative universals through instituted signs provide the foundation for the principle that we can know what we have made *(verum-factum)* and for the concept of common sense, both bound up with social history. Language produces and is in turn produced by society and thus reflects the developmental process, as revealed in etymological investigation. Language is essentially ambiguous and oblique, having been created by naming one thing by terms of another; it is fossil poetry, bearing the imprints of prelogical moments of experience, marked by use of identities and analogies. Vico's linguistic system, a complete repository of social wisdom, participates with society in the ideal eternal history, a perpetual cycle of collapse and rebirth; finally, unlike the progressive teleology of modernity, it is en route to no particular destination.

Vico's *Rhetoric*

Karl-Otto Apel has referred to Vico as the "owl of Minerva" in relation to Italian humanism, coming as he does at the end and illuminating its major themes (qtd. in Struever 173). Rhetoric, primary to Renaissance humanists, underlies Vico's key insights on language and society, not surprising in light of his more than forty years professing rhetoric. Yet work on Vico and rhetoric has come slowly to Vico scholarship, partly because of attitudes such as Croce's, revealed in his remark about Vico's rhetoric manual that "in vain one would look [into that work] for a shadow of his true thought" (qtd. in Giuliani 31). Vico's *Institutiones Oratoriae (Art of Rhetoric)* must be better understood—as must rhetorical thought in general—before the foundational role of sublime civic rhetoric in his philosophy becomes meaningful.

Vico's texts themselves cycle in the end back to his beginnings in legal rhetoric, with his insights on language from *Most Ancient Wisdom* to *New Science,* forging a different rhetoric from modern rhetoric, one emphasizing the rhetorical nature of all knowledge. For that reason, an understanding of the elements of his rhetoric, from his view of the purpose of rhetoric to his presentation of inventional and stylistic arts, can help illuminate the role of rhetoric in Vico's corpus. His rhetoric offers an alternative to the linear, analytic rhetorics of his day that became the dominant template for modern classroom practice. Centering on the public nature of discourse and the essentially nonlinear nature of our accumulative, synthetic thought, his sublime rhetoric begins with the body and is poetically based in the processes of making metaphors and analogies.

As Alessandro Giuliani notes in one of the earliest articles on Vico and the New Rhetoric, Vico reestablished rhetoric's ties with philosophy and law, and the rhetoric of his course manuals is always concerned with the relationships rhetoric-logic and philosophy-rhetoric. Although those who have examined his course manuals have called them a "manual of style," Vico's theory is not one of ornate form nor emotive rhetoric (Giuliani 32) but is a rhetoric of social invention and the logic of status and topics. Giuliani, Mooney, Giuliano Crifò, and Palmer are among those who argue that the influence of Vico's rhetoric can be found consistently throughout his work to the final *New Science*. As Crifò notes in the foreword to Vico's rhetoric course, the lessons "have become the indisputable point of reference for much of the formulation of Vico's thought, culminating in the *New Science*" (xv).

Art of Rhetoric

Vico's rhetoric course aimed to teach extemporaneous speaking in acceptable Latin—of course, preferably refined and eloquent Latin—for beginning law students at the University of Naples. His position was not unlike our contemporary teacher of first-year composition orienting students to effective academic discourse. We should remember Vico's students were advanced but second-language learners. Other parallels to the modern teacher of composition also hold: like the writing teacher, his lectureship was low-status and low-paying, and throughout his career, Vico attempted without success to obtain a better-paying, more prestigious philosophical post. As he relates in his autobiography, his personal triumph in producing *New Science* more than compensated him for his very public career failures. The devotion of his many students must have also consoled him.

His course manual, recently translated as *The Art of Rhetoric,* was compiled from sources including his own lectures and student notes from his years of teaching, 1699–1741. Afterward, the same lectures were repeated by his son Gennaro, and the manual continued to be used in Naples until the end of the eighteenth century. The final sentence of the opening paragraph in chapter 1 explicates the term *rhetoric* and characterizes his rhetoric thusly: "[T]he sublime style of oratory rather prefers speech which is intense, sharp, and engaging, leaving its listeners with much to think about" (3). It is in part because of this passage that I term Vico's a sublime rhetoric. In his course manual, it is clear that Vico taught rhetoric essentially as logic of argumentation, emphasizing the philosophical connection with truth. Because his students were training for law and civic service, he assumes a judicial argumentative situation with accusation and defense, the central problem being what ought to be done as in all rhetoric.

This is consonant with his description of the subject matter of rhetoric as "whatever is that which falls under deliberation of whether it is to be done or not to be done," although he does approve of theoretical as well as practical questions (9). For Vico, rhetoric's work is thus to "persuade or bend the wills of others. The will is the arbiter of what is to be done and what is to be avoided." To Vico the will represents "spirit," which along with the intellect or mind makes up human reasoning. As God is the sole "incliner of wills," the rhetor's task is to speak "appropriately to the purpose of persuading," whether or not this end is met (*Art of Rhetoric* 5). To speak persuasively is to use arts leading to the Ciceronian and Horacean triad to please, to teach, and to move.[9]

Vico structures his lectures by using the offices or departments of rhetoric—invention and disposition in part 1 (much of which is on inventional logic) and in part 2 elocution, pronunciation, and memory. Part 2 concerns itself almost entirely with elocution or style, with only a brief final chapter on memory and delivery. This structural emphasis marks Vico's rhetoric as unique, more classical than contemporary yet responding to contemporary themes and authors. As Giuliani explains, rhetoric to Vico is a methodology of applying words to things and facts "but is a matter of things and facts that can be changed through human choice" (32). Because language constitutes thought, the study of expressive means, that is, style, helps make possible an analysis of the human mind and its social nature. Knowledge of a common social language and its particular cultural resonances is necessary to persuasion.

Vico's rhetoric also differs from traditional classical practice because he emphasizes the mind's propensity to learn by analogy. Although an inveterate compiler himself, he criticizes Cicero and Quintilian for proliferating inventional topoi and propositions; his ideal is an art with few precepts or elements, supplemented by exemplars. Rejecting the fictional exercises of the Roman *progymnasmata,* his pedagogical theory works by analogy or imitation, in harmony with his theories of mind. Like painters imitating models, novice orators should read and imitate existing texts of orators, historians, or poets, meditating on them and translating them into their vernaculars. Vico thereby becomes pedagogically modern in his use of examples and models if he remains ancient in his use of general precepts or arts. In addition, Vico tells his students that "the best yet is to write as much as possible according to that most useful advice of Cicero's—'the best teacher of speaking is the pen'" (*Art of Rhetoric* 23). On the threshold between orality and literacy, Vico, son of a bookseller, remains on the threshold of modernity, overwhelmingly linear and literate.

Although he repeats classical dicta on the elements of success in speaking—natural endowment, the arts, and practice—he sometimes diverges on his advice for preparation for rhetorical study. First, he addresses civil education, which should begin with an education among peers, so that "along with them, he may learn the common sense *(sensus communis)* which is the standard of all prudence and eloquence" (*Art of Rhetoric* 19). Significantly, education should first cultivate "honor and greatness of spirit"—spirit again connoting Vico's rhetoric of sublimity. Most importantly for the oratorical spirit, he advises that the future rhetor be raised in the capital city of a nation: "Truly, such a splendid and magnificent city will mold his spirit as splendid and magnificent" (*Art of Rhetoric* 19). Vico cherishes ideals of civic spirit and pride, classical values that locate the "good life" in citizenship in cities.

The rich and copious development of spirit is Vico's first requirement, not only for producing a sublime rhetoric but to produce a rhetor who must be holistically the real thing rather than a textualized character. Vico early on forecloses the classical issue of whether an orator's virtue need be in the person or whether it is enough to portray his virtue in the speech text:

> Indeed, by itself, integrity of life *(probitas vitae)* brings to the orator his greatest credence *(gravitas)*. And eloquence, which is the discernment of what is to be said and what is to be left in silence, like a handmaiden, will easily follow upon wisdom, which is the guide of what is to be done and what is to be avoided. (*Art of Rhetoric* 20)

This practical wisdom, as we have seen, comes from development of *sensus communis*, the key to Vico's rhetoric. It is obvious from Vico's rhetoric manual that the system of topics as a shared and common dictionary of thought, in particular those dealing with general public discourse, is

at the heart of *sensus communis*. It can be so because it has been distilled into an art over time and circumstance by human use. Thus, in a
circular fashion, commonplaces and common topics derive from *sensus
communis*, and their use produces a knowledge of the common sense.

Next, paralleling advice in *Study Methods* and *Most Ancient Wisdom*, Vico advises students to study with humanistic rather than Cartesian and scholastic methods. Training in geometry that involves imag-
ining figures will help the student learn to creatively imagine the structure
of an oration. Along with this image-centered mathematical training,
which involves both the spatial and figurative imagination, the best
preparation for rhetoric is training in philosophy, music, and acting.
Moral philosophy will help train the spirit. Music's rhythms are essential to develop language production, and acting will help train not only
the voice but also the body. This advice is consistent with his belief that
rhetoric not only is a practical art, holding the auditors by truth, but also
an oral performance transporting the listeners via the orator's body with
its voice and rhythms, truly a sublime, passionate art of the whole.

Inventional Arts

Vico's treatment of invention in the rhetoric manual follows Cicero,
Quintilian, and the Renaissance humanists more closely than Aristotelian invention, although it includes Aristotelian logic. As the aims of
rhetoric are to please, to teach, and to move, in the rhetoric manual he
addresses inventional arts under this framework, rather than through
the Aristotelian triad of ethos, pathos, and logos, although these are
subsumed in his discussion. His classification of arguments to be invented
by the orator has three heads: credibility arguments for teaching, con-
ciliating arguments for favoring the listeners' spirits, and arguments of
arousal to stir the listeners' spirits.

Vico defines invention as the devising of suitable arguments intended
for persuasion, and, like Aristotle, classifies them as artistic, those made
by the orator using topical arts, or as lacking in art, those existing external to the orator such as examples and testimonies (*Art of Rhetoric*
25). He makes the point that topoi for both teaching and credibility
arguments remain in the area of probable reasoning when the question
is one of knowledge, but he includes verisimilar conclusions when the
question is one of a practical course of action. Arguments that deal with
certainties, many of them based on signs, are for judges to use in sen-
tencing, not for orators, Vico believes. Some loci overlap with dialecti-

cal loci while others remain particular to orators. Oratorical arguments appeal to the attitudes and values of listeners or arouse their spirits.

Common loci for both orators and dialecticians include definition, division, etymology *(notatia)*, the etymological connection of words *(verba coniugata)*, genus, species, the total, the parts, the truly efficient cause, the agent, matter, and so forth for a total of sixteen topoi. From the final locus of collateral circumstances come the possibilities, the occasions, and the instruments, and from these three come the antecedent, concomitant, and the consequent, important Vichian considerations over time. The similar and dissimilar and the congruent and opposed are also in this set. Various types of oppositionality are set forth, for a total of just over thirty loci, depending on how they are counted. Vico calls these loci the "elements of argumentation," likening them to an alphabet and the devising of arguments as analogous to reading (*Art of Rhetoric* 29).

He explains that these elements are to be internalized and used artfully as aids in swiftness of extemporaneous argument:

> This is not so you will find arguments in all of the loci (indeed you do not choose all of the letters in reading a word, but select only some of them), but rather that you will be certain you have considered everything which is contained in the question proposed and is relevant to it. (*Art of Rhetoric* 29)

Brief examples—often gnomic in form—follow to illustrate, such as from etymology, "He was a consul; in fact, with his deeds he counseled the commonwealth;" or from the congruent, "It is of the miser to esteem a penny above dignity" (*Art of Rhetoric* 31).

Arguments of conciliation include those drawn from the customs of the orator and other parties involved, the "ways of political structures *(civitas)*" and the situation (43). Here many of the considerations of character such as in Aristotelian *ethos* are found. Arguments drawn from political structures are those such as "liberty in a democratic state such as Holland; the greatness and splendor of an aristocratic republic of nobles such as Venice; the prosperity and glory of a prince in a monarchy such as ours" (*Art of Rhetoric* 43).

In arguments of arousal, Vico recommends Aristotle's *Rhetoric* and *Ethics* for understanding audience psychology. He advises that arguments of conciliation be placed in the *exordium,* those of teaching in the disputation, and those of arousal in the *peroratio,* yet advises that "manners and emotions must be commingled with the issues themselves *(res ipsae),* and, as blood through the body, they are thus diffused through-out the entire oration" *(Art of Rhetoric* 45). This common Vichian metaphor, repeated in several texts, stresses the holistic interweaving of a discourse through fluid elements found throughout. It highlights his biological thought distilled in his lost medical treatise *On the Equilib-rium of the Human Body* and is best remembered by students of Vico as the metaphor used to refer to the axiomatic logic of *New Science.*

Disposition, Art of Arrangement

Following his discussion of invention, he takes up the traditional parts of an oration: the exordium, narration, proposition, confirmation, confuta-tion, and the peroration, giving numerous examples. Yet even in the dis-position, he continues to discuss inventional matters. For example, in chapter 30, "The Confirmation," using military metaphors, he discusses argumentation. The valor of the orator shows best in the confirmation, which he calls the *agon* or battlefield where arguments are exposed.

Here in scholastic terms, he explains argument as "the form and figure *(forma et figura)* by which the middle term is joined with the two leading points *(fastigia)* of the proposed question or major and minor premises." His example centers on the maxim from Sallust: "All things rise and fall, wax and wane." To prove that "the bronze Colossus will perish," students should add the argument "that it is made." One con-nects "that which has a beginning" with "the bronze Colossus. . . . But the bronze Colossus has a beginning;" then connect Colossus with "that which has an end: . . . Therefore the bronze Colossus will wane with the others" *(Art of Rhetoric* 87). This rich example reveals the preoc-cupation of Vico's thoughts with change over time. It also shows the consistent nature of his vocabulary and concern with using aphorisms, maxims, and other linguistic formulae distilling wisdom for making new connections and knowledge, as we will see in his discussion of conceits in the section on elocution or style. Somewhat surprisingly, the axiom, a logical form, is the heart and soul of sublime rhetoric.

Vico places his discussion of rhetorical logic under disposition in the chapter on the confirmation, another example of his tendency for in-ventional theory to circulate through his lectures like blood through the body. In it, he explains further the rhetorical syllogism. Orators may omit familiar axiomatic general statements in order to vary the logical form or engage the listener in supplying the argumentation necessary. This reduces the syllogism into what is called an enthymeme: "If speech has been given to man alone, why does he not cultivate eloquence?" (This omits the middle notion—that the study of eloquence is worthy.) The enthymeme *par excellence* is formed of contraries, but stating it in the form of a question heightens the acuteness: "What trust shall you find in a stranger if you have been hostile to your own?" (*Art of Rhetoric* 89–90).

Speakers may also amplify the syllogism into what seems a more sublime form—an epicheirema, used by orators "who are expansive and copious of speech." Vico calls the five-part epicheirema "a most perfect ratiocination and . . . proper kind of argumentation." It is made by expanding the proposition with a short proof, then amplifying the assumptions behind the proposition in varying ways before coming to a "sharp conclusion" (*Art of Rhetoric* 88–89). Epicheirema are typical of the logic of Vico's *New Science*. Explanation of Socratic questions, induction, the Stoic sorites, and other forms of rhetorical logic are found discussed under disposition as well.

However, the art of *status,* both an inventional art and its own rhetorical logic, is found earlier in his discussion of the "judicial cause," chapter 22 (*Art of Rhetoric* 57). Vico had obtained his chair in rhetoric in 1699 by a disputation on Quintilian's *De statibus caussarum,* an etymology and explication of the term *status,* the theory of judicial controversy that assists the rhetor in determining the center of gravity of a case. Giuliani argues that the classical theory of status made it possible to "go beyond an emotive and irrational rhetoric" because of its "objective, impartial, and neutral value" (*Art of Rhetoric* 38). With the structure of *status,* rhetoric becomes the art of distinguishing the nature of the problem, thus the approach to take in arguing the case. With the art of *status,* the judicial controversy can be seen it all its complexity as containing a plurality of questions.

These questions are based on three traditional parts of a legal controversy: on the fact, on the name, and on the law, "that is, the conjectural, the definitional, and the qualitative" or "Has he done it?", "What has he done?", and "Was his deed just?" (*Art of Rhetoric* 57). In his course manual, Vico primarily discusses the qualitative and secondarily definition. Both center on language—the section on quality, containing legal interpretation, includes a discussion of the ambiguity of language, which Vico presents as beneficial because it makes laws adaptable to varying circumstances; definition centers on the act of human creation in discriminating and assigning value to changing facts and situations. Throughout, analogy and common knowledge play an important part in generating the plurality of questions that characterize Vico's topical thinking.

Elocution, or Style

In part 2 of his rhetoric manual, Vico writes that elocution or style is the most important part of the art of rhetoric in that eloquence takes its name from that. Yet he confounds style with invention by defining elocution as "the proper exposition of the appropriate words *(idonea verba)* and thoughts *(idoneae sententiae)* suitable to the things invented and arranged *(res inventae et dispositae)*" (107). He discusses style under the headings of elegance, words and thoughts, dignity, figures of words and thoughts, and composition of the words, periods, and rhythm. In preliminary discussion, he explores the difficulties of attaining an aesthetic sense of a language that is extinct. In a discussion of the history of Latin, he asks the students to develop a Latin that will allow them not only to pass as Roman citizens, but to "appear the more elegant among the Roman citizens" (109).

In his advice on word choice, Vico speaks of using words related to the common language, emphasizing language as a vehicle of collective experience based on common sense. He includes metaphor in this advice, because he sees metaphor as ordinary language. In addition, metaphor is the premiere trope, having the potential for creating knowledge. In the following chapters, conceits, maxims, and aphorisms are viewed as common wisdom, and figures are not viewed as ornaments of speech but as mental procedures. As Giuliani writes: "Figurative language has a prescriptive, normative function and the human world and its institutions are dependent on it" (37).

At the heart of Vico's sublime rhetoric in the rhetoric manual is his chapter "On Conceits" (chapter 37), responding as much to contemporary concerns as to classical texts as he sets out advice for orators to speak by means of conceits or maxims. This chapter in particular is a crucible for Vichian thought. What interests Vico most are axioms that have a certain brilliance and show ingenuity, or *concetti*. He follows his near contemporaries Matteo Peregrini (1595–1652) and Sforza Pallavicino (1607–1652) in his exposition, especially Peregrini's golden booklet *Delle Acutezze*, setting out how to form an acute saying, by noting the things, the words, and their joining or tying. Peregrini defined acumen, the power of ingenuity, as "the fortunate invention of a medium term which in a certain saying joins diverse things with a wonderful aptness and by the most grand of eloquence" (qtd. in *Art of Rhetoric* 126). These acute sayings are linked to enthymemes or rhetorical syllogisms.

Later in the chapter on conceits, Vico praises Pallavicino, with his golden booklet *Dello Stile*. Pallavicino interests Vico because he explains the delight caused by acute sayings by linking it with the wonder of the new. From wonder come the knowledge of the previously unknown and a complex joining of truth and beauty. Such acute sayings involve the listener by causing him to explore the linked elements and to make it for himself: "Hence, he sees himself to be ingenious and delights in the acute saying, not so much as having been presented by the orator, but as he himself has understood it" (qtd. in *Art of Rhetoric* 128). Vico's concern with the participation of the listener in the discourse is apparent not only here but in the discussion of tropes, distinguishing his rhetoric from one that conceives the audience as a target or mark for the orator's persuasion. Here the listener is an interlocutor, actively seeking and making meaning and delight through his own cognitive acuity. Goetsch provides an insightful perspective on Vico's use of such acute sayings as axioms in structuring his *New Science*. Sublime rhetoric weaves together speaker and interlocutors through the orator's giving the audience the gift of learning something new in a delightful way. Sublime rhetoric marries rhetoric and poetic, truth and beauty, giving rise to that sense of holism accompanied by wonder.

Tropes and Rhetorical Figures

Tropes and figures of speech and thought take on a different cast when placed within this sublime system of civic rhetoric. Consistently with Vico's later work, tropes derive from two causes: necessity or poverty of language and ornamentation, delight, and enjoyment. The four primary tropes for Vico—synecdoche, metonymy, metaphor, and irony—are not themselves singular but are heads under which other tropes may be grouped. It is easy to see why metaphor is the principal trope, because in it "a word is transferred from its proper signification to another by means of a similitude" (139). The greatest metaphors are verbs rather than nouns because verbs give inanimate things life and movement and perhaps greater sublimity. Vico also provides familiar lists of schemata or figures, "illustrious forms in which words and thoughts are clothed" (*Art of Rhetoric* 153), along with plentiful examples.

However, he explicitly blurs his classification scheme once more by such chapters as 57, "On the Figures of Thought for Proving." Hyper-

bole seems to work as a topos: "It is that by which we propose the objections one by one and dilute them one by one," including the proposition, the enumeration of arguments, and their refutation as well as the
conclusion (176). Many of the chapters are explicitly linked to generation of text: "Figures of Thought for Explication" and "Figures of
Thought for Depicting Customs" both have inventional functions. Again,
Vico blurs a polarity, in this case form-content, in his course manual.
Rather than contradicting or having no connection with his philosophic
work, his pedagogical practice as evidenced by the *Art of Rhetoric* lecture material demonstrates that the roots of philosophic thought running well outside his rhetoric are anchored in his sublime rhetoric.[10]

Rhetoric in Vico's Other Works

Inventional arts course through Vico's corpus of work, interweaving
humanistic and scientific thought. Topical thinking to Vico was closely
tied to the construction of knowledge through language; from his earliest work it was set into opposition with the critical Cartesian philosophy of his day. Ernesto Grassi, who does not analyze Vico's course manual, describes Vico's use of topics as a "topical philosophy" that places
Vico on the side of *pathos* in a rhetorical-pathetic, logico-rational split
running through Western metaphysics. At the same time, Grassi sees
topical philosophy as Vico's effort to overcome the dualism of pathos
and logos.

   In his 1708 lecture "Study Methods," Vico reveals his growing anti-
Cartesianism as he protests the neglect of topical arts for Cartesian critical thinking. Two years later in *Most Ancient Wisdom,* he repeats his
criticisms, advising a processual use of topics to generate questions to
probe a matter, listing examples of his topical questions. Vico poses a
number of questions that function as a general heuristic for inquiry:

> And first, he must examine the question "Does the thing
> exist?" so as to avoid talking about nothing. Second, the
> question "What is it?" so as to avoid arguing about names.
> Third, "How big is it?" either in size, weight, or number.
> Fourth, "What is its quality?" under which he considers color,
> taste, softness, hardness, and other tactile matters. Fifth,
> "When was it born, how long has it lasted, and into what
> [elements] does it break down?" On this pattern, he must take
> it through the remaining categories comparatively and set it
> beside everything that is somehow germane to it. The causes

from which it arose and the effects it produces or what it does must be compared with other things like it, or different, with contraries, with things greater, smaller, and equal to it. (100)

These questions, based on mixed dialectical and rhetorical loci, condense and repeat inventional topoi from the rhetoric lectures. The first two questions are obviously from the determination of *status,* issues of fact, definition, or quality. Vico's third question reflects Aristotle's common requisite of degree and Cicero's comparison category. In the fourth, the question of quality, Vico's stress on the senses shows the influence of contemporary empirical science with its sensory emphasis.

Perhaps the most interesting question, both because of its ramifications in Vico's later work and because of its multiple origins, is that which highlights the temporal nature of Vico's thinking, the fifth: "When was it born, how long has it lasted, and into what does it break down?" This pattern of birth and decay shows up in *New Science*'s theory of *corso* and *ricorso,* in which eras of progress regularly degenerate into barbarism. Both Cicero and Quintilian show concern with events in time; Quintilian believes time was important in all types of rhetoric but especially in legal rhetoric. Cicero and Quintilian also view time in terms of cycles, being especially interested in beginnings. Others with whom Vico was familiar who emphasize cycles include Heraclitus, Plato, Herodotus, and Varro, as well as the Egyptian scholar Scheffer, and Vico credits the Egyptians with *New Science*'s three-fold division of ages into divine, heroic, and human. Herbert of Cherbury is named as an important source of Vico's topical system by Nicola Badaloni.

On the final movement in Vico's topical scheme, L. M. Palmer notes that by "putting it beside everything in any way germane to it," one assembles the elements of a mental construction of the object itself. This totalizing perspective links topics to Vico's constructivist epistemology as well as to a Cartesian quantifying methodology—"plac[ing] the thing on every categorical scale in relation to the other things on the scale." Yet the aspect of Vico's topics that Palmer finds important is that the answers to the first two questions—whether it is and what—are given only by proceeding to the fifth question of cycles. This temporal aspect provides the "different concern" of his method, which Palmer sees as integrating Aristotelian, Baconian, and Cartesian philosophy (100, n.). Vico's discussion of topical thinking in *Most Ancient Wisdom* does attempt to integrate the three, serving as a key illustration of his effort to synthesize elements from the old discourse and the new discourse of

science, which can also be seen in his echoing of Baconian texts in discussions of topics.

Vico's use here of a topical system turned to scientific discovery is
more immediately Baconian, having been presented by Bacon as containing the elements of true knowledge or science (but the term retains a
breadth unlike today with Bacon as well as Vico). Using the metaphor
of the alphabet, Bacon writes that the object of a science must be

> to inquire the forms of sense, of voluntary motion, of veg-
> etation, of colours, of gravity and levity, of density, of tenu-
> ity, of heat, of cold, and all other natures and qualities, which
> like an alphabet, are not many, and of which the essences
> (upheld by matter) of all creatures do consist. (2.7: 5)

Here we have come full circle back to the concept of simple natures as
the primary elements, which Vico has transmuted back into a topical
system, echoing Bacon as well as many others in the structuralist metaphor of an alphabet.

Using the same metaphor as in his rhetoric manual, Vico praises the
topics' ability to function as "indices and ABC's of inquiries" so that
researchers can fully survey a problem. Including both jurists and natural philosophers, Vico predicts: "And from the same source from which
well-equipped speakers spring, there also might come forth the best [sci-
entific] observers" (*Most Ancient Wisdom* 101). As in Bacon, researchers are here provided "the beginnings of a lesson whose term will be a
right reading and a true writing of the (alphabetical) order of the world"
(Reiss 210). With the extension of topics—the methods of the old discourse—to the new, Vico blurs the passage to a new discourse of science.
Moreover, he enriches and levels the sciences and arts by means of his
own interpretation of the art of topics, an epistemic linguistic art.

The ability to make connections among disparate elements, the definition Vico gives to *ingenium* in both the rhetoric manual and in *Most
Ancient Wisdom*, represents values from the old discourses of "patterning," seeking resemblances between the divine in the world and the world
of the divine. Linked also with metaphor, which constructs knowledge
through similarities, ingenuity is the power of coming to new knowledge
in Vico. Having rejected both topics and a nonrational association of
ideas, as did Locke, eighteenth-century analytico-referential thinkers are
not likely to find Vico's theories compatible, and indeed Vichian texts
such as *Most Ancient Wisdom* fell on barren soil.

Yet as a member of an Enlightenment community of natural philosophers in Naples, Vico was aware of the growing role science was play-
ing across European society. In the 1710 metaphysical text on ancient
wisdom of the Latin people, he rejects Cartesian science and offers his
own topical science, addressing natural philosophers as well as legal
scholars. In response to Cartesian science, Vico protests that a person
who is sure of perceiving a thing clearly and distinctly is often deceived,
having only a "confused knowledge of it, because he does not know all
[the elements] that are in the thing and which distinguish it from others." However, by going through the topics with a "critical eye," he will
be certain that he has a clear-and-distinct knowledge of the matter, because he has considered it in the light of all relevant questions. By working with the "places" others in the scientific community have so far made
use of, a researcher not only has a framework and a point of departure
but can hope to arrive at a consensus of others trained in the discipline.
However, with Cartesian introspection, all one can know is the *certum*
of one's own consciousness of a matter or data, not a true understanding of causes, *verum*, or knowledge. For Vico, complete topical thinking becomes critical as well as being creative (*Most Ancient Wisdom*
101). Once again, Vico has deconstructed the invention-judgment binary
along with the rhetoric-science opposition.

Topics and Scientific Thought

Atilla Fáj was one of the earliest to argue that Vico was positing his
theories in the realm of science as well as humanities:

> Are the loci, considered as preconceptions, useful for discov-
> eries in mathematics and in the natural sciences or do they
> impede directly every revealing operation? I believe that Vico
> had a notion of the fertility of topoi as preconceptions even
> in fields outside the historical sciences; in fact, in these fields
> he could operate with several cognate theories in ancient
> philosophy and rhetoric. ("Unorthodox Logic" 93)

Fáj believes that the art of topics not only makes allowances for "personal, temporal, local, and other circumstantial factors" but also brings
to light changes of meaning, thereby assisting scientific progress ("Unorthodox Logic" 93). Barnouw also maintains that Vico's work, including *New Science,* responds to the new science of the seventeenth century, arguing that Vico disputes Cartesian conceptions of science and

proposes a new conception of science as a whole, not a separate method
for the study of socially and historically constituted realities (609). This
new science is based on the theories of the maker's knowledge, *ingenium*,
imagination, and topical thinking. The encouragement of the imagination is to help in the cultural pursuit of rational truth and serve as a base
for critical and rational faculties (614).

Yet if Vico is proposing a science suitable for either humanities or
natural science, a unified science, what happens to the realm of probabilities, the sacred space of civic life? In *New Science,* Vico places his
ideal eternal history with its certainty in the realm of science, of universal truth. Has he thereby ceased to maintain the humanistic realm of
probability he defends so staunchly in *Study Methods* and *Most Ancient
Wisdom,* the basis for his forty-year teaching career? His reconfiguration
of the sciences would make the *verum-factum* principle and degrees of
human constructivity the principle of division between the sciences, dis-
placing the divisions of probability and certainty. Yet the notions of
probability and probable judgment are two of the main elements of
Vichian rhetoric.

The Probable Realm

In his early works such as *Study Methods,* Vico describes mathematics
as the most certain endeavor and human sciences such as rhetoric and
history operating in a separate realm of probability. However, by *New
Science,* this certainty-probability dichotomy is more often described in
terms of degrees of certainty, as in Locke, with the history of human
institutions being most certain because it has been constructed by humans. With the placing of natural sciences into the realm of the contingent, Vico essentially rhetoricizes the sciences, transferring them to the
realm requiring the flexibility of thought of the civic world.

In the 1708 oration *Study Methods,* he argues against a critical education, saying that judgments in practical civic affairs must be based on
a consideration of probabilities rather than the certainties privileged in
Cartesian mathematics-based thought. He protests the Cartesian move
to locate everything from science to human affairs in the realm of certainty, noting that the critical method requires that all falsehood, as well
as "secondary truths and probabilities," must be "banished from the
mind" (Pompa, *Vico* 37).

Later in the first inaugural oration, he explains the relationship of
probabilities to prudence, saying that because the "mistresses of human

affairs are opportunity and choice," both uncertain, "those whose only concern is for the truth find it difficult to attain the means, and even more the ends, of public life" (Pompa, *Vico* 42). Public life is dependent on human vagaries and is relativistic and circumstantial:

> [I]t is wrong to transfer to the sphere of practical wisdom the method of judgment which is proper to knowledge. For the latter judges things according to correct reasons, whereas men are for the most part fools, governed not by reason, but by caprice and fortune. Moreover, it judges things according to how they ought to be, whereas in fact, they happen for the most part at random. (Pompa, *Vico* 43)

However, by the time of *New Science,* we see that Vico has changed: though things happen unpredictably, they are, as modern chaos theory shows us, not entirely random; neither are most humans fools for they are guided by an immanent providence. Similar to Vico's early work, however, the development of prudence and common sense overcomes some of the randomness of human life. There, the emphasis on probabilities results from his concern for the development of prudence but also of common sense, because, as he has previously noted, "common sense arises from probabilities. For probabilities stand halfway, so to speak, between truth and falsehood, since they are almost always true and very rarely false" (Pompa, *Vico* 37). In this early work, Vico explains that transferring a method proper to the scientific sphere of certainty to the probable sphere of human civic affairs is wrong; those who do so "have not cultivated common sense." Moreover, "content with a single truth, [they] have never sought after probabilities [and] they fail altogether to consider what men feel in common about this one truth or whether the probabilities appear true to them" (Pompa, *Vico* 43).

For civic life, divergent thinking producing a host of probable causes is preferable to linear thought producing the single cause of science. A rhetorical social knowledge, relative to a time or place, constitutes practical wisdom: With his sharpened mind, the citizen can quickly grasp the reality of a situation so that he speaks and acts spontaneously but with dignity and is ready for anything. This model citizen is both a rhetor and scientist, a flexible thinker who uses language and logic in both problem solving and persuasion. Feminists may seek elements for a revised theory of the citizen in Vico's model citizen, but with caution, for this model citizen is necessarily a man, based ultimately on the male citizen of the Roman republic. Yet the divergent thinking Vico describes as necessary for the contingencies of social life is an element missing from modern communication and political theorists today. Vico's theories of how thought grows from the body have political and moral significance that contemporary feminist philosophers have productively if cautiously begun to explore.

Rhetoric and the New Science

The questions *New Science* leaves with the historian of rhetoric are: "If history is a science based on language, what kind of science is it?" and "What kind of science is rhetoric?" Lachterman believes that Vico never

> confuses a theoretical science of the invariant principles of human institutions and their development with a suppositious science of the contingent actions of individuals or nations. Rhetoric, not science, addresses itself to this contingent realm. (47)

Yet it is possible to read in Vico a blurring of these boundaries, and Lachterman himself notes the conflation of rhetoric and philosophy (science) in Vico. Perhaps this is another case of Vico's principle of history that human intentions are often thwarted by subconscious processes.

In *Most Ancient Wisdom,* Vico begins to conflate scientific with rhetorical methods, if not rhetoric itself, first in advocating topical thinking in science and second in speaking of wisdom as an ability to perceive and react wisely to particulars in diverse situations as a goal for both those in the sciences such as physics and the constructive arts (Palmer 61). With his growing emphasis on *verum-factum* having its degrees of certainty according to its process of making (mathematics being most certain in *Most Ancient Wisdom,* history most certain in *New Science*), Vico subverts his own earlier division of realms into probability and certainty. In conflating science and rhetoric, Vico is in step with the dialectical tradition leading up to Bacon, as traced in Lisa Jardine's work.

In another instance of Vico's conflation of division, Fisch argues that Vico's new science of humanity displaces Aristotle's traditional categorization of the sciences into contemplative, practical, or productive divisions. The new science fits all three, but it is

> in the first place productive as studying signs of our own making and relations among them . . . In sum, the trichotomy of knowing, doing, and making is untenable. What is none

of our doing or making is none of our knowing either. And
not only are doing and making prerequisite to further knowing, but knowing cannot later detach itself from them or be
made to precede them. ("Vico's *Practica*" 429)

Just as Aristotle's theoretical-practical division has been made un-
tenable or irrelevant by the productive epistemology of Vico's *New Science*, so have other taxonomies. As Nikhil Bhattacharya points out:

In Vico's theory of knowledge, all knowledge must be after
the fact, that is, after effecting a construction. Cognitively,
traditional epistemology separates mathematical and empirical judgments in two different categories: Vico does not. . . .
Furthermore, even the traditional distinction between necessary and contingent statements is no longer useful. Since
knowledge is of causes of constructions, and causes are activities, it would seem that since activities appear to be contingent, all knowledge is of the contingent.
 . . . It is perhaps more accurate to say that for Vico knowledge is of hypothetical necessity. (190)

Vichian knowledge is contingent, yet is not random or arbitrary because
it is based on knowledge of causes, "the kinds and forms from which
each thing is made," in short, knowledge of its origins (*Most Ancient
Wisdom* 100). The ability of humans to recollect and construct becomes
the determining principle in the new division—or rather unification—
of knowledge, with the reader's own narration of human history—or
demonstration of it—raised to the rank of most certain. This may be
Vico's parallel to the Baconian recognition that writing—literate experience—is the foundation for science.

How do we know Baconian scientific writing is true? The "proof
of the pudding is in the eating," as Reiss puts it. Bacon says "practical
results" will guarantee truth. How does Vico guarantee the truth of his
historical science in the *New Science*? His sublime rhetoric again comes
into play. He invites his readers to reflect on it, to make it for themselves:
"Indeed, we make bold to affirm that he who meditates this Science
narrates to himself this ideal eternal history so far as he himself makes
it for himself by that proof 'it had, has, and will have to be'" (104, par.
349). This is a form of constructive verification, but it is not transcendental correspondence or coherence. If readers find it consistent within itself
and with their own experience as human beings, they have constructed it

successfully. They have scientifically demonstrated history. They will know even more certainly when they meditate on whether there are more or fewer or different causes explaining human history than he has offered. Vico's inventional thinking through topics served precisely to produce the multiple causes needed to understand reality in the legal or rhetorical realm, which makes this a rhetorical proof. He says that in the process of imaginative reflection, the reader will receive "sublime, natural theological proof" by "experienc[ing] in his mortal body a divine pleasure as he contemplates in the divine ideas the world of nations in all the extent of its places times and varieties" (*New Science* 103, par. 345). Rather than a logical proof, this is the transport that serves as proof of sublimity in rhetoric. Knowledge, which begins with the body through language, is confirmed with the mind-body's assent of delight and pleasure.

The rhetorical implications of this alternative conception of science go to the heart of rhetoric's very definition as a field. For when in *New Science* Vico shifts the ground out from under scientific certainty, rhetoric can no longer be defined in opposition to science. If science is indeed rhetoricized, there is no longer a purely objective way of knowing uncontaminated by social circumstances to serve as a foil for rhetoric. This means that science and rhetoric join in the same realm, with the difference being only a matter of degrees of constructivity in any particular case. Such is the result of Vico's effort to reconcile the old and new discursive practices, recognizing the rhetoricality of science more than three centuries before Thomas S. Kuhn or Herbert Simons explore the revolutionizing concept of science's emergent rhetoricality.

However, Vico does not explore the consequences for either natural science or rhetoric of his new science, and most commentators believe he continues to maintain the same division between human science and physical science throughout his work. Of course, he does maintain a division, but it cannot be the same division as before, and one result is that it elevates the prestige of the human sciences, including rhetoric. Vico writes in his 1731 "Practic" of the *New Science* that the history and theory of jurisprudence—linked with rhetoric and politics in the universities of his time and the prime subject of his history of humanity—should be at the head of the sciences.

Although Vico has provided a rhetoric harmonious with contemporary science, why has not his rhetoric been acclaimed, and why has his work been occulted so that every century must discover Vico anew? These repeated rediscoveries were out of step with earlier eras because they made the purely objective science of positivism an impossibility and did away with the Cartesian vision of the fragmented universe explored by the isolated scientist who doubts. Vichian knowledge is a community production, more harmonious with the vision of communities of scientists some see provided by Bacon.

Struever believes that Vico's communitarian impetus caused him to be out of step with his times:

> I would maintain that Vico attempts nothing less than an epistemological basis for a theory of community. . . . His achievement, I think, illuminates both his isolation in early modern European intellectual history and the basic contrast between the declining Italian Humanism and the French rationalism dominant in the seventeenth and eighteenth centuries. (184–85)

Vico's body of texts manifests a socially constructed rhetorical knowledge that deconstructs dichotomies still entrenched in many rhetorics today, such as the philosophy-rhetoric split, invention-judgment, and signification-persuasion. His theories of rhetoric are not familiarly modern, opposing Cartesian values still dominant, a path on which the boundaries between the arts and sciences and among their disciplines remain fluid and in which disciplinary knowledge does not fragment into the atomistic curricula of most modern educational institutions.

Eloquence, for Vico, as Verene has stressed, is not mere stylistic display. It is wisdom speaking and speaking of the whole, for the "whole is really the flower of wisdom" (*Study Methods* 77). Perhaps the least modern aspect of Vico's thought is this concern for the whole, linked with his effort to create a unified vision of human history. His views on language and rhetoric are central to this encyclopedic vision (but as Battistini points out, this is not the modern sense of encyclopedism emerging in that period in France). On the other hand, if Vico's methods are antimodern or countermodern, his projects themselves are representatively Enlightenment. As such, his sublime rhetoric with its emphasis on the image and emotional arousal of a culturally unified audience can be read with suspicion by post-twentieth-century, post-Holocaust moderns. The double-edged Enlightenment draws fire on both edges: it is both too rational and too aesthetically emotional in its thrust.[11] Vico's classical synthesis attempts to escape dualism in his search for continuities of persuasion and signification despite shifting exigencies and circumstances.

As David Harvey points out, the project of modernity itself is to find eternal and immutable values despite the fragmentation and change of the modern day. This clash itself launches the project of history, for as Harvey notes: "If there is any meaning to history, then that meaning has to be discovered and defined from within the maelstrom of change, a maelstrom that affects the terms of discussion as well as whatever it is that is being discussed" (11–12). Swirled about in that maelstrom, Vico reaches for meaning, a sublime historical significance, making his corpus part of the project of modernity.

If Vico represents the emerging modern filtered and framed by classicism and Renaissance humanism and if he saw the rational modern age as one of barbarity, his solution was to work on the present, not to return to the past, in contrast to Monboddo (see, for example, "Practic of the *New Science*"). Condillac represents a purer strain of modernity, not surprising considering his situation in rationalistic France. His armaments remain classical texts, but his attitude to them has now shifted. He wields their power as needed and takes whatever interests him from them but expends no energy in arguing for them or in conserving their arts. If the Greeks have had their day, if the Roman Empire its glory, and if Italy its glorious Renaissance, perhaps it is now time for France and a new golden age.

5
Condillac and Modern Rhetoric: Across the Threshold

> The business is to unfold their gradual progression, and to shew in what manner they are all derived from one fundamental and simple perception. This research alone is of more use than all the rules of logicians. For how indeed could we be ignorant of the manner of conducting the operations of the mind if we were once well acquainted with their origin? But all this quarter of metaphysics has hitherto lain involved in such obscurity and confusion, that I have been obliged to frame to myself, in some measure, a new language.
>
> —Condillac, *Essay on the Origin of Human Knowledge* (Nugent translation)

> Le commencement était le plus difficile: il n'y avait même de difficulté que bien commencer. [The hardest thing was always beginning: You could even say that the only hard thing was beginning well.]
>
> —Condillac, *Cours d'études pour l'Instruction du Prince du Parme*

Quarrels over modernity coalesced and consolidated against the backdrop of a neoclassical rhetoric that peaked in France at midpoint of the eighteenth century. Montesquieu's *De l'Esprit des loi* of 1748 represents an emergent feeling of contrast between classical antiquity and modernity, yet it sets the stage as well for the discussions of civic republicanism often provoked by neoclassical thought (Wright, 202). From Vico's standpoint nearer to Renaissance humanism, his knowledge of classical texts gave him a less mixed classical orientation. Rhetoric could become more aestheticized, but it could also become more prescriptive and rigid as it took on neoclassical values. Vico's notion of a common sense held by the public body and the practices of his rhetoric retained the shared knowledge and flexible ways of knowing that formed the basis of classical civic culture. As modernity progressed, classical ways of knowing tended to lose ground to a more individualistic, mentalistic form of knowing, produced and verified by what would become modern experts. Rhetoric's traditional social epistemology and civic wisdom would be condensed into a straw figure to be tossed aside in the modernist momentum to grasp and represent scientifically a reality outside human social life.

On the threshold of modernity, Vico returns to beginnings to understand human development and thus to augur, to divine, and to prophesy the future. He has little faith humans can avert the providential cycles of history and becomes a Cassandra, warning of catastrophic events with little hope of being heard or actually bringing about change. In contrast, the future seemed brighter and full of promise for the more modern Étienne de Bonnot, Abbé de Condillac. In his philosophy, a return to origins to retrace events could serve as the proper method to put things back on the right course if, indeed, they had gone astray. This process optimistically affirms that one can accurately judge historical deviation, that progress is possible, that the right knowledge will emerge from the right method, and that human mental structures will perfectly match the structures of the universe. Nonetheless, just under the surface, Condillac's powerful human passions would seem to undermine this optimism, which is based on faith in human reason.

It is clear that Vico's situation and problematic are not Condillac's: Condillac enters upon an intellectual scene in which a thoroughly French modernity had long since been proposed and accepted, in theory, if not always in practice. Thus, he assumes the positive values of the modern while attempting to retrace, refine, and extend the project of modernity. He perfects his modernist method first in his *Essay on the Origin of Human Knowledge* revising John Locke and consistently applies it in his voluminous and wide-ranging philosophical and pedagogical inquiries. The social and political consequences of his philosophies were ambiguous, especially in his language and educational texts. However, in his Lockean and sensualist moments, he represents the radical Enlightenment. He was also an economist and a younger brother of Mably, a classical republican often regarded as a founder of socialism.[1]

Condillac accepts many of the shifts that have occurred in rhetoric over time as necessary and rational. If the art of rhetoric long ago collapsed into poetics, so be it. Moderns can scarce understand the force of Demosthenes' speeches anyway—that is in the course of things. We should no more imitate the ancients than we should dress like them (a statement that might be read as an argument against his classical republican

brother Mably if it were not so strictly linked with language arts). French
has its own beauties, its own national course of development, its own
national genius. After the often perplexing baroque style of Vico, the
clear and distinct prose of Condillac feels like a return home after a diz-
zying trip to Naples.

The modernist Condillac advises in undertaking any problem a re-
gression to the *germe* of the problem, a return to origins. This method
becomes a standard move in the modern progressive repertoire. Thus,
in deciding issues of writing and rhetoric, Condillac returns to the origin of language.

Kenneth Burke's notion of transformation, the subtle shifting of
elements over time until they are positioned quite differently, helps describe the cumulative effects of Condillac's texts, which work to shift
or transform what Thomas S. Kuhn has called "antecedently available
terms," in this case, moving away from neoclassical rhetoric and toward
belles lettres. Condillac's works repeat classical terms, especially from
Ciceronian rhetoric, but with a difference, and they also add to rhetoric. Jacques Derrida's notion of the innocent supplement that comes to
supplant is exemplified in Condillac: a recommended return to an origin becomes a universal method, a Newtonian law. Discoveries made by
that method also become laws, such as the discovery that all language,
that is, all knowledge, is transformed sensation expressed originally
through natural gesture and developing through the connection of ideas.
Condillac has devoured the ancients as well as their French neoclassical
proponents and makes use of them for modern purposes. Like Vico,
Condillac also describes a rhetoric of science: each discipline is comprised
by its rhetoric, for a science is no more (nor less) than a well-made language. This modern transformation of rhetoric to rhetoricality can be
found in germ wherever language and meaning are examined.[2]

Because his philosophical essays work out essential problems of
modernity—although there is little interest in him today in France—
Condillac remains an important philosopher of modern rhetoric and
language. For this project in particular, his widely published logic and
course of studies are also significant because they revolutionized education and educational philosophy at the end of the eighteenth century.[3]

In his narrative of language's natural origin and progress, his pedagogy based on a language-centered theory of cognitive development, his
cultural view of literary progress, and his explanation of how anything
new ever comes to exist, Condillac reveals both his modernity and the
continuing presence of the past. At the heart of his translation of the past

was the creation of a system of rhetoric via repetition of and analogy to both John Locke and Isaac Newton.

By returning to origins, correcting Locke, and working out a linguistic analogue to Newtonian scientific theory, Condillac discovers the law of the attraction of signs, based on analogous concepts such as attraction and force. This law becomes Condillac's principle that in the search for truth and certainty, signs should always be strongly linked or rationally connected in the right order, his principle of greatest analogy (Aarsleff, *Condillac* 187). But, ultimately, analogy to what? And whose definition of analogy? Vico's analogy, as with Platonic analogy, has an otherworldly resonance along with its secular, modern, scientific purpose. This concept becomes the crossroad of old and new in Condillac and reveals his hybridity and hesitation on the threshold of modernity.[4]

Despite Condillac's contradictions and the hybrid nature of his texts, scholars have often read Condillac in a one-dimensional way, and Michel Foucault has continued this tradition. Although there are many discourses in the multidimensional Condillac, the best work seriously takes on more than one of them, acknowledging both the sensory-empirical and the rational-spiritual strands of his thought. Hans Aarsleff's recent introduction to Condillac's *Essay on the Origin of Human Understanding* best accounts for the complex dimensions brought about by the ratios of passion and intellect in the essay.

This dualism is mirrored in the sociology and history of France where Condillac can be located at a crossroads socially and historically in France. He reflects and refracts a dualistic classical tradition from seventeenth-century France synthesizing a plainer-styled rhetoric with ties to the parliamentary, the bourgeois, and the future revolution with the more elaborate, courtly Ciceronian rhetoric associated with the monarchy, with an emerging sublime science of poetics, and with salon culture. This courtly rhetoric had existed earlier as an art of education or advice to a prince (an Italian prince), a tradition Condillac builds on with his educational program for the Prince of Parma.[5] Notwithstanding the sensual and courtly strain of his rhetoric, Condillac is still primarily regarded as a mechanist or empiricist advocating the plain style. He is stereotyped as reducing everything to a mechanical response to sensation. (On the other hand, it is also possible to stereotype him as reducing everything to the sign.) His repetitions of the past and his striking innovations produce an oscillation between mechanism and organicism (see Derrida's *Archeology*), alternatively scientism and Romanticism, that complicate his theories of rhetoric.

The English had captured the European imagination in the first half of the eighteenth century. British thought—that pragmatic constitutionalism and empirico-rationalism embodied in diverse ways in Locke and Newton—excited minds working on myriad problems bequeathed by René Descartes. The Abbé de Condillac, like his exemplar Locke, serves in ways as a mere underlaborer collecting and documenting already existing theories and practices of seventeenth- and eighteenth-century France. At the same time, his texts serve as the knot fixing those practices and beliefs, attitudes and values into a coherent and recognizable, if not consistent, set. This set reappropriates French theory from the English (after all, Locke began with Descartes and Pierre Gassendi) and revises it for the glory of French nationhood.

Condillac's body of work revolutionizes by repeating and appropriating the past. He enters discussions of method begun by medieval educators and Francis Bacon. He champions the properties of linearity and analysis in language—both purifying moves elevating philosophical or scientific discourse—all the while resting his theories on nature and naturalness through an emphasis on natural language rooted in analogy and in the origin of language in natural gesture. The stress point in his work by which I attempt to prize out his rhetoric is this contradiction between analysis or purification symbolized by rational connection and uncontrolled associationism, networking, or translation.

Transformation by analogy, or an "ana-logic" linked with nature (Leavey 17), becomes the point of greatest stress both in his philosophy and theories of rhetoric. If a modern rhetoric of real force relies on analogical principles based on nature and an original natural language, humans may make themselves unnatural, alien to themselves, by using language in philosophical-scientific ways. Thus, a form of nostalgia lies at the core of Condillac's expressive rhetoric, which must be developed as such in order to return us to ourselves and to compensate for our losses in becoming scientists (even of language). This is at the heart of Condillac's dual systems of rhetoric: (1) a discourse of analogy-organicism, sensation, nature, and emotionality and (2) a discourse of mechanism, cultivated humans, and rationality. The two are never clearly separated because they are two ends of a developmental spectrum. The natural is the base, God-given, and common to all while the philosophic or scientistic is the developed human analogue to original creation. Humans and their society move out of and away from nature, whose forces they cannot control, and toward controlled, rational connections. However, paradoxically, even what is natural in rhetoric must be learned and perfected through observation and reflection on the greatest connection of ideas, using a perfected Lockean method.

Language and Organic Nature in the *Origin* Essay

Exactly four decades after the posthumous fifth edition of Locke's *An Essay Concerning Human Understanding,* Condillac published a text whose explicit purpose was to revise and perfect Lockean theory. This was his 1746 *Origin* essay *Sur l'origine des connaissances humaines (Essay on the Origin of Human Understanding).* This essay (translated into English by Thomas Nugent in 1756) and Condillac's later works, including a multivolume educational program written for the Prince of Parma, add to Lockean theory what Locke himself suggests but never fully carries out—a developmental account of human understanding.[6] Following Locke's "Historical, plain Method" (*Essay* 1.1.2: 44), Condillac focuses on tracing the origins of human understanding. In the process, he discovers a missing link in Locke's chain of logic, the *liaison des idées* (linking or connection of ideas, his version of something like Newtonian attraction) that becomes a founding principle of all his later work.[7] Condillac's great insight into language and understanding is that "the use of signs is the principle which unfolds the germ of all our ideas" (Nugent 11). This is because "ideas connect with signs," and it is, as I will show, only by this means that they "connect among themselves" (Aarsleff, *Condillac* 5). Therefore, the connection of ideas through signs becomes the route to understanding.

Although Condillac's attempt to provide a genetic account of the understanding leads him to language origins and the insight that human thought is impossible without signs, he later explores how much of thought is possible without signs. He writes in a letter to French scientist Pierre-Louis Moreau de Maupertuis, "I . . . was mistaken and gave too much to signs." Aarsleff argues that Condillac meant "he had failed to give sufficient emphasis to the equal necessity of social intercourse"[8] (Introduction, *Condillac* xxvi). In Condillac's later *Treatise on Sensation,* he explores how much active human judgment is involved in even the lowest sensory stimulus.[9] This combination of ambiguity, oscillation, and duality of Condillac's work is a signature. In language theory, his body of work maintains a Lockean theory of language as representative of ideas or things, grafting on to it a neoclassical or belletristic theory of language as expressive of feelings, feelings of passion or transport, as in Longinus. This results in (at least) two theories of language at work in his texts, theories that can be seen as the end points of a developmental spectrum with the originary or primitive expressive language on one end and the cultivated or mature philosophical language at the other. These dual strands at the heart of Condillac's language theory—and particularly the often-overlooked aesthetic expressivism—grow out of his speculations on the expressive origins of language in nature, the origin of force and powerful rhetoric.

Condillac came from a family of administrators to the crown. Mably, one of his older brothers, was a famous socialist and republican. Jean-Jacques Rousseau was a tutor in the family of the oldest brother, Jean. Condillac's social position as a member of the nobility of the robe, as a representative of the Church—although he was a nonpracticing priest—and early in his career as an active participant in Parisian salon life embodies many contradictions. In particular, his roles entailed the tensions between the eloquence of courtly rhetoric and the less elaborate parliamentary rhetoric espoused by the aristocrats vying for power against the monarchy. His dualistic language theories reflect the synthesis of courtly and parliamentary language described by Marc Fumaroli, and he also respects the delicately balanced stylistic compromise of the French classicists. By embracing Lockean rhetoric—with its aim of seeking not rhetorical probabilities, but the greatest certainty in truth, a linear inferential order, and a scientific plain style—Condillac creates a new synthesis. Instead of a rhetoric built on a tension between public parliamentary and private courtly discourse, he sets up a tension between an increasingly arhetorical scientific discourse and an increasingly privatized poetic discourse. This is not unlike the later split between poetic and scientific discourse that we know best from the New Critics. This paradoxical split and hesitation between scientific and expressive rhetoric, based on a Newtonian universal law of connection and attraction, comprise Condillac's modern rhetorical system. It is not only modern because it echoes Newton and the new science, but it is also modern in Bruno Latour's sense because of its constitution founded upon unexamined contradictions, isolated concepts that mingle despite efforts to keep them conceptually pure.[10]

Organic Language at Its (Natural) Origin

In the *Origin* essay, Condillac follows his historical method, which states that if we would understand anything, we must return to its origin in nature. He then constructs his dual rhetorical system on the grounds of a speculative narrative in which language originates in the instinctive emotional expression of human needs and desires. This ancient narrative, common in classical texts, is similar to those of other language theorists of his day, having many obvious parallels with Vico, whose work he probably had not read but that was known in France; the two share many common sources. Condillac acknowledges his debt to Bishop William Warburton, primarily *Divine Legation of Moses* (1738–1741) and *Essai sur les hiéroglyphes des egyptiens* (1744). Like Warburton (and earlier Vico), Condillac avoids criticism on theological grounds and emphasizes the human role in language production by beginning his origins story after the Biblical Flood. In this linguistic state of nature, Condillac imagines two children each wandering alone in a desert long after the Flood. They encounter one another and join ranks, assisting one another through an instinct of sympathy or empathy. They express their feelings by "natural cries" in the manner of beasts, accompanied by violent motions, or "natural" gestures, which correspond instinctively to their physical or mental states. There is no possibility for dissimulation in this expression—all expression is immediate truth.

If our body retains traces of this natural language today, the domination by the body is nearly complete in the earliest language of gesture and action. Gesture itself "analyzes" reality, and significantly, gesture works and develops through analogy. This earliest language is innate, powerfully expressive, and not under human control. However, as the two early humans continue to interact by gestures and cries, eventually, by habit and repetition, they begin to associate signs. With that crucial turn to concentration, language and mind begin to develop dialectically. The earliest speech is mixed with the language of gesture and from the poverty of language is necessarily metaphorical and poetical. Signs accumulate significantly, always invented by analogy to other signs in the same system of language.

As humans gradually accustom themselves to naming things, a process that segments or analyzes the more holistic language of gesture, through habit they find speech more efficient and slowly give up gesture altogether. Significantly, Condillac connects the origins of dance with this earliest natural "language of action" and links the varied intonations of the earliest speech with music (*Essay* 118). The historic proximity of speech to expression and the arts leads him to classify eloquence with music and poetry, with aesthetics rather than with logic or jurisprudence, as do, for example, Vico and later Richard Whately.

As language continues to progress, it becomes less poetic and more prosaic so that the human mind becomes less imaginative and more analytic. In this way, Condillac's developmental history posits a system in which both the individual and species are spread out between two poles—that of childhood, poetry, and imagination and that of maturity, prose, and analysis. The development of the sign serves as the threshold joining the one to the other.

Attractions of the Sign: *La Liaison des Idées*

As has been noted, Condillac's revision of Locke primarily entails the organicist attempt to retrace a matter in an unbroken genealogical line to its germ, seed, or origin. To help explain the origin and progress of the understanding, Condillac's *Origin* essay posits the development of three kinds of signs, elaborating his narrative of language origins and development. First, signs may be accidental or of the type that may be the "objects that some particular circumstances have connected" with some of our ideas" such as a particular kind of tree with a fruit (Aarsleff, *Condillac* 36). Signs may also be natural, facial expressions, cries, or gestures of passion established by nature. Condillac's views of this natural body language bear striking resemblance to our contemporary research on nonverbal communication. These two kinds of signs are all that our imaginary early children possessed before the crucial development of the true sign. Repetition of rudimentary signs over much time, partly because of habit, revealed to the children the possibilities of the arbitrary or *instituted* sign, one that is made up of conventional words or other arbitrary means of signification.

For Condillac, it may be possible to think using accidental or natural signs, but the faculties of (long-term) memory and higher intellectual functions absolutely require instituted signs. This tripartite theory of signs leads to Condillac's great insight into language and understanding, *la liaison des idées,* or the idea that "the use of signs is the principle which unfolds the germ of all our ideas" (Nugent 7). This great insight was that "ideas connect with signs, and it is as I will show, only by this means that they connect among themselves" (Aarsleff, *Condillac* 5). Therefore, the sequential connection of ideas through signs becomes not only the origin of the understanding, but the very process of coming to knowledge, or method itself.[11]

This three-part analysis of the sign precedes and somewhat parallels Charles Sanders Peirce's familiar division of signs into icons, indexes, and symbols.[12] Derrida's *The Archeology of the Frivolous: Reading Condillac,* an introduction to Condillac, stresses the teleology of the sign as it moves from the involuntary natural state to the final freedom of the instituted, arbitrary sign. Nonetheless, Condillac never ceases to value the originary, expressive reality, because the prelinguistic state of nature remains a touchstone for truth. It is a higher truth than human-made (or socially made) truth of later cultures. In the early state of nature as well as early in the development of language, humans had no need or ability to lie—the instant expression of emotion was true and universally understandable. Yet with the progress of language, although we gain in analysis and mastery, we also lose, because language loses its capacity for instantaneous communication of certain truth.

Therefore, dance, music, poetry—and eloquence, with its arts of rhythm and gesture—remain closer to the body and to truth than in later philosophical or scientific discourse. This dialectically pulls the teleology of the sign away from the freedom bequeathed by its arbitrary institution. Indeed, as Condillac makes clear in his later work, signs are never purely arbitrary, primarily because they must be formed in and through analogy to previous signs or to words in the linguistic system.

In part because of this Adamicist natural language (in Aarsleff's terms), Condillac's philosophies can honorably maintain ties with courtly and aristocratic rhetorics. This is at a time when some *philosophes* (Rousseau and Denis Diderot, for example) rejected salon life and its elaborate art of conversation as being no more than flattery, seduction, and artifice. Condillac—an aristocrat if only a minor one—admits to some degeneration of contemporary language. Yet in contrast to his contemporaries, he avoids too pointedly criticizing the overly stylized discourse of the salon.[13] This was a moderate stance for one whose standpoint was midway between the church and society, the aristocratic and the rising middle classes. However, an elaborate style in Condillacian rhetorical theory would appear more natural than the extremes of plain style. Finally equivocating, he advocates a conventional naturalness in his work on belletristic style, producing a hybrid of nature and culture, muddying the waters of neoclassical and modern rhetorics.[14]

The Sign as Seed of the Cognitive Machine

In his inquiry into the understanding after Locke, Condillac announces his significant discovery: Human understanding absolutely requires instituted signs. This theory of the sign becomes the basis for his model of cognitive operations outlined in the *Origin* essay, an early developmental psychology. Condillac attempted to follow Locke's genetic method, but he was dissatisfied with the discussion of innate ideas therein because Locke simply assumes the existence of higher mental operations, such as reflection, without explaining them. Although accepting primary faculties, such as the understanding and the will, Condillac wanted to set their processes into motion rather than reifying existing concepts, especially reflection. Thus, Condillac begins his *Origin* essay with an explanation of the progressive operations of the mind, showing how they produce themselves from their "first cause."

In Lockean manner, this first cause is perception, or the impression in the soul from the agitation of the senses. Condillac's second operation is awareness, the elementary consciousness of perception, and the third is attention. The stage of attention brings in subjective elements because "Things attract our attention by the aspect that is most relevant to our disposition, our passions, and our condition of life" (Aarsleff, *Condillac* 24, par. 14). The crucial stage of attention makes a purely representational theory of language an impossibility. The act of attention becomes the crossroads for the biological and psychological, for the individual and cultural. Human particulars oscillate with human universals in this Enlightenment philosophy. The fourth operation, reminiscence, informs us we have had these perceptions before, and it is at this stage that natural signs come into play. This stage, which Condillac separates from true memory, introduces a concept similar to what we today call short-term memory. The fifth stage, imagination, works closely with reminiscence and revives the image of the perception. However, Condillac has much more to say about imagination, which also functions in a richer manner than that closer to reminiscence, bringing in two concepts of imagination, similar to the Romantic fancy and the true creative imagination. The sixth operation, contemplation, extends the life of our imaginations, and the seventh, memory, brings us control over all our mental operations through giving us the power to revive a perception with arbitrary signs and dispose our attention for ourselves (Aarsleff, *Condillac* 25–28). Despite the linearity of the operations, we also see a certain spiraling or mirroring of some operations—such as, reminiscence, attention, and imagination—on a higher level.

True to Longinian values, Condillac tells us the operation of imagination is key to the human use of signs. True memory, developed only through arbitrary or instituted signs, gives humans power over their imaginations, which is necessary to make them fully and creatively human. Yet imagination is the operation that offers up signs to the memory, serving as a connective hinge between the lower and the upper stages of mental operations.[15] With memory, we can frame or conceive of our ideas. All this chain of cognitive activity, from perception to conception, throughout dependent on the connection of ideas through arbitrary signs, makes up the understanding. The three late operations—imagination, contemplation, and memory—require signs of some type, but memory absolutely requires the instituted sign. The instituted sign links the understanding with the will and the power to control our thoughts and minds.[16]

As in Vico's work, where civilization begins with the human ability to still their bodies, bodily control becomes important because humans are naturally out of control. Condillac's human bodies are always being moved from without and seem powerless to control their immediate natural passionate responses to their worlds. As Condillac later makes clear in his *Art of Writing* for the Prince of Parma, despite our progress, we are still creatures of passion and dominated by our bodies.

> The passions have command over all the movements of the soul and the body. We are never in a state of total tranquility because we are feeling creatures; calmness is nothing but the state of being relatively less moved.
>
> It is in vain for man to flatter himself that he can evade this domination: everything in him is the expression of feelings: a word, a gesture, a glance reveals them, and his soul is disclosed.
>
> It is in this manner that our body, in spite of us, retains a language that manifests even our most hidden thoughts.[17]
> (*Oeuvres* 1.15: 578)

Yet Condillac seems to say that even those who have gained the most control over themselves through instituted signs cannot control the body language that threatens to reveal them to their social worlds. Even cognitive rationalism must bow to the priority of the passions.

The Machine in Motion: Analogous Realities

For Condillac natural or prelinguistic thought—those mysterious and elusive ideas before the sign—has no succession in time but is static and holistic, like a picture. Because it is free of analysis, it is strong in imagination and emotionally powerful, similar to the earliest language. Therefore, the best language for imaginative, expressive texts is one that tries to recreate this all-at-onceness, this powerful tableau effect of prelinguistic thought.

Conversely, the very linearity of instituted language forces us to decompose thought or the holistic visual world into discrete, linear units that are spoken or read over time. This moves away from the aesthetic pole of language and toward the philosophic. For example, in his pedagogy, Condillac liked to place his young pupil, the Prince of Parma, before a window with shutters that were opened to give a brief view of the landscape. Aarsleff summarizes:

> In remembering and talking about this landscape, the young man was forced to analyze the instantaneous unitary tableau into elements he recalled as single units—trees, shrubbery, bushes, fences, groves, and the like. He was forced to think sequentially because discourse is linear. It was on this basis that Condillac in his later writings developed the principle that good science is language well made. (*From Locke to Saussure* 30)

In this philosophical rhetoric, the linearity of language serves as an adequate analogue to external reality, primarily apprehended by the eye; language becomes a human supplement to decompose reality and convey what is really seen out there in the world into an individual mind, where we once again recompose it to represent the holistic world. Of course, for Foucault, it is this very difference between what can be seen and what can be said—between the world and language, the visible and the articulable—that poses an unbridgeable epistemological rift. If these two systems do not correspond, then language cannot possibly represent reality. This lack of correspondence should be true as well of Condillac, but what enables Condillac to bridge this rift and synthesize the two systems is his theological world view, more representative of Foucault's Renaissance resemblance than eighteenth-century classical episteme where Foucault locates Condillac. For Condillac, both systems, verbal and visual, have been created analogously in a harmoniously ordered universe where ideas and words, words and things (including people) have similar structures. His religious views, as well as his Neoplatonism and vestiges of Leibnizian philosophy, operate to smooth over the threatened epistemological break between his dual rhetorics. Until quite recently, his early work on monadology was unknown. Yet this is the work that won Condillac intellectual respect and entrance into the Berlin Academy. Although he later criticizes Leibniz in his critique of systems of philosophy, Condillac was apparently initially a believer in monads, atom-like particles that resulted from the fragmentation of the original matter of the universe and carry the memory of originary unity. Monadology postulates that matter is essentially one, and substance is protean, capable of taking many forms. Language takes the role of the monad in Condillac's later texts.[18]

In the expressive rhetoric of Condillac's *Art of Writing,* language works because of this assumption of an originary natural harmony, correspondence, or empathy between individuals. This more feminine bodily rhetoric, maintaining ties to orality and an elaborate Ciceronianism, also presents a different sensory emphasis—the ear is as important as the eye. As Condillac explains in a later addition to his writing course for the Prince of Parma, each passion has an "inarticulate cry that is transmitted from soul to soul," and music can actually copy this passionate vocal inflection. When music imitates this passion closely, it gains the highest possible expressivity, and accordingly, a language that can imitate music is most expressive: "Each measure, each inflexion in music has then a particular character, and a language has more harmony and becomes more expressive as it is capable of more variety in its rhythms and inflexions" (*Oeuvres* 1: 612). Harmony and expressivity become for Condillac another form of connection, one that seems to work outside the rational principle of the connection of ideas. Condillac seems to characterize this nonrational association of ideas that Locke had linked with madness as possibly an even more effective system of liaison. This rhetoric includes values such as inversion, abundance, intensity, and subjectivity in language, expressing the internal emotional tableau rather than representing the external landscape. Therefore, the expressive function dominates over the representational or mimetic function of language in aesthetic genres. Condillac argues in the conclusion to his writing course, just after discussing the body's natural language, that

> our body in spite of us, has a language that manifests even our most hidden thoughts. It is this language that the painter studies: for it wouldn't be much to design familiar features. In fact, what do I care to see a mute figure in a painting: What I want to see in it is a soul that speaks to my soul.
>
> Thus the man of genius does not limit himself to designing exact forms. He gives to everything the character that belongs to it. His sentiment passes on to everything he touches, and transmits itself to all those who see his works. (*Oeuvres* 1.15: 578)

As Aarsleff points out, with this passage Condillac abandons the classical ideal. An expressivism tied to notions of original creation, which I code as feminine, pervades Condillac's sublime, aesthetic rhetoric. This expressivism allies itself with painting and other aesthetic arts, and other expressivists often refer to descriptive writing as painting. However, as this passage demonstrates, *to paint* does not always equal classical or neoclassical mimesis. Painting here is not representative but expressive, although it can be said to depict the emotional landscape of the writer.

Nonetheless, Condillac's historicism functions as a network to undermine the polarity of any linear-masculine–holistic-feminine binary or representational-expressive binary we might set up. He values analytical language for its discriminating ability but at the same time privileges eloquence and poetry because they, along with genius and imagination, reenergize a culture's language. In a circular or dialectical movement, masculine analysis breaks down complex abstract ideas to return humans to their feminine senses and social roots. Yet paradoxically, the feminine pole of the language spectrum produces language with maximum energy and force[19]—qualities traditionally linked to masculine writing or speech. It is not just that Condillac cannot keep his conceptual categories clear and distinct: like Vico, his vision is holistic and his philosophies interwoven, networked, and essentially hybrid.

Condillac's failure to separate nature and culture is holistic and premodern. "Art (or culture) seizes us in the crib" (*Oeuvres* 602) so that we scarcely know our nature, the natural state of our society, or our language. What we do know is more and more based on language in Condillac's early and late thought (as in his *Language of Calculus*). Once humans grow "out of nature," language is based chiefly on social convention and contract. Nonetheless, we remain essentially natural beings—thus Condillac's need to make frequent use of the hybrid phrases "conventional naturalness" or "naturally conventional" (*Oeuvres* 602, 609). Nature and human conventions share an analogous reality.

Rhetoric and Condillac's *Art of Writing*

The analytical and the aesthetic and the masculine and the feminine can be traced as they intertwine in Condillac's writing course for the Prince of Parma, which serves to illustrate the pedagogical practice of Condillac's earlier language theory in the *Origin* essay. An early belletristic rhetoric, the writing course shares many common sources and features with Hugh Blair's later *Lectures on Rhetoric and Belles Lettres,* in particular the goal of training the student's taste with an emphasis on models of both good and bad sentences and longer passages from contemporary writers.

Like writing aids in bookstores today, Condillac's course of studies for the Prince repeats familiar advice—in this case from the Port Royalists and other bestsellers—and it was popular. It was finished by the early 1760s and printed in 1775, republished the next year, and again in 1780, 1782, 1790, 1798, 1803, and 1821. As François Heidsieck notes, all Europe for two generations went to school with the Prince of Parma until critiques by Maine de Biran and Victor Cousin caused the course to lose favor[20] (71).

Condillac's work with the prince also proved innovative, deviating markedly from previous pedagogies. It broke from classical education from the moment the teacher decided to make the practice of his own developmental theories the cornerstone of the education. For example, in Condillac's first experience with the prince, he initially observed him, then joined him at play, guiding him to reflect on or analyze what he did there. Montessori-like, he made the prince's own experiences the basis for his teaching, leading the student in a chain from experience to analysis to experience to higher analysis. In his language course, Condillac continues to follow his genetic method of a return to origins and a retracing of the connection of ideas.

As for 'traditional' or classical rhetoric, an obvious, but nonetheless significant, historical shift is apparent from Condillac's very title of an *Oeuvres* section, *The Art of Writing*, which no longer refers primarily to oratorical eloquence but to print literacy. Only one brief, superficial *précis* of eloquence (which is, after all, a Ciceronian term for rhetoric) remains in this treatise of the classical arts of public persuasive speech. In Condillac's *Course of Study for the Prince of Parma*, analysis—a rational breaking down of elements to make possible new combinations—becomes the rhetorical equivalent of the classical canon of invention. Method—the principle of order that long before Descartes was the second rhetorical canon of *dispositio*—has been transformed into the principle of linearity, cohesion, or the linking of ideas. Derrida points to a passage in *La langue des calculs* (a section in *Oeuvres*) in which Condillac calls analogy itself "the method of invention" (*Archeology* 83), equating linearity and linking with analogical thought.

In practice, Condillac's method instructs a writer or inquirer to begin with phenomena best known or closest to the senses and to move out in an unbroken chain to those least known. For Condillac, unlike most earlier theorists, including Bacon, the method of presentation to a student or reader should be in the same order as that encountered in the process of discovery. Using attraction, linking, analogy, and repetition of the same—those elements of the natural universal law of knowing and writing, Condillac attempts to repeat the successes of Newtonian law in natural philosophy for human culture.

The fourth canon of rhetoric, the art of memory, is also made entirely unnecessary by the proper linking of ideas. Nonetheless, memory itself (closely connected with the imagination) becomes central to Condillac's account of the cognitive process of knowing. Likewise, the classical arts of delivery are declared no longer relevant, although their force is recognized in shadow by the privileging of the language of action.[21] This leaves Condillac's *Art of Writing* with the third canon of style and with aesthetic theory, both aimed at developing the Prince's taste through the criticism of classical and contemporary models of belles lettres.[22]

Throughout the writing course, Condillac's aim is to reconcile clarity and precision with beauty and passion, a further echo of his urge to balance, harmonize, and synthesize. This synthesis can be seen from the treatise's opening, in which he advises the Prince to consider two things in forming his style: clarity, aligned with linearity and liaison; and character, synonymous with emotion, voice, and tone, deriving from both the writer's subjectivity and the subject under consideration. These two elements together make up the beauty of style for Condillac.

The writing course builds on the principles of linearity and liaison, itself progressing linearly from words to sentences and building to more global concerns as in many later school texts. In general, section 1 acquaints the Prince with the necessity for clarity and distinctness in constructions, and section 2, consisting of schemes and tropes, shows how to vary sentences to represent the character of thoughts. Section 3 concerns itself with coherence, the "weaving of the fabric" formed of principal and subordinate thoughts. Each section builds on a few principles copiously illustrated not by Latin or Greek authors but by French classical and contemporary literary models from such figures as Boileau, the Abbé DuBos, and Mme. de Sévigny. Frequently, Condillac analyzes a sentence and revises it to show how it might have been done better. Throughout, he stresses order and cohesion—each idea must be naturally linked with those before and after. This discussion of coherence and cohesion may be the most sustained attention given to these elements of written prose until modern discourse theory.

His advice depends heavily on a theory of genre. In his long fourth chapter, "Observations on Poetic Style and Incidentally on What Determines the Quality That Belongs to Each Genre of Style," Condillac begins with an abstract taxonomy of belletristic discourse by genre, resembling later uses of the modes in writing: didactic, narrative, and descriptive.

In didactic writing, such as philosophy, the writer poses questions and discusses; in narration—history, stories, poems—the writer relates facts, whether real or imagined; and in description, which Condillac discusses under the separate headings of eloquence and poetry, the writer "paints" what he sees and feels.

This collapsing of eloquence and poetry is consistent with Condillac's earlier statement in the *Origin* essay. There he notes that besides the fact that eloquence is not allowed "some particular figures and phrases which are admitted in poetry," eloquence and poetry "are sometimes confounded in such a manner, that it is no longer possible to distinguish them" (236). Thus, he collapses rhetoric into a belletristic poetics, one foregrounding literary taste and expression and occulting public persuasive discourse.

Roland Barthes has traced earlier conceptions of such literary rhetorics to Ovid and Horace, to Dionysus of Halicarnassus with his concern for rhythmic value of sentences, and through *On the Sublime* to pseudo-Longinus's Second Sophistic work repopularized in France by Boileau's seventeenth-century translation (27). Eric William Skopec also describes similar rhetorics of the period, belletristic works by DuBos and Fénelon, for example, that ally rhetoric not with logic and jurisprudence, but with aesthetic arts—music, painting, drama, sculpture, and architecture (Skopec 124). His point in doing so is to describe a system of eighteenth-century expressionist rhetoric, a rhetorical system of which Condillac's expressionistic rhetoric is very much a part. With such an expressionist system, Skopec can focus attention on eighteenth-century rhetoricians and poeticists in their own right without applying the stock labels neoclassical or pre-Romantic.

In *The Art of Writing,* theories of expression and genre ultimately become not theories of rhetoric but theories of aesthetics, as poetics takes priority. There, in the longest section, which is on poetic style, Condillac fleshes out his theory of the cycles of progress and the genius of language he has earlier discussed in the *Origin* essay. The chapter opens with the question whose answer leads to the very duality between language at its origins and cultivated language: "How does poetry differ from prose?

This question, so difficult to resolve, will raise many others that are no less difficult; there is no question that is beset with more complications" (600). In exploring this topos, he speculates on the differences in the aims or functions of poetry and philosophical language, the styles of both, and the arts of both, concluding, "The greatest difference thus is between the style of the philosopher and that of the lyric poet" (601). The philosopher uses images only incidentally, in support of a linear argument, while the lyric poet's language is the nonlinear, imagistic, hieroglyphic language of tableaux. Again the spectrum is drawn out, with the two poles identified as the aesthetic and philosophic.[23]

However, just as the ends of prose and poetry—the Horacean to please and instruct—can be confounded, so at times can the styles. Condillac therefore concludes that the primary difference is in the "art": the poet must write with more "art," but yet appear "natural." How to accomplish this is a problem, however, especially so in times when language itself is not what it once had been. Condillac firmly holds that "no language succeeds better than the language of action itself" or the holistic poetic language next to it. Yet the historic decline of the language of action brings about dissimulation:

> Originally, we couldn't speak about anything except what we felt; and today we most often speak of what we do not feel! ... What remains of this [language of action] is nothing but over-refined expression which is not understood the same way by all. (*Oeuvres* 579)

Condillac again reveals his nostalgia for an Adamic language, which cannot lie but instead powerfully and truthfully expresses. Thus Condillac's work cannot be read exclusively in terms of either progress or of degeneration.

For art itself provides an important compensation or remedy for the decline of language. Condillac's classical notion of art as collective strategies for performance is premodern. It helps bridge the gap, recreating the power of the natural or the original language—if the art is perfected by practice and habit.

In the discussion on poetic style, Condillac's insight into progress of the arts grows out of his pre-Kantian puzzlement over the relativity of the terms *natural, beauty,* and *taste.* He begins by exploring the binary of art-nature. Accepted judgments of what is due to nature and what to art are often flawed because humans credit more to nature than is due, he argues, contending that most of our arts and habits are conventional:

> But nature doesn't make us with this or that habit; it only
> prepares us, and as we come from its hand we are like clay
> which, having no fixed form of its own, assumes all those that
> art gives it. . . . Art . . . seizes us in the crib, and our studies
> begin with the first exercise of our organs. (*Oeuvres* 602)

Nature here collapses into the conventional; however, in this Renaissance
strand of Condillac's thought, humans and their conventions remain a
part of nature. Naturalness itself becomes a phenomenon decided by
human convention. Thus, poetry for Condillac must be natural, but it
is a conventional naturalness and, moreover, one that varies from one
culture to the next. In Condillac's genre theory, there are as many kinds
of naturalness as genres: the true test of naturalness is the successful
address to the passions.

As in classical rhetorics, but just as strongly in courtly rhetorics such
as Baldassare Castiglione's, practice and habit work to perfect or natu-
ralize an art. In a familiar metaphor, this works the same way in writing as in dance:

> When, for example, we admire the naturalness of movements
> and postures in a dancer, we do not think that he has formed
> himself without art; we merely conclude that in the dancer
> art is a habit, and that he no longer needs to study in order
> to dance, just as we no longer need to study in order to walk.
> But art unites itself with the natural in poetry just as in danc-
> ing; and the poet is, in some manner, to the prose writer what
> the dancer is to the walker. (*Oeuvres* 603)

As in Aristotle, after having studied an art, one internalizes it through
practice until it becomes habitual. Thus, an art imbricates itself with
human bodies and cognition, participating in their construction. However, the process must be erased for an art must be invisible: In *On the
Sublime* as well as the courtly advice books since the Renaissance, art
does not—and should not—be visible.[24] For this reason, it often comes
to be taken for nature itself. Moreover, art "unites itself with the natural" and at its peak is nature itself (*Oeuvres* 602). This alone produces
art capable of moving human passions.

For this reason, for the purposes of training the taste, it is important to be able to pinpoint the high point of an art. Condillac here returns to something close to his theory of cultural cycles from the *Origin* essay. If art is only the "collection of rules we need to learn to do

something," an art is only fresh and valid when those rules are newly discovered and observed. Later, after they have been formulated and become rigid and less natural, they do not serve to advance the arts. Artists begin to ignore them and their art declines. Therefore: "We end where we began, that is to say without having any rules. Thus, art has its beginnings, its progress and its decadence" (*Oeuvres* 603). Although Condillac concedes that taste and beauty are relative, in part due to these cycles, he still believes that rules can be formulated by observing the three stages and comparing them.

Therefore, he explains, in the first age of arts, humans conceive of beauty and taste but with little invention and "still less correctness." In the second age, we find more invention and correctness, intuit rules, and judge works against them, growing in our pleasure. Masterpieces of this second age give us, with some faults, models of the beautiful, *"la belle nature."* However, by abstracting and clearing away these faults, we can begin to imagine the ideal. Unfortunately, this very act involves analysis, which opposes imagination and inhibits it. Therefore, in the final age, our judgment extinguishes the sentiment of beauty:

> Here it is with analysis in art as it is in chemistry: it destroys the thing by reducing it to its first principle. . . . the beautiful consists in an agreement we can still judge when we decompose it, but which can no longer produce the same effect. (*Oeuvres* 605)

This Kantian pronouncement on the noncognitive nature of the aesthetic response is a predictable outcome of Condillac's opposition of intuition and the imagination and analysis or judgment. As a consequence, taste begins to decline as soon as it reaches its peak in the second age, and "its decadence is the period which believes itself to be the most enlightened" (*Oeuvres* 605). Thus, Condillac provides a relativistic view of aesthetic taste and judgment, somewhat stabilized by models from the high point of each culture's cycles.

Significantly, it is necessary to limit these models to each culture's own productions to maintain the linguistic analogy that develops historically with each people or nation as the language itself comes into being.[25] Therefore, Condillac does not advise using classical Greek or Roman models for French poetry, because "if we today had no other talent but to make use of their belief, it would be as ridiculous to consider oneself poet as it would be to believe one was well-dressed with the clothes of the ancients" (*Oeuvres* 606). This echoes his earlier stylistic relativism in which he banishes the classical ideal, validates the vernacular, and helps construct Romantic values:

> If you ask which ideas are noble and elevated, I tell you that nothing is more arbitrary: the decision lies in accepted usages, in manners, in our received opinions. If reason ruled our judgments, utility would be the law, and the state of the laborer would be the most noble of all; but our opinions judge otherwise. (*Oeuvres* 558)

This statement is of a piece with Condillacian values throughout *The Art of Writing* and the *Origin* essay. The arbitrariness of the linguistic sign is extended to the realm of art and taste, allowing for linguistic and cultural change, primarily to be driven by the man of genius. However, because humans are ruled by passions, utility is not the law; for Condillac, poetic genius makes the law of language and takes the position as "most noble of all" (*Oeuvres* 605).

This is also consistent with Condillac's resolution to the issue raised by the chapter title as to the proper choice of styles for each genre. As the chapter and *The Art of Writing* conclude:

> In general, it is enough to observe that there is in poetry, as in prose as many kinds of naturalness as genres; that one doesn't write an ode, an epic poem, a tragedy, a comedy, in the same style, and that all the same these poems must be written naturally. The tone is determined by the subject one treats, by the design proposed, by the chosen genre, by the character of nations and by the genius of the writers who are made to become our models.
>
> Thus it seems to me that it has been demonstrated that the naturalness that belongs to poetry and to each kind of poem is a conventional naturalness which varies too much to be capable of definition, and which, consequently, it would be necessary to analyze in all possible cases if one would explain it in all the forms it takes; but one feels it, and that is enough. (*Oeuvres* 603)

This late-eighteenth-century view of the rules of art, expression, taste, and of genius becomes Romantic, especially in the emphasis on emotion, but at the same time, it holds to a classical social base and remains rhetorical in conception much in the same spirit as the treatise by pseudo-Longinus. The social and bodily base upon which Condillac's superstructure of analytical thought comes to rest is the realm of the physically intersubjective, to which humans must constantly return if they are to remain human, in the sense that they remain a part of and not separate from, nature. Yet this is a nature that was long ago overlaid by the cultural, as is seen by his theories of language and culture.

The Cultural Character of Language and Genius

For Condillac, every language expresses the character or genius of the peoples who speak it, yet a national language develops because of its great writers. Every nation of people combines ideas according to its own particular genius, controlled by the analogy that determines its unique character. However, Condillac judges that the best language is produced by a people whose character or genius demonstrates a balance of imagination and analysis. Importantly, genius and imagination account for how anything new ever comes to be. However, as in Locke, the imagination can also be a disruptive faculty in need of counterweights.

Genius is an individual yet also a cultural phenomenon. The character or genius of a people and a language is influenced somewhat by its climate but especially by its government. Just as the form of government influences the character of a nation people, "so the character of a nations influences that of languages" (Aarsleff, *Condillac* 185, par. 143).

Condillac's linguistic and cultural history (similar to Vico's) partakes of patterned cycles of progress and decline, following a natural course. He uses this history to explore individual-social interaction and to speculate why arts and sciences do not flourish equally in every country and why great writers often cluster in the same historical periods. He arrives at the answer that both sciences and great writers depend on the development of language, especially the number and variety of analogous expressions in the language. It can be shown that "superior geniuses cannot arise in nations until their languages have already made considerable progress" (Aarsleff, *Condillac* 185, par. 150); "[t]he success of the most gifted geniuses who have had the happiness even of the best organization, depends altogether on the progress of the language in regard to the age in which they live" (Aarsleff, *Condillac* 187, par. 147).

Genius in Condillac's system is to change what the imagination is to the sign system. To use Derrida's metaphor, it is the hinge,[26] the moment of liaison that occupies a central place and sets the system into motion: the imagination offers up new signs to the memory and determines the progress of the mind; a genius offers new elements to a linguistic community and makes possible a natural cycle of birth, flowering, and decay.

Analysis and imagination are described as opposites that usually retard the progress of each other, similar to the way Thomas Hobbes and Locke believed that judgment and wit do. Nonetheless, each language has a point in development where analysis and imagination each reach a golden mean. This is described as the middle of three cycles and that Condillac judges to have taken place in French classicism of the seventeenth century.

The first age is when language begins to have "fixed principles and a settled character" and favors the development of "eminent men" (Aarsleff, *Condillac* 187, par. 146). In the second age, these great writers (usually some eminent poet) enrich the language with a variety of expressions, making the second age the most fruitful for future writers and the best age from which to choose models for stylistic imitation. However, in the third age, trying to surpass previous writers, the next generation "tries to break a new path:

> But since all the styles analogous to the character of the language and to his own have been already used by his predecessors, he has no choice but to keep his distance from the analogy. Thus in order to be original he is obliged to contribute to the ruin of a language whose progress a century sooner he would have hastened along. (Aarsleff, *Condillac* 193, par. 158)

As Derrida points out, the deviations of genius make possible the new in the culture, just as the deviations of the arbitrary signifier produce linguistic change. They are the linguistic equivalents of the original swerve of the atom that created the universe in early Greek atomism. Because of these deviations, we have real history instead of the deterministic cycles of natural law.

Because each linguistic community develops its own analogy, language cannot be a mirroring of reality but is from the beginning an interpretation of reality or a sort of an analogue to it. This concept of analogy makes Condillac's linguistic theories unique as well as relativistic. Although he never discusses languages outside the Western tradition, he does not rank or judge languages according to a universal measure. Less-developed languages with more imagination are better for poetry, while more-cultivated analytical languages are better for philosophy. However, Condillac makes it clear that in gaining the precision and clarity needed for philosophy, these languages also lose something important to human culture. Although his work as a whole emphasizes progress, his discussions of writing and culture emphasize his nostalgia and determination to hold on to the human values at the origins of language.

In sum, for Condillac, the seeds of language lie in social circumstances with our biological constitutions and our needs that give rise to our passions and the language of action and by analogy instituted language. This narrative of origins is based on an organicist metaphor of development from the germ of sensation culminating finally in the flowers of the arts and sciences. Because the arts, including eloquence, develop early in human history, they remain close to the natural language of the body, which is the source of energy, knowledge, and pleasure and, thus, of strong and forceful writing. Because these rhetorics grow naturally out of their own cultural circumstances, when they are left to naturally grow and develop, they develop their own particular beauties and deficiencies. Condillac is, therefore, willing to break with past cultures such as Greece and Rome because rather than helping develop French literature, these might actually impede the progress of the arts and sciences. His nationalist values also come to the fore in promoting what will later be called the French golden age of literature. And, in his defense of vernacular languages and literatures, he inaugurates comparative literary history and theory.

Reception of a Rhetoric on the Threshold

If Condillac's metaphors oscillate between the organic and the mechanistic, the seed and the rose, the soul and the fulcrum, his two rhetorics present philosophic truth in an oscillating relationship with aesthetic truth—sometimes with philosophic truth resting on a foundation of aesthetic truth and sometimes the reverse. This ground, actually a formulation of a new poetics, begins to usurp the traditional ground of public, civic rhetoric, moving toward private, emotional expression. Like classical rhetoric, however, and like early Romantic theory, this expressive rhetoric is both subjective and social. Universally felt, this emotion-centered poetic substitutes for the pathetic appeals of traditional rhetoric. However, because this eighteenth-century expressive rhetoric is presented in literate form, rather than publicly and orally, over time a more and more privatized process of reading may have acted to produce a more radically privatized expressivism.

This convergence of literature with private expression coincided with the consolidation of print culture, which includes a historic rise of women's literacy and writing and a more profound identification of literature and the feminine. Conversely, at this moment, scientific discourse extended its effort to divest itself of privatizing metaphor and figurative language and became even more identified with a public masculine rhetoric. These new configurations of scientific and poetic discourses both arose and developed at the same historic moment. Raymond Williams explains the emergence of the affirmative "aesthetic" response during this period as a healthy reaction to the emerging dominance of the utilitarian and commodifying forces of capitalism. However, he also points out that the rise of a new "science of aesthetics" led to "new kinds of privileged instrumentality and specialized commodity" (151), that of taste and a more narrowly defined sense of literature. Nonetheless, the oppositional, yet complementary relationship between scientific and poetic discourses was not at the moment of its emergence and has never been one of simple binary opposition.

Condillac has been better known for this masculine, scientific rhetoric than the affirmative, feminine aesthetic expressivism. This has in part been due to his followers, the *idéologues* (a group at the salon of Mme. Helvétius) including DeStutt de Tracy, Cabanis, and Volney, who promoted a reductive but utilitarian version of Condillac's theories during the French Directory (1795–1799) as a model for educational reform in the aftermath of the French Revolution.[27]

After the Revolution, with the Napoleonic backlash against the *idéologues,* even Condillac's masculine rhetoric would be suppressed and almost forgotten, sedimented into a unitary sign of empiricism. The tradition of Condillac would itself become a hieroglyph, a symbol of his work in prelinguistic sensation—the image, perhaps still memorable to French schoolchildren, of a rose-smelling statue. Conversely, as followers of Rousseau and Pestalozzi took up Condillac's pedagogical methods and his logic, the hard edge of empiricism would soften into a student-centered, experiential curriculum that especially appealed to those interested in child development. The importance of the sense of touch, learning through play, and early exposure to the belles lettres forms a signature of modern education usually traced to the educational philosophies of Pestalozzi or Montessori. Theories most often traced to Rousseau can be found in Vico and are exemplified and operationalized in the pedagogical practices of Condillac.

Writers as dissimilar as Foucault and Aarsleff make Condillac and French language theory central to linguistic speculation in the late-eighteenth and early-nineteenth centuries.[28] However, Condillac's influence is little recognized in Anglo-American histories of rhetoric. Wilbur Samuel Howell's only reference to Condillac is a brief mention that Hugh Blair cites him as a source for his discussion of the rise and progress of language in his *Lectures on Rhetoric and Belles Lettres* of 1783 (*Eighteenth-Century British Logic* 652). Aarsleff's "The Tradition of Condillac" in *From Locke to Saussure* traces some of the accidental and deliberate omissions and misreadings of Condillac, many of them by German linguists evaluating Condillac at second hand through Herder's 1770 essay on language origins. Later, conservative suppression of philosophers popular during the French Revolution and rejection of speculation on the origins of language for more positivistic methodology have also contributed to his neglect.

Along with Foucault, postmodernist Michel de Certeau interprets Condillac as a stereotypical empiricist, ignoring the expressivism in Condillac's language theory. Primarily leaning on Condillac's later work, he argues that a Condillacian linguistic philosophy stood behind the efforts of the French Directory (1795–1799) to "fabricate a national language after the Revolution.

> For Condillac, constructing a science and constructing a language amount to the same task, just as for the revolutionaries of 1790 establishing the revolution required creation and imposition of a national French language. This implies a distancing of the living body (both traditional and individual) and thus also of everything which remains, among the people, linked to the earth, to the place, to orality or to non-verbal tasks. (138)

On the contrary, Condillac's texts contain an expressive aesthetic rhetoric that refuses to do just what Certeau criticizes him for: his expressive rhetoric refuses to banish the body, the people, and the elements of language linked to orality, such as sound, repetition, rhythm, and tone. Yet unlike the linking Certeau implies—the association of these bodily, sensuous elements to the proletariat, historically these elements connect to the elite tradition of courtly language that in the eighteenth century were expressed through the more socially fluid belles lettres tradition of salon conversation and literary production. Since the 1960s, similar rhetorics of the body have been assimilated by French writers such as Julia Kristeva, Luce Irigaray, and Hélène Cixous.[29]

The organic and the mechanistic in Condillac are in some ways unfortunate metaphors in that the two poles of his developmental spectrum seem to differ more in degree than in kind. The organic feminine determines the masculine as a seed does the future plant. Although the masculine may at times seem more powerful, it must always return to the feminine to replenish that power. In a move familiar to us today, this renewal in Condillac primarily takes place through an aesthetic experience that returns us to our physical and emotional roots.

Condillac's *Origin* essay and his widely adopted educational program designed for the Prince of Parma maintain in tension both halves of what twentieth-century thinkers took as a natural opposition between referential scientific and expressive literary language. This dual system lies at the heart of modernist rhetorics, with each system ignoring the disjunction and contradictions between the two. Yet just as quantum theory has not banished Newtonian physics, postmodernism has not done away with modernist writing theory or aesthetic machinery. This may be because like still-relevant Newtonian descriptions on the level of the everyday world, modernist aesthetic theory continues to work for us at some level in our classrooms. Mixed as they are and tolerant of contradictions, our polyphonic discourses more resemble deposits from melting glaciers—scoured debris picked up over centuries and dumped with the climate change at the end of an era. The glaciers of early-modern and modern discourses of science, politics, rhetoric, and sublime poetics have left their sedimented rubble conveniently at hand.

6
Lord Monboddo's Antimodernity: Scottish Marginalia

> I do not know what meaning classical studies could have for our
> time if they were not untimely—that is to say, acting counter to our
> time and thereby acting on our time and, let us hope, for the ben-
> efit of a time to come.
>
> —Friedrich Nietzsche, "On the Uses and
> Disadvantages of History for Life"

> I must own, I think there is some truth in Dr. Cudworth's observa-
> tion, that the philosophers of this age are seized with a kind of
> *pneumatophobia* and *hylomania*, a desperate aversion to *mind*, and
> a passionate love for *matter*.
>
> —Monboddo, *Antient Metaphysics*

Historically marginal figures and their texts become historically marginal
in part because their thought is especially impure. Often it carries elements
on the developing edge of thought within a frame of traditional, conservative, or even reactionary thought. This impure combination brings to mind
the New Testament proverb warning of the dangers of putting new wine
in old wineskins—it was feared those skins would burst and the wine
would run free. As a metaphor of historical rupture, this image holds on
one level for the Scottish judge James Burnet(t), Lord Monboddo, whose
eighty-four years, ending in 1799, spanned the eighteenth century. Yet,
even as a marginal figure in philosophy or rhetoric, his texts have flowed
strongly in the main channel of historical linguistics, continuing a line that
insists we in language studies and rhetoric contend with his marginality.

The second epigraph shows Monboddo's reaction to modern philosophical thought, to what appeared to him a phobia about matters of
spirit and mind, *pneuma* referring to breath, spirit, nonmaterial psyche,
and soul; or a mania about *hyle,* originally the Greek word for wood,

also matter. The first epigraph might have been written by Monboddo himself despite the gulf between the countermodern Friedrich Nietzsche—who ultimately dispensed with the classical paradigm—and his even more countermodern Scottish forefather. The term forefather, while surprising or perhaps even shocking at first, is apt because of Monboddo's impact on German language theory and Romantic philosophy after Johann Gottfried Herder and others read his six volumes entitled *Of the Origin and Progress of Language (1773–1792)*. The influence of this linguistic connection was immense, if only as an unattributed sheaf in the archive and impossible actually to gauge. Both men emphasize a rhetoric whose philosophical roots are inextricable from their brilliant insights into language. Despite their wide divergence, the very untimeliness of their turn to the Greeks marked both their difference from their contemporaries and opened up new possibilities for future thought. Like Nietzsche's, Monboddo's rhetoric is at once radical and radically conservative or, more precisely, reactionary. It represents an antimodernity of an intensity not seen in the modern-countermodern philosopher Vico or in the exemplary modern *philosophe* Condillac.

Monboddo is not interested in preserving an existing neoclassical tradition or in straining out useful concepts and practices from the past but in a complete return to an originary Greek rhetoric and Platonic view of language as participating in a real but abstract and nonmaterial reality. Yet in his day, Monboddo was in most ways in the mainstream of British *ancien régime* thought and society. He represents a central line of British reaction to the Enlightenment, a reaction that would intensify with the coming of the French Revolution. His rhetoric, linked with his narrative of return to an imagined past, becomes eclipsed, while the Scottish narrative of loss folds into the very foundation of modern literary studies.

Marginality and Contradictions in Monboddo

This chapter represents a grappling with Monboddo's contradictions and an attempt to understand his simultaneous centrality yet marginalization in the republic of rhetoric and letters. Paradoxically, he was everywhere the central Scottish and English thinkers were, both socially and intellectually, except for his being, as Foucault has written, "in the true."

For example, Monboddo knew well his contemporaries in language philosophy but used his ancient philosophies to produce what he believed to be new and superior theories for a modern age. He argues that humans are first social but without language; next, they spoke barbarous languages; and finally, their philosophers consciously formed true languages of art. Thus, he drives a wedge between natural and artificial human states in order to show how everything (of value) that humans have is rationally constructed, a notion that would appear in any other context to be a modern theory. With Jean Jacques Rousseau, he believed nature was not a state of war and that man in his natural state was both political and rational—but Monboddo did not believe humans could organically, naturally, or analogically develop anything truly civilized. As in Plato's *Republic,* philosophers rationally planned all advances, yet Monboddo was not always a rational. His elitist views—consonant with traditional elitist ideology—and not a few wild, speculative notions make his thought seem untimely and eccentric. Yet, some of those elitist and recognizably colonialist characteristics are ingrained into modern linguistics. Among the eccentricities of his six volumes on language, replete with polemics against Francis Bacon, John Locke, and Isaac Newton, there exist some remarkable insights of the genius—especially concerning the genetic relations of language families—that form the foundations of modern linguistics.

At once a pessimist and an optimist, he had little hope to win over his contemporaries but had faith that his philosophical arguments would convince future generations. His belief in cultural degeneration was somewhat hard to stomach for the progressive moderns of the Scottish Enlightenment. Edinburgh was a uniquely rich intellectual environment, the "hotbed of genius," the title of David Daiches, Peter Jones, and Jean Jones's book, where one might meet a genius on every street corner. Monboddo contributed to the brilliance of the city, socializing and entertaining widely. However, after his work began to appear, he was considered an eccentric figure, one outside the mainstream, becoming perhaps even more at home in London society than in Scotland.

His grammar and his Aristotelian rhetoric in volumes 2 and 3 of his *Origin and Progress* (the third volume came out in 1776, the same year as George Campbell's *Philosophy of Rhetoric*), examine language and tell how its use can be made into an art. However, his appropriation of classical rhetoric takes on a reactionary cast as he consistently sees history degenerating, making it necessary to return to past truths most clearly revealed to the Pythagoreans and known by the Egyptians, then by the Greeks. He is especially concerned to hold onto the arts of public discourse, which he sees as passing away with the death of rhetoric. His stance on conserving public discourse has some parallels with later cultural critics such as Jürgen Habermas.[1] Yet Monboddo, the classicist and Scottish aristocrat, was no democrat.

One key gauge of modernity used throughout this book has been the turn to the vernacular from Latin language culture. Monboddo wrote in the vernacular, but it was not *his* vernacular—it was neither the Scots dialect nor Gaelic but a Scotticized English, an attempt at the English of the center, of metropolitan London, and Monboddo took it up diligently and for the most part adroitly, in his writing at any rate. He valued his London connections, traveling to London each spring and taking active part in intellectual life there. Yet unlike the Augustine humanists he met and conversed with, he valued Greek language and literature and seemed to consider himself above the "mere Latinists."

This is a surprising stance for a reactionary Scotsman, considering the importance of Latin as a literary language to that country. After 1603, the old literary Scots of the court poets had diminished, leaving Latin as the chief intellectual language and linking that country with international thought. However, with the decline of humanist culture, Scotland was left without a literary language and with a crisis of national identity. The implications of this for rhetoric were immense. As rhetoricians chose English as the primary literary tongue, they devised new rhetorics, grammars, and elocutionary arts to achieve a powerful literary standard. They formed clubs to debate and discuss sophisticated language issues, and they can be said to have invented the modern study of English literature. However, in England, there was still prejudice against Scotticisms and the brogue. Monboddo wisely chose to write in English, although he chose Greek as the superior classical tongue. He never completely purified his tongue. Did he turn to Greek because his Scots pronunciation of Latin was ridiculed, as often was the case with Scots Latin, or was it his metaphysical commitment to a Platonized Aristotle?[2]

Monboddo's Life and Guiding Philosophies

If his philosophies are often contradictory, Monboddo's very life was buffeted by opposing forces, not the least by the conflictual ties of Scotland and England. He was born in 1714 of a peace-loving mother and a rebellious Jacobite father who had spent time in prison for violently protesting the 1705 Act of Union. Thus, Monboddo, a bit like Locke, claimed to crave peaceful studies and swore off political enthusiasms. (However, like Locke, scholars suspect papers have been destroyed that would link him to the political activity of his day [Cloyd 14].) However, he once wrote that he scarcely lived in his own time, and so it might seem from the ancient books he read and his own philosophies. Nonetheless, he spent six months of every year as a judge and was as active in Edinburgh and London literary society as any other Scottish philosopher, if not more so. Yet he compulsively cites Homer's work as the finest literature ever written[3] and rarely mentions contemporary literary texts (except perhaps for *Tom Jones*), and he wrote in one letter that he had never even heard of David Hartley (W. Knight 126). He did have many friendships with like-minded contemporaries; perhaps the most important was with James Harris, another Neoplatonist critic of Locke and author of *Hermes: Or a Philosophical Inquiry Concerning Language and Universal Grammar* (1751).[4] On the other hand, even the very topics Monboddo chose, including a final critical work on Milton left in manuscript, were what everyone in his circle—particularly Henry Home, Lord Kames and Hugh Blair—concerned themselves with. (However, unlike Blair, he was never persuaded by the Macpherson-Ossian ploy, somewhat amazing as he so often believed the textually unbelievable.)

Educated partly in a local school and later with a tutor, he attended King's College, Aberdeen, reading at one point with William Blackwell. He then studied international law in Holland, settling in Edinburgh thereafter to practice civil law. (The 1705 Act of Union allowed Scotland to keep its legal and educational systems intact, and Scotland's culture in many ways centered on values and principles from Roman law.) Active in literary society, he loved the theater and was an active member and a president of the para-Parliamentary Literary Select Society and curator of the Advocates Library when David Hume was keeper. He wrote many of his early papers on language using the classical sources in the Advocates Library. In 1765 to 1766, he made three trips to Paris in connection with the famous Douglas court case, making notes about dictionaries of barbarous languages—in particular, Huron—in the royal library, seeing a stuffed orangutan in a case in the royal cabinet, and meeting Abbé d'Epée, de la Condamine, de Jussieu, and a feral girl named Memmie Le Blanc. These events were key in his beginning his major works on language. In 1767 he was named to the Court of Sessions and taking the title of his estate became Lord Monboddo. His younger friend James Boswell—who might have chosen Monboddo over Samuel Johnson to memorialize—helped to celebrate. In many of these roles, he may have found himself situated problematically between England and

Scotland as well as the old and the new; yet he deftly negotiates the chasm by maintaining conservative Scottish values while embracing England and contemporary culture as well.

In most ways, he was a traditional, civically active member of the Scottish landed class. He was an agricultural improver and a benevolent landlord who worked to conserve the wildlife, and increase the population on his estate. He belonged to the camp that believed humans could know their own minds and order their lives rationally. This put him at odds with the moral skepticism of a Hume, for example, and aligned him on many points with Boswell, Thomas Reid, and James Beattie.[5] He objected to the materialism of Locke and his followers and worked with Harris and other Neoplatonists to reestablish abstract and Platonic Aristotelian categories in natural philosophical and linguistic studies. Aristotelianism was the only way to maintain connection with reality, which Monboddo viewed as the Scale or Great Chain of Being, an ordering of material reality as well as the intellectual hierarchy that extends from it.[6] Thus an abstract, universal grammar could come nearer to reality than studies of mere matter could do.

His lifetime of studies in Greek convinced him that ancient Greek society was the golden age of human development. After all, in Homer's day, men were taller—at least twice the size of the Lord's bare five feet— and much hardier than his son who had died at age eleven, or his favorite daughter, who died at twenty-five. Moreover, the Greeks well knew those arts and sciences necessary to protect and develop both the body and the intellect. Thus, Monboddo led a healthful life with a carefully regulated natural diet, exercise in the nude, and a regime of cold baths followed by oil rubs before the fireplace. This Spartan regimen worked for him but may have weakened his wife and other family members, who, except for one daughter, died young. Monboddo held that progress in one area leads to degeneration in others[7] (Cloyd 71). Unhappily, the progressive, scientific moderns had turned away from classical learning to indulge in wealth, comfort, and luxury, leading to a softening and degeneration of humankind (Cloyd 126–28).

Never completely losing his Scottish mysticism and credulity, his capacity for rational thought made him a brilliant speculative linguist who, in correspondence with Sir William Jones, helped found the modern science of comparative-historical philology. Paradoxically, the development of this modern science—which Hans Aarsleff well characterizes as "factual, descriptive, classificatory, empirical, comparative" as well as objective and disengaged from mysticism—would serve to both obliterate the speculative Monboddo's fame and to ensure it. It would also, as the newest "model humanistic discipline" (Aarsleff, *From Locke to Saussure* 32), play a role in the decline of rhetoric, linked with what the nineteenth century saw as the outmoded unscientific theories based on classical learning.

Considered an eccentric from the earliest publication of the first volume of *Origin and Progress,* he stood up to public opinion steadfastly. In this first volume, this early evolutionist speculated that the orangutan was of the same species as humans and credulously passed along a Swedish sailor's tale of seeing on the Nicobar Island men with tails that they swished like cats (235–39). (Once in Edinburgh society, his rival, the older Kames, granted him precedence in a doorway, saying, "By no means, my lord; you must walk first that I may see your tail.")

From Monboddo's earliest days in his aristocratic family, his thoughts had been tuned to a different pitch from his more progressive contemporaries. His advanced education had been conducted at home under Francis Skene, later professor of civil and natural history at the University of Aberdeen, whose guidance gave Monboddo a historical turn. As he and his biographers tell us, his method when any new question arose was to first collate what had been said by Greek and Roman authors. Only then would he begin to construct his own views. We have seen the same method in Vico's encyclopedic thought, for the Aristotelian method advised first collecting others' opinions through the use of topics. Obviously, this increasingly bulky method of inquiry, more attuned to the search for knowledge in an earlier age, was precisely what irritated the moderns, with their more direct empirical epistemology. Such thinking is closer in spirit to Michel Foucault's Renaissance episteme than to his description of the classical episteme in *The Order of Things.* No doubt this is one reason Monboddo remained on the periphery in the eighteenth-century Scottish republic of rhetoric and letters. Rather than feeling out of step with the times, he prides himself on having the proper method of reaching truth by beginning with first principles, not isolated facts.

It did not help his standing with his peers that he taught that the invention of the syllogism by Aristotle was the high point of human intellectual history or that he said before the elder Kames that no knowledge of any value could be created without a knowledge of Greek, when that literary lion, who was his greatest rival and whose work apparently set the agenda for most of Monboddo's inquiries, did not know Greek. However, Monboddo did know Greek texts by Greek authorities—the heavyweights he could brandish perhaps to ward off feelings of inferiority for his diminutive size. Perhaps he also felt diminished as a colonized Scot in an English empire—we do know he used his Greek to put down London's Augustine humanists.

A critic of both Locke and Newton and in the spirit of Vico, Monboddo believed one solution to this dilemma of degeneration would be to connect the scientific progress of the moderns with the wisdom and arts of the ancients. In this way, Monboddo's stance toward classical learning seems to mirror Vico's, but it is more reactionary and more hopeless. There is no possibility of a new cycle beginning after the inevitable collapse of civilization. What threatens Monboddo is no less than the end of humanity. When it comes about, Monboddo believed we can take slight comfort in the fact that we have, at any rate, most likely fulfilled God's purpose for us.

Language and Rhetoric

It has become a commonplace for historians of rhetoric to write of the decline or decay of rhetoric. This narrative of decline usually begins in the seventeenth century, continues through the eighteenth century, and ends in the putative "death of rhetoric" by the late-nineteenth century.[8] Yet, as we know, the mainstream of eighteenth-century Scottish rhetoricians did not perceive themselves as part of a decline. They felt rather on the threshold of the new, at a scene of birth, not of sickness and impending death. A new day had dawned, and the intellectual pioneers who woke to it felt up to the challenges of constructing, in a new language, a new rhetoric more suitable to their own studies and times.

Those figures include, of course, first Adam Smith, then Blair, Campbell, and Kames, many of whom had adopted or critically adapted one form or another of a Lockean view of language and rhetoric based on Newtonian principles. With some rational but primarily empirical motives, they began their lectures on rhetoric with inquiry into language and human nature, language and the human mind. Language- and aesthetics-based French belletrism became an especially popular source from which to draw or often to plagiarize, judging from our own historical perspective. These rhetoricians, especially Campbell, worked out the implications for rhetoric of newly emerging psychologies and epistemologies compatible with Cartesian and Lockean empiricist thought. As Howell notes, these inductive thinkers rejected as particularly irrelevant to the needs of their day the intricacies of the syllogism. Not just the leading edge, these figures represent the center of Scottish Enlightenment thought on language and rhetoric.

If these transformations of rhetoric into modern scientific rhetoric represented progress to the central figures, their contemporary Lord Monboddo championed the narrative pattern of decline. To Monboddo, the golden age of rhetoric in Greece—Periclean rhetoric—had passed. The practices of this peak moment were best preserved in the texts of Aristotle; therefore, if human culture were to develop, moderns should return to these texts and this past. This pattern of returning to the past, especially to the origins of a matter to trace its progress as we have seen in Vico and Condillac, was an old move reappropriated by moderns, and along with his contemporaries, it led Monboddo to language origins.

Origin and Progress

As Monboddo admits in the second edition of volume 1, he was inspired by Condillac. He later tries to distance himself from the materialist implications of that connection. Aarsleff points out that Monboddo learned of Condillac's work through excerpts in a review he read of Nugent's 1756 translation of Condillac's *Origin* essay, "the review correctly giving the subject of chapter 2 of the *Essai*'s II, i, as 'origin and progress of language'" (*Study of Language* 37). Condillac's expressive origins of language provided a naturalistic foundation for his own belletristic writing program for the Prince of Parma. Blair and others take their language-origin accounts from Condillac and the French encyclopedists. Although Monboddo learns much from them, he attacks their populist, organic, natural processes of language development. One reason he began his *Origin and Progress* was to argue against these elements in Charles de Brosses's *Traité de la formation mechaniques des langues and des principes physiques de l'etymologie* (1766). Similar to Condillac's account of language origins, Monboddo's narrative pinpoints the roots of language in the cries of the earliest humans. From this beginning, because of having the God-given *capacity* for language, humans developed the *habit* of oral expression through natural cries of emotion. Gradually, by habit, humans developed the faculty of speech, with the crucial turn being articulation. He defines language as "the expression of the conceptions of the mind by articulate sounds" (*Origin and Progress* 1.1: 5).

Thus, Monboddo deemphasizes Condillac's placement of the origins of language in facial expressions and the language of action. For Monboddo, not the use of signs (which he believed animals used) but meaningful articulation is what sets human language apart from animal communication. Although as we have seen, Condillac also has a qualitative shift with internalization of signs by repetition and habit. Articulation is not natural to man but was developed by him over time. Arguing against Lockean theory, Monboddo believes that the "greater part of words are not natural signs for ideas" and further asks, long before Ferdinand de Saussure, "What natural connection is there between the idea of a tree and the articulation of sound?" The making of ideas audible through articulation was as great an achievement to Monboddo as the making of sounds visible in writing (*Origin and Progress* 1: 304). Articulation, he notes, is itself a metaphor from the joints:

> [A]rticulation breaks and divides the continuity of the voice, which otherwise would go on in the same tenor without any distinguishable parts. And it is in this way that all the variety of sound is produced, by which men have been enabled to express their conceptions, and to mark every conception by a different sound. (*Origin and Progress* 1: 330)

This explanation of systematic linguistic difference was one of the earliest, and it was widely circulated among the first scientific linguists. Typically hierarchical and interested in separating barbaric from civilized languages, Monboddo seems to use the concept of articulation primarily to judge the age and development of a language. For example, he argues that the long vocalizations and simpler sound systems, such as in the Huron language he studied in Paris, belong to the barbarous tongues, which included Chinese. The long words derived from natural cries, full of vowels and having musical tones. These long words were later broken down into shorter sounds but in more developed languages of art systematically recompounded and differentiated.

After articulation was established, humans must have begun to invent words rapidly, until finally, language was in chaos. Monboddo believed that then a group of philosophers rationally, consciously refined the barbarous language, creating a language of art. In Chinese, a very old language, these learned men began to systematize but must have stopped short, leaving that a crude language. Early languages of art, including Celtic, were invented by a few countries; if barbaric languages showed any art, it was because the higher languages had spread to them and influenced them.[9] Languages were nonetheless related: "Flection, or analogy as it is commonly called, gives what may be called the *form* of languages; and makes them appear so different, that it is only the critical eye that can see the resemblance" (*Origin and Progress* 1.2: 436). However, the perceptive Monboddo could see these resemblances, noting those between Gothic and Persian, taken together, are the "parent of Celtic." Significantly, this analogy revealed itself to him, and he in turn discussed analogy and language families in letters with Jones, collaboratively assisting the foundation of what would be a key modern discipline, historical linguistics.

From Language to Rhetoric

In his narrative of *Origin and Progress,* the art of language progresses as it is refined by men of science, rising from grammar and style to rhetoric and poetics. As always, the progress of the human mind is from instinct to art, from natural capacity to acquired faculties. The stress is always on what humans have made of themselves—of culture or art over nature, a belief closer to the progressive Scots and common in Renaissance humanism. Culture or custom is "second nature," he believed: "I add that it is more powerful than the first, and in a great measure destroys and absorbs the original nature" (1: 25).

I. M. Hammett has investigated Monboddo's early papers preliminary to *Origin and Progress,* including a "Discourse on Language" probably prepared for the Select Society early in the 1760s when discussion of language there was at its height. Hammett believes this paper and others are consistent with *Origin and Progress* in that Monboddo never changes his elitist, primitivist views. A Stoic view of reality embedded in Roman law is that "knowledge consists of the conformity of our ideas with the real thing in nature" ("Early Monboddo Papers" 145). The real things in nature were abstract ideas to the original Stoics and to Monboddo.

Rationalism and a rationalist epistemology lead Monboddo to reject the view that innate, unconscious behavior of developing social beings produces unintended social outcomes. This idea can be found in Vico's notion of providence, but in Monboddo's day it was prevalent in many writers—the invisible hand of Smith, for example—but it is also present in Kames, Dugald Stewart, and especially Hume and Adam Ferguson. Another source for this was Bernard de Mandeville's *Fable of the Bees; or Private Vices, Public Benefits* (1728). This work told a naturalistic tale of language origins emphasizing signs and gestures organically developing into language. Monboddo objected, believing that "nothing happens by chance" and holding to rational, conscious motivations (qtd. in Hammett, "Early Monboddo Papers" 147). The growth of language needed art and conscious contrivance, he maintained.

Because they are consciously and rationally constructed, elitist culture and custom are significant to civilization, and the associated classical concept of art is key. As in classical texts, an art is something that can be taught and learned, not the post-Romantic mystification of art that cannot be taught. There is none of the tension between art and intuitive practice that is found in Condillac here. Monboddo states in the introduction to *Origin and Progress* that "whoever thinks that by his own genius and natural parts he can discover what is necessary to the arts of rhetoric and poetic need not read this book." The art of rhetoric is something admittedly not unlike cookery so "It cannot be denied that it will be better practiced by certain rules and observations, collected and digested, than without rule" (1: 20). Thus, he precedes to give the principles of his Aristotelian rhetoric, an egg laid in this nest woven of speculative origin of language theory, a philosophical grammar, and a stylistic, belletristic rhetoric.

As James Irvine argues, Monboddo's earlier letter on rhetoric—with its emphasis on art's first principles and rules, drawn not from observation, experience, or human nature but from ancient texts—is an implied slap at Campbell and other empiricists formulating rhetorics (27). Yet, Monboddo is not an antiempiricist here. He recognizes that Aristotle collected observations and scattered rules together in forming his system of rhetoric. However, to Monboddo, Aristotle lived in the peak period for rhetoric and also "possessed the art of making Arts more than any man;" therefore, his principles were best as the foundation of the arts of matter, invention, diction, or style (Irvine 30). Monboddo shows no historical sense here—for him, once observations of successful rhetoric have been made and their principles drawn up, as Aristotle did for Greek rhetoric, it is done for all time, and there is never a need to do it again. True historical change does not exist—only a falling away from an earlier, higher standard.

In his language volumes, the matters discussed above are prefatory to his abstract of Aristotelian rhetoric in the sixth volume of *Origin and Progress* (1792). As the title implies, the whole series of volumes begins with the origin of language in primitive society and ends with the progress of language arts, at the pinnacle of which stood apparently Aristotelian rhetoric. What is not apparent is that had Monboddo lived longer than his eighty-four years, this rhetorical peak of progress would have been superseded by poetics, for Monboddo greatly admired Aristotle's *Poet-*

ics as well as his rhetoric and wrote some seven hundred manuscript pages of criticism on John Milton in preparation for a final volume never published. Nonetheless, much of the content of the existing final volume of *Origin and Progress* comprises a philosophical grammar and stylistic rhetoric finally emphasizing style rather than invention, despite his criticism of the Sophists for making just that move. Yet, theoretically, he is devoted to Aristotle and his logic, calling, as I noted earlier, Aristotle's discovery of the syllogism the "greatest discovery in science ever made by any one man" (qtd. in W. Knight 50). This sort of paradox is emblematic of Monboddo.

His appropriation of classical, particularly Greek learning, served as a bulwark against the encroachments of religious and moral skepticism that he saw as contributing to human degeneration. His linguistic studies in particular supported his effort to explain the progress of the human understanding to counter this decline. Accepting the Cartesian cogito, he wrote Welbore Ellis in 1783: "We know nothing of the Divine Mind but what we know of our own—therefore the study of our own mind is the foundation of Theology" (W. Knight 50).

The resonance of this use of mind is, of course, Platonic, and as mentioned above, his Platonism was influenced by Harris. Yet he had to reconcile Plato with his earlier regard for Aristotle. As Monboddo writes Richard Price in 1780,

> [a]s to Plato, he was certainly a great genius, and a Philosopher truly Divine. But he was not so learned in Metaphysics, as his scholar Aristotle; nor does it appear to me that Metaphysics, any more than Logic, was formed into a science in Greece in his time. It was reserved for his scholar Aristotle to make a science of both . . . for Aristotle decides what Plato only disputes about. (qtd. in W. Knight 125)

And again that year, writing to Samuel Horsley,

> I think that the philosophers of the Alexandrian School did perfectly right in joining the two Philosophies together, the one being imperfect without the other; but Plato I think more imperfect without Aristotle than Aristotle without Plato. (qtd. in W. Knight 138)

However, he centers his metaphysics on Plato's doctrine of ideas and an abstract essentialism: "I will maintain that there is not only in every species of things, but in every individual thing, *something*, that makes it what it is, and distinguishes it from every other thing." It is the Platonic idea of the thing that "gives permanence and stability to everything here below, without which all the material world would—according to the doctrine of Protagoras and Heraclitus—be in a constant flux, like the stream of a river." Monboddo refused the Cartesian introspection that made every man "a standard of truth and falsehood to himself" (qtd. in W. Knight 139). Thus, as Cloyd notes, for Monboddo, Platonism served as one point of a triangle, with the Great Chain of Being and Christianity the other two corners, the tripod a strong foundation of his theories of language and rhetoric (175).

Because of Aristotle's acuteness in setting out first principles, he becomes a touchstone for rhetoric, and Greek rhetoric remains the peak of rhetoric. Monboddo differs from other British intellectuals of his day because he has a negative reaction whenever Latin authors are named. Those who are accepted, like Horace or Herodotus, inevitably model their style on Homer. An early undated, unsigned letter on rhetoric bears testimony to this:

> Sir, You must not be surprised that I have recommended to your perusal on this subject only Greek books. I really know none, even in Latin, and much less in any modern language, from which you can get any good instruction. I cannot judge of Quintilian, because I have not read him; but I am persuaded you will do as well to learn from his masters as from himself. (Monboddo did read him by the time he wrote volume 6.) As for Cicero you may profit by reading him, after you are taught, but he will not teach you; and, in general, I do not find that any of the Arts and Sciences are to be learned in the Latin language, so that a mere Latin scholar has always appeared to me contemptible. (qtd. in W. Knight 274)

With this as criteria, he lets his opinion of Dr. Johnson sink even lower. In a letter advising Boswell against writing the life of Dr. Johnston, Monboddo argued that Johnson "has no fine Taste nor correct Taste of Writing, and even as to his Learning, He is no Greek Scholar" (Cloyd 62). This stands as much as a rejection of the centuries of Scottish Latin scholars as it does the British Oxbridge tradition. In turning away from Latin, Monboddo curiously becomes a modern, signalling the next century of Greek worship by archaeologists, humanists, and linguists.

Rhetoric in *Origin and Progress*

To Monboddo in his rhetoric volume, rhetoric and dialectic are a more ancient art than poetic and more useful, if less pleasurable. In his typical way, he cites anthropological evidence from "barbarous peoples," including the Indians of North America, "among whom a chief, though he may be very eminent in war, is not regarded, if he cannot speak" (iv).

In his introduction to *Origin and Progress,* Monboddo writes of rhetoric and poetic as two types of style, albeit style that is most beautiful and produces the greatest effect. Other types of style he has earlier treated have been four: the epistolary, dialogic, historical, and didactic. However, his actual definition of rhetoric is much broader, if only generally Aristotelian:

> An art of persuasion without science or demonstration, upon subjects of deliberation, of judicial decision, or of praise or dispraise, by arguments taken either from the nature of the subject, from the person of the speaker, or the persons of the hearers. (5.2: 29)

This definition marks off a space for persuasive discourse upon issues of general public concern. His qualifier "without science or demonstration" is meant to stress the primacy of persuasion and to protect general discourse from the narrowness of expert discourse, as in Aristotle, by limiting it to arguments drawn not from specific fields but from common opinion and knowledge. He admits that science and demonstration partake of persuasion but agrees with Aristotle that rhetoric has no determinate subject, partaking of all. Yet particular arts or sciences may be treated rhetorically by using continuous discourse instead of dialogue and by using persuasive rhetorical style and general arguments drawn from "things that everybody is supposed to know" (5.2: 30) instead of a didactic style and particular arguments drawn from the mysteries of the art or science.

In short, rhetoric does not have an art but is one; it has to do with the manner of treating a subject but not the subject itself. It is, as in Aristotle, an art for public discourse. Thus it is, as Plato's Gorgias said, a most dangerous art, but all depends on the use made of it. The subjects of other arts are limited, but "rhetoric comprehends all the affairs of men, and the whole business of human life" (5.2: 33), but the subjects relate to civil or political life incapable by their nature of being reduced to an art of science and depending often upon future events, concerning which we cannot guess or conjecture. So rhetoric is the art of persuasion without demonstrating or teaching any art or science. (6: 11)

Inventionally, rhetoric persuades not by words and style but by arguments, drawn from the person of the speaker, the persons to whom he speaks, and the subject itself, the original "Aristotelian triangle" linked to *ethos, pathos,* and *logos.* In discussing arguments, Monboddo notes the difference between dialectic and rhetoric, explains topics, and goes on to summarize the three types of discourse: judicial, deliberative, and epideictic. Throughout he gives only principles of Aristotle's rhetoric, admitting that he intends only to provide readers with a

> general plan of this fine work of Aristotle and to direct the attention of the reader to the several parts which I think are of the greatest importance. . . . And indeed my chief design, in all that I have written upon the philosophy or the learning of the antients, is to revive, if possible, the study of antient arts and sciences, . . . and to show the reader that he cannot perfectly understand any art or science without the study of those unfashionable books to which I refer. (6: 88)

However, after these eighty-eight pages (brief in relation to six volumes) comprising a *précis* of Aristotle, he concludes that this is the end of the *matter* of rhetoric (invention), which he had earlier deemed the most important part. He goes on to discuss at greater length style, then pronunciation, and delivery. Thus, Monboddo's rhetoric, while protesting against his contemporaries and their new rhetorics, becomes, like Smith's, Blair's, and many others', a rhetoric emphasizing an analytical and interpretive belles lettres approach as opposed to an inventive, generative, sociopolitical civic rhetoric. It also weights rhetoric in the direction of formalism and stylistics, a phenomenon for which his contemporaries have been criticized (see Miller, for example). He himself also criticizes rhetorics that emphasize formal matters over invention and thought.

Rhetoric and Style

In Monboddo's undated letter on rhetoric, probably written early in his career, he forecasts his later treatment of rhetoric in the *Origin and Progress,* providing a rationale for his emphasis on style. He tells his correspondent that the art of rhetoric is limited to three parts—matter, or invention; diction, or style; and pronunciation, or delivery. He rejects the systematizing of pronunciation into an art and ignores delivery, so important in Condillac and that dismisses elocutionary rhetorics like those of Richard Brinsley Sheridan and Gilbert Austin, popular with the Scots eager to rid themselves of rusticisms. (Of course, these elocutionists were strongly linked with the cult of taste, which dismissed Aristotelian principles.) Monboddo then advises his correspondent, who apparently wishes to prepare a course of lectures on rhetoric, that although matter or invention is more significant, it will be too difficult for most hearers. He then writes that what a teacher must work chiefly on is "the Diction [style], for as to the matter, it will be too difficult for most of your hearers and perhaps for yourself, till you have gone through a very regular and severe course of study of Aristotle's works" (Irvine 29). He advises this study to include not only the three books of rhetoric and eight books of topics or dialectics but significantly the book of categories, interpretations, and much of the analytics. This would ensure that the reader would garner Aristotelian theories of matter, form, and abstract hierarchy. This becomes the advice he later summarizes in volume 6 of *Origin and Progress*.

In his stylistic advice, his one principle of composition throughout remains variety. This primary excellence in composition and style is seen relative to the opportunities each particular language provides for variation. The more ability to provide variation, the more highly he ranks the language. Of course, he measures all languages against Greek. However, he pays high tribute to another language, Sanskrit, admitting of even more variety. As he values diversity and variety in the human species, he holds to variety in language and composition. After giving examples of excellence in oratory, he ends with an analysis of Lord Mansfield's lost oration on the subject of Demosthenes' speech *de Corona* (commonly analyzed by Monboddo's Scottish and English contemporaries). Monboddo also spends much time discussing Greek history and analyzing Demosthenes, whom he considers the greatest orator of ancient times, except for Pericles, despite the fact that Pericles left no written texts.

Monboddo's criterion of variety is the plenitude of the Great Chain of Being, capacious enough to include tailed men. However, it is a variety in very little danger of getting out of hierarchical order. Variation, the primary excellence in composition and style, is seen relative to the opportunities each particular language provides for variation. The more opportunity, the more highly he rates the language. Again, as in his earliest papers, the semi-barbarous Chinese fare poorly in his gradings, rating as difficult, awkward, undeveloped, and unsuitable to discoveries in the arts and sciences, despite their early inventions of paper, gunpowder, and printing. For some reason, variation in tones in Chinese goes unappreciated by Monboddo, who wrote that it is more musical than "any language ought to be" (*Origin and Progress* 1: 252).

To sum up, Monboddo's theories of rhetoric build fairly consistently on the principles he lays out in his discussion of language. He claims his study of language began in part in reaction to Locke's theories of sensation and reflection, which he felt denigrated the mind, making it too passive, receptive, too materialistic, and too dependent upon the body. Ideas come from the mind, whose self-moving power is its essence, he believed. This is why Monboddo returns to Aristotle for his developmental theories to wield against Locke. This move is ironic because Locke's theory of senses and his inchoate developmentalism were also from Aristotle; moreover, Monboddo criticizes Aristotle for the same materialist flaw as Locke. (Locke's Platonism goes unremarked by Monboddo.)

Finally, Monboddo's discourse on the matter of rhetoric is as mixed and varied as the Aristotle he appropriates. Both men's discourses contain the germs of a radical, nonessentialist, even epistemic rhetoric such as is appropriate to a democratic society. However, both also contain elitist, hierarchical rhetorics much more suited to aristocratic, agrarian—slaveholding—societies. Perhaps this is not surprising as both men were aristocrats in a rapidly changing, agrarian, slave-holding society in which the nobility were being challenged by rapidly rising merchant classes. This conflict produces discursive rifts and tensions throughout his texts. Monboddo's veneration for Aristotelian rhetoric and thought makes him in some moments a progressive, but more frequently a reactionary, much like the mixed texts he embraced.

If the theoretical differences between Monboddo and his contemporaries are great, the question remains: What were the practical differences in rhetoric between them? Assessing his work across the multiple volumes of his *Origin and Progress* and *Antient Metaphysics,* perhaps not much. If invention is the center of traditional rhetoric, Monboddo does little with it other than to synopsize Aristotle and send the reader on his way to the classical texts. Because of his interest in competing with his contemporaries on issues such as speculative language theory and literature, he ends up much more a belletristic rhetorician like Smith and Blair than it might at first glance seem. Blair begins his rhetoric with a theory of language origins quite similar to Condillac's, the starting point for Monboddo's language origin theories. Blair, Kames, and many others end up closer to English literary studies rather than to rhetoric, and so does Monboddo. Nonetheless, the meaning of rhetoric is different to Monboddo because of his Platonic metaphysical values: rhetoric can achieve knowledge of truth in human decisions as it can in natural philosophy because the hierarchy of abstraction of language approaches the real.

Language in Society

Monboddo's rhetoric weaves in and out of his encyclopedic view of humans, based on his story of the development of human civilization, mind, and language. For him, humans in the state of nature are both rational and political—they fit Aristotle's definition of a political animal in that they associate, have a system of communication, even before speech, and carry on a "common business" (279). If humans *were* once solitary, a great cause must have brought about the change to social and political life, and for Monboddo that great cause was simply necessity or want. Necessity was the original cause for the invention of all the arts and sciences. After the rudimentary arts of hunting and fishing or supplying foods were invented, and basic needs were met but not in a state of luxury, humans invented arts for pleasure and amusement. Finally, with their minds cultivated, the desire for knowledge produced the sciences.

Language was the "instrument of instruments," without which mankind never would have proceeded far in the invention of other arts (*Origin and Progress* 1: 249). Ultimately, the old chicken-and-egg problem arises concerning language origins, and Monboddo offers to straighten out Rousseau on the matter. Which came first, language or society? Rousseau seems to doubt that society could have existed without language, although language could not have been invented without society for there would have been no cause to invent it at all. However, Monboddo argues that societies—not mere herds but political units— may exist without language or at least without speech. Some method of communication would be needed, however, and animals use cries, facial expressions, and gestures. He names bees and ants as counterexamples—he is not talking about associations made on the basis of instinct but of sagacity.

As examples of animals that have political life, he names the beaver as exemplary, citing Buffon's *Histoire Naturelle*. Citing Cardinal

Polignac's *Anti-Lucretius* Latin poem, he offers the example of the *Baubacis*, a foxlike creature that made wars and took slaves to help them in foraging. They made the slaves lie down on their back and packed hay on them; having thus loaded the "living carts," they dragged them along by the tails, he explained. "I think it can hardly be doubted" that such a sagacious animal would in time have invented language, he writes (*Origin and Progress* 287). He also tells of sea cats whose males would keep in line with strict discipline their very humble and submissive wives. The sea cat had no use of speech, "but it appeared that without it he can practice the most difficult of human arts, that of government over females, in which most men have failed" (*Origin and Progress* 288–89). These sorts of entertaining examples and bon mots must have gone over well in papers for the Select Society and other social gatherings.

Another example in *Origin and Progress* is that of the orangutans, who, he notes, walk erect, live in huts, join in company to attack elephants, and do many other things together but have not the use of speech. The insight Monboddo expresses with these examples is that humans associated in political life for a long time, and the art of articulated language—his definition of true language—only developed slowly and gradually. His point stops short, however, of saying that development happened organically or naturalistically, particularly in the higher stages.

Language and Understanding: Monboddo and Mind

Monboddo's metaphysics, consistent throughout his lifetime, permeates his views of mind, cognition, and knowing. Mind itself is the first principle of the universe for Monboddo: existing by itself or joining with body, it pervades the universe. It becomes clear in his *Antient Metaphysics* volumes that his entire system of language and rhetoric rests on a foundation of Aristotle-like hylomorphism (*hyle*, matter; *morphe*, form). This Platonized Stoical system includes matter and form as well as the hierarchy of forms. Form is the privileged member of the binary form-matter; universal forms exist first, and matter can take any number of forms. As Monboddo repeatedly stresses, mind itself is the first principle of the universe; existing by itself or joining with body, it pervades the universe. The universe has plenteous matter to fill a hierarchy from the smallest forms to the most abstract idea of the mind of God.

After Monboddo produced three volumes of the *Origin and Progress* series, he turned to his series *Antient Metaphysics*, producing three volumes before returning to his *Origin and Progress* work. Because the final three volumes of *Origin and Progress* are a philosophical rhetoric, it concerns us to see on what this rhetoric rests.

In the *Antient Metaphysics,* one can read his reactions to the criticism that must have stung from the earlier project. For example, Monboddo begins *Antient Metaphysics* acknowledging

> the subject is altogether unfashionable, not only among the vulgar, who ridicule it under the name of *metaphysic,* but even among the philosophers of the present age, who are so much conversant with particular and individual things, as hardly to believe that there exists a science of Universals. (i)

He prefaces many later explanations with a forthright admission that readers will no doubt think his system "absurd and ridiculous" (228). He declares from the outset that the style will not be fashionable, will have no modern "spruceness and trimness" (i). Later in that same volume, he critiques Newton: "I know very well that, in the age in which we live, the authority of the antients goes for very little" (507). However, in his preface to the first volume, he boastfully predicts that modern French and English writers such as Hume will be forgotten, so that he need not take particular notice of their controversies (vii). Monboddo learned quickly from the response to his first *Origin and Progress* volumes, if not from his debates at sociable dinners, that he was swimming against the Scottish Enlightenment tide. Writing for posterity, he therefore warns the reader and plunges ahead.

Evidence also can be seen in the metaphysical volumes supporting a possible shift in Monboddo's personality following a critical illness. During his crisis, a woman philosopher came to him in a dream and lectured to him for hours in French. His emphasis on Platonism, the reality of ideas, second sight, and dreams in the *Antient Metaphysics,* while thoroughly Scottish in tone, differ from the scientific view of language and anthropology in the earlier three volumes on language. However, if the tone and emphases are more profound in the *Antient Metaphysics,* Monboddo's theories of mind and cognition remain the same, and he frequently references these in the latter three volumes of *Origin and Progress.* Monboddo's critiques of Locke and Newton are also clearly articulated in *Antient Metaphysics.* For metaphysics to Monboddo is the universal science of causes that comprehends all other sciences. Yet, it ultimately seems to be based on extralinguistic phenomena, for example, the (Platonic) image or an imageless mathematical conception itself.

In his rationalism, Monboddo's metaphysical view of the mind encompasses the mystical and nonrational. A freemason in the land that produced the earliest nonguild masonry, Monboddo shared the respect for Pythagoras and the wisdom of ancient Egypt that earlier humanists and his fellow masons held. However, despite his wide knowledge of ancient history, Monboddo was scarcely historical, holding that the ideas from the Pythagoreans, as refined by Plato and Aristotle, were universal and eternal.

In this system, the movement of analogy again plays a starring role. "We proceed from *Nature* to God through *Man*," reasoning analogically, he argues (*Antient Metaphysics* 226). As for the mind of man, it has "powers and faculties independent of the body and which probably will be exerted to much greater advantage when it is disencumbered of the body" (*Antient Metaphysics* 163).

Mind, essentially the principle of all motion that runs through nature, is "what people call life," and body is what is moved. This works through the vegetable and animal minds of nature to the rational-intellectual mind of humans and up to the First Cause, the Supreme Mind. This Platonic Supreme Mind is the first principle of motion in the universe, eternal, immovable, unchangeable. Citing Plato, Monboddo writes, "Everything in nature is *body* or *mind* or their accidents" (or accompaniments). He makes the point again and again that mind can exist with or without body.

What moves body must always be mind because body cannot move itself is another frequent refrain in Monboddo. His criticism of modern science is thus that it is nothing more than "metaphysics without mind," his critiques of Locke and Newton echoing this point (*Antient Metaphysics* 11–12). As in Aristotle, nature-mind always has an end: "the perfection of its nature" (*Antient Metaphysics* 15). Thus we see the Aristotelian vocabulary of potentiality, power, and capacity, linked especially with custom and habit in Monboddo.

He cites Plato and Aristotle but reminds readers that "antient theism" is older than both of them, going back to Egypt, close to Asia Minor where the human race began (*Origin and Progress* 1.2: 254). This is not the theism of Descartes and Newton, as the Mason Monboddo is quick to point out, but is ancient theism, based on the concept of Mind, "the prime efficient cause of every thing in the universe" (*Antient Metaphysics* ix). As for the universe, it is, for Monboddo, one body, an idea that traveled from the Pythagoreans to Plato. "Man is in himself a little world," as he likes to repeat, encompassing the four elements as well as the three substances of vegetable, animal, and intellectual life (*Antient Metaphysics*

1: viii). Man is therefore not just part of the system of the universe but is a model of the whole system.

Cognition

His explanation for mind and cognition not only intertwines with his system of metaphysics, it also serves to reveal the bones of the classical schema for mental operations, making clearer Condillac's sources and highlighting Condillac's more modern departures from this classical material. Condillac's modernity may have been in his "crossed-out God" (Latour 32) or his truly historical view that classical texts referred to ancient times and were not necessarily applicable to the modern era. In contrast despite his wide knowledge of ancient history, Monboddo was scarcely historical, holding that the ideas from the Pythagoreans, as refined by Plato and Aristotle, were universal and eternal.

Most of his Scottish Enlightenment colleagues—Hume, Reid, Campbell, Kames—worked on the problem of knowledge and human sensation. Many of them shaped and practiced the Common Sense tradition to avoid just the sort of speculative muddle Monboddo chooses to place himself in when he asks, How can we know reality, when it is beyond human senses? Like Condillac, Monboddo turns to what Plato has called "a bastard kind of reason," answering that we can only know reality indirectly by analogy (*Antient Metaphysics* 55). For example, we must study our own minds, because by analogy we can contemplate and come to know the Superior Mind (*Antient Metaphysics* 101–2). While we are in our bodies, we see "as it were dreaming," shadows and images, like the men in Plato's cave. While the true object of intellect is to apprehend the idea or form, more mundane cognitive operations work in the manner of a bootstrap operation to rise to this level. Because of the faculty of abstraction, whose level can be seen in the language of a people, humans can gradually rise to a level just below the angels.

The model of this bootstrapping mind, for Monboddo, followed Philoponus, a Christian commentator on Aristotle. Mind was divided into the gnostic and oretic powers: gnostic for knowing and perceiving and oretic for desiring or having aversion. For Monboddo, there are two overall gnostic powers of the mind: the power that perceives the particular objects of sense and the power that abstracts from sense and produces generals or ideas. Abstractions from sense become objects of the intellect, but there are also immaterial substances that have no need to be abstracted but have real existences. Thus, while it is true on one level of mind that there is nothing in the intellect that was not first in the senses, it is not necessarily true for both levels.

The various powers described by Philoponus become rearranged into mental operations for Monboddo in a rather haphazard fashion. He separates *sense* (organ of sense or the impression bodies make upon the organ of sense) from *sensation* (the power or faculty that the mind perceives). Likewise, he defines the *phantasia,* imagination, or the power of capturing sense impressions, using the Platonic vocabulary of painting. These two capabilities are shared with brutes, along with a certain amount of reason or the ability to compare sense impressions. Together, these three—sense, *phantasia,* and comparison or reason—make up the sense. The part of the gnostic powers he calls intellect, the generalizing power or the discourse of reason, he divides into opinion or science, depending on the nature of the subject or the manner in which the inquiry has been conducted. It first abstracts; second, it apprehends ideas alone or joined into propositions; and third, it investigates and discovers connections of ideas concluding in science or opinion (*Antient Metaphysics* 118). He also discusses Aristotle's division of the intellect into practical or speculative. Unlike Condillac, his analysis does not become segmented into a clear process, nor does it depart radically from his sources. What seems to be important to him is to explain sensory apparati without losing the plane of the ideal. In the process, however, he produces a constructivist theory of the senses, both classical and modern in its perspective.

Mind and Cognition: *Phantasia,* Language, and Beyond Rationality

Perhaps most importantly to Monboddo, the intellect can act without the sense: it can apprehend "what has neither *colour* nor *shape,* and what *eye hath not seen, nor ear heard,*" or incorporeal substance (*Antient Metaphysics* 148). Thus "man is an animal superior to any other upon this earth in *power* and *capacity,* as well as in *energy* or *actuality,*" and although he shares even *phantasia* and a certain amount of reasoning with animals, animals do not share an intellect, a self-moving mind that can contemplate objects that exist only within the Supreme Mind can study itself and come to know the Supreme Mind (*Antient Metaphysics* 148). Thus, brutes and humans are not different by degree but absolutely distinct (*Antient Metaphysics* 132). This careful explanation seems to be a reaction to earlier criticism of his consideration of orangutan and humans of the same species. Despite the dividing line, Monboddo still places humans in nature and therefore close to animals and disparages Descartes and mechanists who would make animals machines. They are not machines, but they do lack higher intellect.

Brutes as well as humans preserve in phantasia the perceptions of sense and therefore can be said to reason on a basic level. However, they only revive the images stored in their imaginations when prompted by "bodily appetite," while humans can do so at will, "making of his imagination a kind of magic lanthorn, by which he exhibits to himself pictures of all kinds, beautiful and pleasant, or ugly and frightful" (*Antient Metaphysics* 113). The imagination is tied to the senses, however, but the objects of the human intellect are quite different for Monboddo. For humans, the first operation of the intellect is abstraction, which forms ideas. The second is the apprehension of ideas alone or joined in propositions, and the third is the discursive, which has the original notion of passing back and forth and making connections of ideas, concluding in science or opinion (*Antient Metaphysics* 115, 118).

Despite the attention he pays to the discursive intellect, Monboddo does always not center the development of cognition on language development as do Vico and Condillac. However, finally, as an afterthought, at the end of his description of cognitive operations, he adds that "without the use of speech, humans wouldn't have become intellectual creatures at all" (*Antient Metaphysics* 148). Cognitive development for Monboddo, however, centers on the image as captured in phantasia and on proving that the intellect can work separately from the body to reach a sort of extralinguistic truth. He believes the human mind can emerge from matter and transport itself into the ideal. Thus, there is a natural progress of humankind from the womb and the vegetable, to the zoophite, to an irrational animal, and then to a civil being and finally perhaps rising to achieve a spark of the divine.

Monboddo values sight as "our most excellent sense, to which as Aristotle says we owe the greatest part of our knowledge" (*Antient Metaphysics* 150). His views on seeing tend to be both modern and scientific. He believed in the latest theory—that rays of light reflected by what we see, strike the pupil of the eye, where they are refracted and converge so as to form a picture of the object in the retina, and that picture the optic nerve conveys to the brain. The Epicureans were right, he believed, because we do not apprehend the thing itself but only the images it produces. All senses work like sight so that through the use of our senses, we do not know the nature of anything. Like Locke, he uses the analogy of the mind to a kind of camera obscura (151). Importantly, the imagination can replay without the use of sense the images that are captured. Images can also come from previous sense encounters, or they can come from superior minds, as they do in dreams. He quotes Milton's *Paradise Lost:* "Millions of spiritual creatures walk the earth/ Unseen, both when we wake, and when we sleep" (4. 5: 678). We dream, and invisible minds communicate with ours; we wake and have visions. Greater minds are in communication with our minds, Monboddo believed. He also believed in second sight: "A way of foreseeing things by *vision,* in which they are represented in the manner they happen. It is well known in the Highlands of Scotland, and as I have been informed, among other nations, who are nearer the natural state than we" (*Antient Metaphysics* 157). This is another instance in which Monboddo seems to regret that humans are moving away from nature into culture. The "folk," as Herder would call them, seem to hold onto these residual natures and serve as proof that mind can affect bodies without the senses.

Monboddo gives us the paranormal case of the sleepwalking girl: A fifteen-year-old girl who lived in his neighborhood had a disease well known in the country. Monboddo explains that the affliction, called *louping* or the *jumping ague,* seizes its victims in their sleep and makes them "jump and run like persons possessed." After being awake several hours, this particular girl would be seized at about seven or eight in morning. Suddenly a heaviness would come upon her, and she would close her eyes and be in apparent sleep. She then leapt up on stools and tables and ran out of the cottage "with great violence" to a certain destination that had always been revealed to her in a dream the night before. She then came back. However rough the road, she never fell although her eyes were "quite shut," as testified by a brother whom the family sent to run with her. Monboddo tells how she could run atop a wall around her garden or leap up onto objects. Finally, after announcing that she would make three more runs, which she did, and the phenomenon ceased. This is like sleepwalking, Monboddo writes, arguing that it proves the mind can perceive objects of sense without using the organs of sense (*Antient Metaphysics* 159).

Critiques of Locke and Newton

Much of his metaphysics lays the groundwork for or centers on his critiques of Locke and Newton. Both critiques rest on a profound antimodernism grounded in an unwavering, if suspiciously pagan, view of theism, despite the transcendental nature of his Episcopalianism. Of Locke, he complains that "our great author of the philosophy of *mind*" writes that he has no idea of substance, the "very elements or chatecism [*sic*] of philosophy." However, Locke thinks he has "clear ideas of different qualities inherent in substances" (*Antient Metaphysics* 49). How? Monboddo asks. Is it not by abstraction? Locke, however, seems to doubt there is any such operation of the human mind as abstraction or at least abstraction in the Platonic sense Monboddo means it.

For Monboddo, Locke's main problem seems to be that he confounds ideas and sensations: ideas are after all abstractions, higher up the ladder of abstraction than sensations. This is a materialist, atheistical tendency Monboddo is certain he did not intend:

> And as, through his whole book, he confounds ideas and sensations, it is plain that he had no notion of the mind's having any perception, except by the senses, nor knew that it could operate by itself, without the assistance of the body or its organs; that is, in other words, he did not know what an idea was, though he has written a whole book upon the subject; and has given us a system of the philosophy of mind, without making the distinction, which is the foundation of that whole philosophy, betwixt the mind operating by itself, and operating by the assistance of the senses: And, because the mind must of necessity at first operate by the means of the senses only, he has from thence rashly concluded, that it can never operate in any other way. (*Antient Metaphysics* 1: 49–50)

As we have just seen, for Monboddo, the mind is not dependent upon the physical senses but has sight given to it from another realm, on a higher plane.

Monboddo also attacks Newton because he is not consistent with Aristotle or classical authorities. Monboddo protests that no body actually has a tendency to remain at rest, for bodies are either moving or have a tendency to be in motion. Newton provides no beginning or cause for motion either. Attraction supposes an active principle in matter, with which Monboddo disagrees. Newton cannot explain gravity, which is for Monboddo an occult cause. When Aristotle uses *occult causes,* it is to profess his ignorance, in Monboddo's astute opinion, but Newton's system is *built* on an occult cause, that is, attraction (185). "A philosophy of this kind does not explain nature, such as God Almighty has made it, but creates a new world, and makes new laws of *matter* and *motion*."

The very same arguments as were used against Descartes's system of vortices apply here: "*first*, . . . there is no proof of its existence, and *secondly*, if it did exist, it would not answer the purpose" (*Antient Metaphysics* 189).

Monboddo opposes yet sincerely tries to understand Newton's universal laws—but always from within his own philosophical system. It is as if he insists on remaining within his own paradigm and resists all efforts to shift perspective. Later, in 1783, in a letter to Samuel Horsley, we see him trying to work out how Newton's theories of motion could be comprehended or disproved from within his own universal philosophical science. He is still puzzling over the problem of the motion of bodies not moved by mind but, apparently, purely mechanistically by "projection and gravitation. . . . But I ask them [the Newtonians] for what purpose they lay down such principles as must startle every theist, and, if they are not downright materialist, have at least a tendency to it?" (qtd. in W. Knight 237). Monboddo was not entirely wrong pointing out these tendencies to materialism in modern scientific thought. However, once again, his rigid either-or thinking means that he was in most cases wrong in questioning the religious sincerity of his contemporaries.

Implications of Monboddo's Philosophy and Rhetoric

Monboddo's metaphysical system represents a holistic vision of a science encompassed in an overarching philosophy. It is different from Condillac's because Monboddo's theism is openly foundational while Condillac and to a lesser extent Vico have a "crossed out God" (in Latour's terminology), overtly setting traditional religious theories to the side while working out their philosophies. Like Vico, Monboddo wants to take the new problems of science into the old paradigm, to put new wine in old wineskins. Unlike Vico, he is not willing to reinterpret or readjust the frame one whit to accommodate new problems, methods, or perspectives. If Vico's system fails to be wholly modern, it does not fail through his applying a rigid and repetitive version of classical thought.

Both Vico and Monboddo are valuable because they see problems with modernity and accurately point them out. For example, Vico prophesies that the individualism of modernity will reduce the capacity for social thought as well as restrict linguistic cognitive capacities and the imagination in the humanities. Monboddo accurately forecasts that mechanistic views of the earth and universe will result in environmental damage as well as decline of animals. Both see modernity in terms of ethical problems. Yet Monboddo, for all his historicizing of language, at times has no sense of history; for all his use of travelers' tales, has no sense of geography; for all his explorations into diversity of human life, no sense of the value of diversity in and to human societies or cultures.

Monboddo ends up a British Scot, from the peripheries, orienting his compass toward London. When home, he reflects the agricultural-improving mind of his day, making efforts to modernize and boost production on his estate. His agrarian benevolence on the estate was renowned—he gathered and tended "his people" as he called them and liked to have them on the land at a time other landowners began to enclose and throw crofters and tenants off, burning the land and starving them out until they left for America or other lands. He was allied with the proto-Victorian Christian benevolence of Hannah More, to whom he more than once proposed after meeting her with other blue-stockings in London. (Despite her advocacy of marriage and family for others, she, perhaps not surprisingly, turned him down.)

Literature on Monboddo leaves us the image of a rustic Scots farmer, a Greco-Anglophile antiquarian, often described on his annual spring pilgrimage to London, made until he was into his eighties. Once called an "Elzevir Johnson," an "elegant miniature" version of Johnson (Cloyd 57), or what would be more apt an Elzevir Aristotle, he was committed to the health-giving properties of fresh air and exercise. Thus, he never entered a carriage but always rode horseback even in the worst of weather in his cocked hat, jackboots, and scarlet cape, peering nearsightedly at a pocket Homer. Behind, leading an extra horse, walked his black servant Gory (W. Knight 9; Cloyd 39).

However, this portrait is as well the picture of a Scottish judge, who, in volume 3 of the letters of Johnson, in the Court of Sessions was one of the few voting against the freedom of an African, Joseph Knight, brought to Scotland as a slave. Other justices, Lords Auchinleck and Hailes, voted that blacks were free in Scotland, but Monboddo voted they were not. Monboddo's devotion to the Great Chain of Being and classical hierarchy rests at the base of such a reactionary, racist decision.

In a note in the *Origin and Progress*, Monboddo writes, "As some men are by nature incapable of a liberal education, they are those who, as Aristotle has told us, are by nature slaves" (3.4: 15). The discussion at that point is on education and leisure, but Monboddo quickly complicates his previously straightforward statement:

> And indeed, the greatest good fortune that can befall a man
> who has not education is to have no leisure at all, but to be
> constantly employed, especially in bodily labour, for which
> by far the greater part of mankind are only fit. So that men,
> not properly educated, are by nature designed to be slaves and
> drudges, or else to be miserable. . . . As some men are by
> nature incapable of a liberal education, they are those, who,
> as Aristotle has told us, are by nature slaves. (*Origin and
> Progress* 4: 450, n.)

Aristotle's *Rhetoric* and its later adherents including Vico divide
society as a body into the head and stomach, those with intellects and
those with appetites. It is often the case in Aristotle and throughout
rhetoric that the theorist-orator states he would prefer to use intellectual arguments but for "the vulgar" for whom the emotional and lower
arguments are used. In light of this hierarchical, classical foundation and
his previous division of society, there is no doubt that Monboddo believed most men were not fit for education, and only a few rational souls
like himself were designed and born to be men of science, leaders, and
thinkers. This way of thinking, buttressed by classical texts, is not only
undemocratic but underlies slavery and colonialization.[10]

Studies of Monboddo frequently end in aporia. On the margins of
the Enlightenment, Monboddo stood at the confluence of the classical
and the modern. His reluctance to turn loose of the old, coupled with
the inevitability of his unconscious absorption of the new, produced an
inevitable hybridization productive of new theories of language and new
anthropological sciences of language. However, these sciences themselves
would be implicated in colonialism and inequality. As communication
historian Paul Heyer writes upon leaving Monboddo,

> For any discipline in search of ancestral figures an inevitable
> problem arises regarding what to do when someone like
> Monboddo turns up who yields insights centuries ahead of
> his time, yet commits blunders that throw doubt on his ba-
> sic common sense. Should he be exalted as a seer or dismissed
> as a buffoon? We are not yet ready to pass judgment. There-
> fore we must preserve the legacy. (37)

Perhaps it is time to pass judgment on Monboddo. He was a hybrid figure, at once racist and reactionary, brilliant, benevolent, farsighted in some
respects, and, yes, sometimes a buffoon. As peripheral and marginal, as

he was, these contradictory traits are perhaps finally only different in degree from some of his Enlightenment contemporaries crowding the center of eighteenth-century linguistic and rhetorical studies.

In refusing to consider the significant differences of his day from the Greeks or to see change as progress on any front, he ultimately isolates himself intellectually. He remains significant for historians of many disciplines, situated as he was at the crossroads of many strands of thought. One wonders whether some of the residual strains of rhetoric might more easily have contributed to the formation of new rhetorics if characters such as Monboddo had not marked them as monstrous residues.

Finally and again paradoxically, in rhetoric, Monboddo repeats the past theoretically in his Aristotelian rhetoric but ultimately makes the modern turn to a formalist, belletristic theory of language. This is despite his rejection of the cult of taste as anticlassical. The heart of classical rhetoric had been invention because of the primary need to produce a probable judgment and persuasive case in speaking in the law courts, legislature, or public forum. Rhetorical arts had secondarily been used as hermeneutic tools for reading literature, but even Aristotle's *Poetics* was oriented to the production as well as the reception of literature. With the spread of printing and the rise of literacy, the use of rhetoric as a tool for reception grew, especially seen in belles lettres and theories of taste.

This turn to belletrism was not in itself pernicious. As we have seen, the development of taste was central to polite learning and at the heart of the turn to essentially standard written dialects of centralizing vernaculars, in both France and the United Kingdom. And, as Andrew Hook argues, primarily with Thomas P. Miller, this pragmatic end was worthy: "Good taste and politeness in the areas of literature, language and style are bound up with good taste and politeness in modern, civilised society as a whole. Self-improvement in the first can lead to advancement in the second" (47–48). How good taste and politeness served to complement or counterbalance the culture of one of the most militaristic nations on the globe in this period is outside the scope of this study, but the intertwining of both at the end of the century of Enlightenment should be noted.

Hierarchy, Progress, and Loss

Nonetheless, finally, it is not Monboddo's belletrism that ends up being dangerous as an influence, but his combining a hierarchical, if seemingly beneficent scale of being with comparative historical linguistics and his foundationally biased cultural anthropology. His foundation of thought based on ranking languages and peoples along with the belief that few were destined to think complexly underlay the belief that some were to be thinkers and doers and others to serve. In light of Monboddo's worship of Greeks, his adulation of Home's sentimental tragedy *Douglas,* his dedication to feudal models of benevolence, his belief in the set qualities of primitives and the "folk" on his estate—as well as myriad other evidence— Monboddo ends up like a crab, scuttling backward into the Romantic and Victorian future. Monboddo's gives us ultimately a historical prototype of reactionary Romantic rhetoric based on a narrative of a return to a Past That Never Was.[11] It is a rhetoric we will see again and again, nearly always posing dangers for liberal and progressive thought.

Both Vico and Monboddo see modernity in terms of juridical and ethical problems and recognize a natural collectivity to human life. Both men's texts are valuable because they see problems with modernity and accurately point them out. (For example, Monboddo accurately forecasts that mechanistic views of the earth and universe will result in environmental damage as well as decline of animals, which he wisely refuses to see as Cartesian machines.) Yet Monboddo, for all his historicizing of language, at times has no sense of history. For all his use of travelers' tales, no true sense of place or the impact of geography on culture. For all his explorations into diversity of human life, no real sense of the different values held by human societies or cultures. In these traits, if not in his rhetoric and language theory, it easy to see that he was more mainstream in British culture of the late-eighteenth century than marginal.

In his rhetoric and language theory, Monboddo often takes up theories potentially useful to a wider democratic life. However, his social position and rigid notion of hierarchy constrain him to favor theories that are elitist and exclusionary. Thus, he reproduces the worst of Aristotelian rhetoric and civic humanism instead of filtering out particular concepts such as *phronesis* (practical wisdom) as did Vico, and later Habermas, with the goal of extending them to a wider group. Monboddo divides languages into barbarous and civilized, along with the world's peoples. Perhaps not unwittingly, this paves the way for a future colonialism based on English language, literature, and values. In Monboddo's rhetoric, to colonize the primitive would be benevolent, as contact with more civilized language allows colonized peoples to improve their linguistic abilities and rise in the scale of abstraction—although remaining well behind civilized nations. Such a linguistic-based teleology fits hand in glove with the goals of an empire on which the sun would never set. It makes explicit some of the unspoken residual beliefs underlying his colleagues' views on rhetoric and language study, beliefs that studying such things as Anglo-Saxon literature and learning proper English will make one "more fully human." These beliefs would infiltrate American literacy and writing instruction in the next century.

Not much more than a century after Monboddo died, T. S. Eliot theorized a rupture in English literature after the metaphysical poets. This break was premised on a historical "dissociation of sensibility" that made it impossible for later poets to equal the quality of the earlier rich and sensuous metaphorical language. Scottish Enlightenment thinkers were also drawn to such sublime poetry, and the touchstone in British eighteenth-century culture for this linguistic achievement was the poetry of Milton, cited by most of the leading lights for its sublimity.[12] Similar ideas were later assimilated by Samuel Coleridge into his theories of imagination and the sublime, again with reference to Milton. The need to posit a state of unification in the past based on a holistic thinking-feeling-sensing bringing mind, body, and reality together has been with us from our earliest literature, but it intensified in reaction to Enlightenment modernity and its persistence in dividing the mind and body.

The waxing of this call for a unified sensibility on the part of the metaphysical poets might profitably be assessed in light of the waning of sublime rhetoric. Dissociation of sensibility may have been no more or less than the sensed loss of a culture promoted by orality and sublime rhetorical arts, in particular, the kind of metaphor-rich arts we see in Vico's sublime civic rhetoric and revered in Monboddo's ideal Greek rhetoric. Perhaps Monboddo ultimately turned to Milton and poetics as the culmination of his *Origin and Progress* out of nostalgia for sublime rhetoric. The narrative of loss continues to haunt poetics as well as rhetoric.

7
Twenty-First-Century Language and Rhetoric

> Nothing so well marks the modern urge as this utopian dream of transparent language, of language so perfectly fitted to the world that no difference could insinuate itself between words and things. The modern age is characterised by this anxiety about language, this recurrent and irrepressible worry about the form of discourse and its fit with thought and things.
> —Stephen A. Tyler, *The Unspeakable: Discourse, Dialogue, and Rhetoric in the Postmodern World*

> If some unfamiliar kind of discursive class is emerging here [today], it has yet to do so with any clarity. Perhaps it would involve the movement of what one might call a processive communicational network, where fixity, discrete denotated objects of knowledge, analytical knowledge itself, discursive transparency, objective grasp, absence of the "subject" would all be strangers.
> —Timothy J. Reiss, *Discourse of Modernism*

How can one trace a genealogy of an ancient tradition, rhetoric, often assumed not only to be dead but to have died in the late-eighteenth century without issue? The three case studies investigated here address this issue in part, examining the transformations of rhetoric as it disperses its cultural wealth into literary study and linguistics. Moreover, the texts on rhetoric and language examined here illustrate three different eighteenth-century approaches to received texts in rhetoric that stood ready for others to incorporate and transform over the next two centuries. If we cannot trace or appreciate these figures' contributions in later rhetorics, it is not that rhetoric was dead or of no interest for newer as well as traditional texts and practices lived on. Not only did rhetoric not die, but it was transfigured while broadcasting its seed on the newly rising disciplinary winds. Other possible reasons exist for the marginalization of these texts: first, these texts are paradoxical and complex; second, these authors may have been marginalized in Enlightenment thought itself; and third, they have not fit our historical paradigms. Yet all of these reasons entail obvious circular reasoning. These figures were marginal because they were marginalized—we do not see these figures because we do not re-cognize them because they are not already seen. Scholars scanning the historical horizon for the clear-and-distinct pinnacles of modern rhetorics have often overlooked these low-lying fellows in the hedgerows, even along the main roads.

Histories that attempt to chart lineage or progress choose their key figures according to criteria that make these figures stand out and above the contemporary base of thought—Adam Smith, Hugh Blair, and George Campbell, for example. Repeatedly encountered and familiar figures become visible to historians like glacier peaks rising above the oceans while others who toil in the sea of commonplaces of their day, however industriously, tend to be left submerged.[1] While none of these three has been ignored *tout court,* they have failed to be included in major historical narratives seeking the roots of a modern rhetoric. They became a minor strain historically perhaps because they did not fully join the chorus of modernity.

If an exemplary modern rhetoric is that which sees language as an instrument to communicate a reality separate from the speaker or writer, none of these figures is truly modern. They did not believe rhetoric hampered progress or that it was what is irrelevant or even dangerous to the process of communicating truth, a modern attitude that locates truth in the individual. A modern view is said to detach language and rhetoric from the social life of a community, privatizing both, as the individual and his interior perception of reality become more important. Obviously all the rhetorics examined here share social aspects of rhetoric. Each philosopher-rhetorician tells a narrative of language originating so deep in the body and in society that an objective realist rhetoric becomes unlikely if not impossible. If such a modern rhetoric rose to hegemony in the nineteenth century, these three cases show it was not yet clear at the end of their century that it would entirely gain hegemony.

Nevertheless, at least for Vico and Monboddo bookending the century, modernity and its orientation to rhetoric were worthy enough opponents to be taken very seriously. Monboddo reactively felt that a loss of the arts of public discourse would further diminish the quality of civilization. He could not accept that a newer version of rhetoric might develop to function in the place of traditional arts. Somewhat similarly, Vico early in his career spoke out presciently against the kind of citizens a Cartesian education might produce—logical and analytical, yet without an ability to imagine, empathize, and persuade based on an understanding of what others in the community might feel and believe. Lacking the ability—and no doubt interest—to project themselves fully and emotionally into public decisions, they also would lack the art of discoursing with passion. Thereby, the most educated of modern citizens would be the paradoxically least able to function effectively to offer leadership in communal crises. They might know clearly and distinctly what they felt but be bereft of the communal feeling and the values of common sense. However, Vico recognizes the possibility—even the necessity—of developing new rhetorics for new historical times. Modernity should be critiqued and new arts drawn from the old transmuted and transformed. The purpose of humans creating the good life together should nonetheless be conserved along with arts necessary to produce effective citizens.

Alternatively, Condillac celebrates rather than decries modernity and holds the most modern perspective on rhetoric. He is also less interested in the active citizen in society, choosing rather to emphasize taste and order in his writing instruction. Alongside elements of a modern conception of language and rhetoric as representation of reality emerges that of a social language as a system of expression. This focus on expressivity is linked with the insight that language is a process of active construction. Nonetheless, the energy from that insight is often channeled into the activity of private expression, that is, representation of an interior landscape. Yet despite effacing this interior-exterior binary, Condillac begins splits between referential and emotive, denotative and connotative, and ordinary and literary language. These divisions have come down to us so that we contemporary moderns have perceived it natural for language to divide into poetic and scientific language.

Vico sees language not as an object or instrument but as socially constitutive activity necessary to carrying on civil society. This view is allied with a broad view of rhetoric linked to poetics, but both are tied to various aspects of social life including religion and politics. Vico's rhetoric also contains an expressivism that finally becomes epistemological, as the body itself and its transport or rejection are the surest guides to narrative truth. In general, his language theory looks back to classical wisdom, yet it is paradoxically from that source that he draws his postmodern notions of rhetoricality and linguistic system. Vico's semiotic, constructivist view of language and rhetoric draws from the pre-Socratics but can be found in diverse forms running through Francis

Bacon, Thomas Hobbes, and John Locke and on to Johann Gottfried Herder, Karl Marx, and Charles S. Peirce. Nonetheless, it remains a marginalized perspective in English studies' writing pedagogy until late in the twentieth century. When moderns began to feel some of the pinch Vico had predicted a modern rhetoric would exert on public discourse, we returned to salvage some of the civic humanist ideals from traditional rhetoric and interested ourselves in his discourse. Having shown how the past could be transformed in light of the present and future, his culturally aware rhetoric—albeit carrying some elements we should no longer tolerate—was a more helpful archive of rhetorical common sense.

Only Monboddo's rhetoric attempts to repeat the past in the face of modernity, a move he grandiosely boasts about in his texts. Of the three figures in this book, Monboddo attempts most intensely to maintain a purity in rhetoric, advising an emulation of Greek rhetoric hybridizing Plato and Aristotle. Classical rhetoric's associations with a hierarchical, aristocratic society have long been noted, and all three thinkers share aspects and values of their hierarchical societies. The poorest, Vico, was aligned in many ways with the Catholic hierarchy but was the son of a bookseller. The belletrist Condillac was of the lesser French nobility and became an estateholder and agrarian. Monboddo was clearly a gentleman, a landed aristocrat, sharing and helping construct a version of the agrarian ideal. Yet, Monboddo felt quite at home in London, with the conservatives of the English *ancien regime;* late in his career, he turns to something newer than classical studies—modern vernacular literary studies of Milton. Monboddo's conservative chain-of-being theory paradoxically served to further modern linguistics by contributing to thought about the evolution of language families. Even conservatives like Monboddo could unwittingly extend the modern by responding to contemporary interests in language and rhetoric.

Historical Change in Language and Rhetoric

The preceding chapters have explored how each figure participated in language study in his own time and place. Their views on language were imbricated with their theories of knowledge. Each figure serves to exemplify one approach to the transformations he perceived to be taking place around him. Each figure began by devouring and transforming existing discourses, rather than by rejecting past discourses in what might be called a Cartesian manner. These case studies help to reinforce arguments that throughout the eighteenth century, change in language and rhetoric was not dramatic and visible but may have frequently appeared as slight repositionings of existing practice, that is, further extensions, or even as repetitions of the old.

Essentially in different generations of the eighteenth century as well as from varying nations, languages, and social networks, Vico, Condillac, and Monboddo reach many parallel conclusions and hypotheses about language and knowledge. If their work is often viewed as marginal and even eccentric, they nonetheless draw from the main stream of the cultural archive of their times, sharing the commonest of textual networks that produced a common mental dictionary, to use Vico's cultural terms. With admitted differences, they devour and incorporate first a common Renaissance humanist and classical archive, including neoclassical, neo-Epicurean, and texts associated with republican ideology and discourse. Rationalist accounts of new epistemologies and methodologies such as those of Descartes and the Port Royalists and Locke's Newtonian transformations and consolidations of earlier British and French texts were known to all three. Finally, Condillac and Monboddo in particular shared an interest in French belletristic texts, such as those by Rollin, Fénelon, and DuBos. These strands provide differing but often parallel or convergent accounts of language and rhetoric. They show that various strains of linguistic and rhetorical theory can all be present at once, like Vico's three ages. Nevertheless, they are not all valued or used alike by their cultures. While there are dominant, emergent, and residual rhetorics, there are also hybrids of these three.

Vico, from his earliest inaugural orations at the University of Naples, tried to integrate old and new discursive values. Although his texts include elements of the scientific approach to the world, they tend to privilege values and processes of the Old World of patterning as well as the discourses of humanism and classical rhetoric. Most importantly in Vico, truth becomes a process of making as opposed to being fixed and stable, based on his theory that language is constitutive of humans. His emphasis on topical thinking, which he sees as a form of operationalism or a constructivist experimentation, emphasizes process and an epistemology opposed to representationalism: we can know only what we make. This is different from mainstream modern realist epistemology where seeing is knowing. Vico also stresses knowing as a social process, unlike the individualism of analytico-referential discourses. All this is what Ernesto Grassi calls Vico's "topical philosophy," a lost alternative in the sweep of modernity.

Yet while Vico was willing to accept and integrate some new elements and values, often the emerging modernist discourses, striving for hegemony, could not honor a truce with the old. As Timothy J. Reiss puts it: the old "could accept, indeed precariously absorb, experimentalism. . . . Experimentalism could not reciprocate. . . . [T]he father can accept the son, but the son quite rejects his progenitor" (379). Although not himself as interested in natural as in the human sciences, Vico remains open to experimentalism, although he redefines it under his *verum-factum* epistemology so that experimenting becomes constructing, not merely observing and representing.

Vico's epistemology effectively denies pure representationalism, as does his theory of the metaphoric foundations of language. Metaphor to a modernist-representationalist stands for a loop in what should be a linear chain of signs coinciding with the structure of the world. It is therefore an abuse of language. Vico took from the medieval educational reformers and others the notion of the four master tropes, decried by Brian Vickers and celebrated by Hayden White, Paul de Man, Jonathan Cullers, and other literary theorists at the linguistic turn. Like these late-twentieth-century theorists, to Vico, all language is figurative and metaphoric; words carry more than a reference to the world—they even bear the imprint of past social history. As Percy Bysshe Shelley and Ralph Waldo Emerson believed, Vico first proved that language is fossil poetry. Thus, Vico could use the history of language to forge new theories to understand human history in constructing his new science. Unlike analytic theories of science, Vico's grew out of a historical, perspectival view of truth, imbricating the old arts of language—rhetoric and philology—with the new philosophies that ended in modern scientific thought.

His arguments for combining rhetorical inquiry and topical invention with Cartesian scientific thought most likely only irritated or perplexed his contemporaries. Vico peremptorily dismisses the Cartesian cogito, arguing that such navel gazing fails to impart any knowledge the inquirer did not already know. He argues for the anthropology of a common mental dictionary of cultural thought unifying human societies. Associated subjective processes such as imagination and memory, also important to Condillac, were deeply rooted in their cultures. Vico's rhetoric also attempts to recuperate syllogistic thought rejected by the Cartesians and Port Royalists, showing that all thought involves a syllogistic linking, with the *imagination* furnishing the creative leaps providing those links. Vico's *New Science* is a working performance of rhetoric in its aspect as a theory of sublime human creativity, how anything comes to be seen and to be expressed.

In theories of imagination as later mystified by Romantics and Victorians, vision becomes the pure idea, stripped of body—but it was never so in Vico. Imagination or *phantasia* was as powerful as it was primarily because it was closer to the body. Childhood—of the individual, the culture, or the race—was a time strong in memory and imagination; adulthood and old age relied more on intellect, logic, and the concept. Yet, successful rhetoric was not possible with only the rational concept: pure intellect could never address or move an audience of the mixed public, and neither could a rhetoric of bodiless ideas nor pure images. For Vico, rhetoric was always visual, always gestural, passionately moving through the body, and never reducible to the idea. Vico's strength is his flexibility—which he claims to have learned from inventional arts—a combinatory art taking various rhetorics for creative transformation. However, this flexibility did not extend to rhetorics that left out visible, material bodies. This is one reason why his and other eighteenth-century rhetorics are gaining attention today—we again live in a visual world where graphic and bodily elements are as important as before the dominance of mass print literacy.

Taking up the discourse of modernism, Condillac's expressivism appears to form itself on the representational view of human nature as "permanently at one with itself," universal, and objectively knowable (Reiss 39). Yet in his aesthetic rhetoric, the emphasis on expressivism tied to language and the rhythms of the body—a feminine rather than masculine influence— also works to undermine representationalism. For if there is a feminine rhetorical surplus of meaning where language actively bears emotions and other values, language does more than just stand in for reality, it creates meaning, various plural meanings. Like their French predecessor Condillac, theorists Luce Irigaray, Julia Kristeva, and Hélène Cixous locate this rhetorical surplus early in human development, bringing in a language source ignored in these theorists—the mother. In the texts of most eighteenth-century rationalist theorists, women inhabit the supra-imaginative, emotional world because they remain closer to their bodies. Therefore, they are excluded from full rationality and can never be full citizens. With some postfeminist thinkers, the overvaluing of reason is reversed, and women are credited with special powers because they dwell in their bodies with awareness. The myth that Enlightenment men dwelt as autonomous and disembodied rational creatures is exploded. Sometimes their theories retrace language origins to the prelinguistic site of the womb, with its bodily enfolding, soothing sounds, and heartbeat rhythms. Literary modernism and its experimental, expressivist discourse best capture the bodily quality of language for these theorists.

Alternatively, exemplary modernist discourses, especially bureaucratic, seem to emanate from a bodiless, anonymous site and thus suppress the sound and rhythm in writing. A godlike voice from nowhere helps to authorize such texts. This is not the kind of discourse Condillac taught the Prince of Parma, who became a literary gentleman of fine taste. If teaching the prince is viewed as a language experiment, a wild child trained in belletristic rhetoric, the outcome can be seen in the Prince. He was a good man, a cultivated man, *poli* (both polite and polished)— but not one especially interested in government. Despite its volumes of historical study, Condillac's pedagogy displaced the civic from the curricular center of language studies, even in the program of a future leader.

Yet, Condillac's rhetoric was not a purely representational one transcribing the exterior world into language. His tendencies to view thought and language as coimplicated and language as based on metaphor undermine the representationalism of his texts, as does his admission that we see the world holistically, although discourse is linear. If thought and language develop together and if language is a system, then words are more than names, and more is going on in language than just referring. Language involves the creation of meaning. His admission that seeing is a different system from language implies that a linear language can never adequately represent the world apprehended by a different sign system. In *The Order of Things*, Michel Foucault pigeonholes Condillac as a narrow and asocial thinker while absconding with some of his key insights, such as the incommensurability of the verbal and visual.

The new vernacular emphasis in writing instruction championed by Condillac entailed much translation and transformation—from Latin to French or from visual to verbal, translation was always a concern. In such a system, students quickly became aware that translation is partial and that writing never fully reproduces the text or phenomenon at issue—it is always transformed. This worked to keep early-modern rhetorics less epistemologically arrogant than later New Rhetorics or nineteenth-century texts of writing instruction. The need to translate helps explain the central concern with analogy, the explanations of how transformations occur analogically. Everything in Condillac happens by analogy—language develops by that principle as do specialized languages such as calculus or economics.

For, like Monboddo's mind, which Aarsleff translates as soul in the *Origin* essay, the mind works principally by analogy in Condillac. Ideas are forged and cultivated by analogy because they are linked by signs, which are formed analogically. Systems of signs are developed by analogy to other signs in the language—words, patterns of tenses, and other grammatical patterns form on the principle of analogy. Condillac's aesthetic expressivism is founded on an original language of gesture, the language of action, developed by analogy and valued for its emotional force. Yet, from this gestural theory comes the linear process of cognition, with attention, imagination, and memory as key steps in his theories built on a foundation of rhetoric and language. The foundation of cognitive activity is language because the sign becomes the link between attention and memory. Rhetoric works on the linear principles of the mind, which forms itself by language. Therefore, no special training is needed, outside of training in consciousness of one's own reflection and attention to the highest models of style. Much like cognitive linguists today, Condillac believes the mind works by pattern matching, by analogy. This settles him in his modernist writing pedagogy of working formally from models. Nonetheless, Condillac's most important legacy may be as an experimental educator, the first whose theories begin with the student and extend the student's own active experiences. This modern line of theory, usually credited to his colleague Jean Jacques Rousseau, extends to Johann Heinrich Pestalozzi and Maria Montessori down to our own time.

Monboddo, perhaps inaugurating modern reactionary rhetoric, hearkens back didactically to the Greeks and classical rhetoric for his exemplars. In this, however, he paradoxically becomes quite modern, representing both the achievements of historical comparative linguistics in his philosophical thought as well as exhibiting traits that are proto-Romantic through his turn to the (Greek) past. The hybrid nature of his language and rhetoric ensures that strains will continue as familiar, recognizable in textual practice today although at the same time making him as eccentric and unapproachable as the earlier Neapolitan Vico, if less immediately likable as a figure. This historical view of Monboddo could be labeled Whiggishness, if not for the fact that when his contemporaries dismissed him, it was for similar reasons.

Proteus, a figure emerging from Condillac's early infatuation with Leibnizian monadology, becomes an appropriate image, signifying shape-shifts in language and rhetoric through the times and places of the three lives. Such a turn to myth and mythical thought serves well as a prelude to Vico, whose rhetoric equates myth with true history. Myth becomes at once an important theme in modernism—as in literary countermodernity—and a sign of the primitive, the archaic, the antimodern that forms the other face to an inescapable modernism. As such, myth, this Janus-faced figure, stands in much the same relation as rhetoric does to modernism, as Vico, Condillac, and Monboddo do to modern rhetorics.

Twenty-First-Century Transformations

Each of these case studies can be read as a stance available today in response to new discourses of language theory or cultural studies. Those positions are first, a conscious attempt to use the old in the service of the new, as with Vico's efforts to adapt topical thought to scientific discovery. Sometimes such hybrid attempts are useful and innovating, although from the point of view of paradigm thought, they risk not making sense, just as Vico seems to have made no sense to those who embraced modern thought in the first half of his own century. Vico's flexibility did not extend to changing the humanist framework he worked within. Second, Condillac reasons historically that we must acquiesce to change, arguing that the modern French could scarcely understand the eloquence of the ancients even if they were to see a perfect performance of classical oratory in their contemporary speakers and speeches. What he believed was needed was a complete rethinking of theory and practice of eloquence that revealed the taste and aesthetic values of his own nation's and class's culture. Only Monboddo dared hope openly that his work would one day revive the study of the ancient arts of language, even though they lay unappreciated by his contemporaries. He had faith that Greek philosophy would stand the test of time. Thus, the three stances—to creatively transform the past using the tools at hand, to devise a new system and phase out the old, or to conserve and repeat an ancient system seen as having universal and timeless benefits—remain potential positions for us today.

From the 1960s' revival of New Rhetoric, those such as Edward P. J. Corbett, Janice M. Lauer, Richard McKeon, Richard Young, and others wished to transform classical arts or to cannibalize them as energizing elements for new rhetorics. Others in the field rejected the very term rhetoric as outmoded and irrelevant and turned to modern composition studies for concepts such as *process* or for *scientific* cognitive models to fashion rhetorics for new times. In the twentieth century, what was ancient was more likely to be put to the service of modern rhetoric. Formalist rhetorics associated with the modes or forms of discourse, clarity, and correctness of grammar were modernist, loosely grouped into what was called for a time *current-traditional*. Those who call for a return to the past often have the 1950s' and early-1960s' rhetorics in mind, and like early classical rhetorics, today these have become associated with hierarchy and closed systems. If they were once designed to foster inclusivity, these rhetorics were called into question when they failed to meet the needs of open-admission students of the 1960s and 1970s.

Despite nominal attention to poststructuralist and postmodern theories, most academic rhetorics today remain ensconced in dominant modernist values. They share traces of Reiss's analytico-referential discourses found in varying degrees in the eighteenth century. Much college writing is still taught emphasizing a primarily referential theory of language with a philosophic (scientific) model and exemplar for discourse, and most emphasize clarity, correctness, and a plain style of presentation. Belletrism would seem to offer relief from this rhetoric, yet as Condillac's rhetoric demonstrates, it shares historical links with modern representational rhetoric and has been criticized for its exclusivity and elitism. Belletrism comes to form the foundations of a science of taste and aesthetics that runs parallel and complementary to the natural scientific discourse of the eighteenth century. Yet, belletristic rhetoric is itself impure, as it can serve to undermine the realist representational rhetoric still component in many respects in our culture. It also addresses the strong visual dominance of today's rhetorics with its inclusion of gestural, architectural, and landscape elements.

One aspect of my narrative about the eighteenth century is that it addresses in a much-earlier moment S. Michael Halloran's question: How did we get from the civic-rhetorical tradition to later classroom rhetorics paying little attention to public discourse? The growing hegemony of analytico-referential discourses might account for this trajectory away from public discourse. Halloran's article points to the rise of individualism, belletristic rhetoric, and specialization of curricula to explain the decline of public discourse in college composition. All these elements are central to the environment that fostered modern rhetoric.

Halloran's early focus on public discourse, that is, on rhetoric that deals with public social and political issues, primarily turned back to civic humanism for its models. That emphasis has only recently been given new life by a combination of rhetorical and cultural studies working in the vanguard of a new discursive class, with a constructivist epistemology and rhetoric of social process more compatible with the values of feminist and marginal groups in society and the university. I refer here to rhetoricians such as Susan C. Jarratt, John Trimbur, Susan Wells, Ira

Schor, and Elizabeth A. Flynn. Halloran early on protested that contemporary classroom rhetorics address students in three aspects of existence—personal, intellectual-academic, and professional—but not as political beings, as members of a body politic in which they have a responsibility to form their judgment and to influence the judgments of others on public issues. Yet, older models of public discourse have been linked with an emphatically rationalist philosophy that has lacked the ability to address issues of pathos and ethos dominant in contemporary media and consumer culture. Newer discursive practices must be capable of enabling students to explore and develop new insights about their cultures, as opposed to an emphasis on control, order, and meeting society's demands for productivity and efficiency in writing. Such new practices might resemble the rhetoric that Covino defines as "intellectual free play" (46), citing Vico as a "renegade advocate" of such open discourse, but one with "scarce influence" in the history of rhetoric:

> While writing competency in the academy and the marketplace currently remains identified with formulary obedience, a "well-made box" (Weathers), the importance of developing speculative imagination and critical inquiry, and the danger of valorizing communicative efficiency, are urgent issues. To challenge what the aims of discourse have become in a data-possessed, technocratic society, we can reconsider the history of rhetoric for alternatives to received ways of thinking, reading, and writing. (12)

Yet, as we have seen, Vico also viewed rhetoric as a critical art that could lead to good judgment about public debate and moral action. His art was a semiotics of cultural common sense that served as a basis for meaning, persuasion, and critique.

Ongoing transformations in media help produce new forms of discourse. Walter Ong's "secondary orality" manifests itself more clearly, and secondary literacies continue to emerge, parasitical on traditional literary culture. Creating the new from recycling the past has become an everyday, if ironic, contemporary trope. What will be usable for future generations from the new hybrids? What rhetorics for new public life are now emergent from past strains? The future is not just an extension of the past; it lies somewhere between fate and chance and cannot be measured. However unpredictable the new discursive values and patterns, elements overshadowed in the literate rhetorics of Vico, Condillac, and Monboddo may be found there. Among these shadowy elements are notions of language as more than just transcriptions of already formed reality accompanied by broader rhetorics of human discursive practice.

Postmodern Cultural Rhetorics

Revisiting rhetoric at the rise of modernity can help us envision the transformation to newer rhetorics more easily than by looking back on the often narrower and more rigid nineteenth-century varieties. We have seen that the elements of these older, marginalized rhetorics include a sense of imagination not yet fully Romanticized and mystified, a belief that arts of rhetoric and language could be taught that could help socialize and moralize citizens, and a constructivist notion of language and culture. In the 1990s, there was an admitted convergence of rhetoric and composition with postmodernist theories of language and culture that struggled against the sedimentation of modernist practices in English.

Many in rhetoric and composition at the end of the twentieth century agreed with what James Berlin had termed "epistemic rhetoric," a socially constructivist view of language that became dominant in the field (*Rhetoric and Reality* 16–17). Epistemic rhetoric for Berlin was ultimately political, "an effort to prepare students for critical citizenship in a democracy" (31). Many of us remember his life's work in an effort to theorize and put into practice similar pedagogies for production of democratic citizens at the juncture of communication, composition, and cultural studies. In rethinking these issues, we turn to rearticulations of old rhetorical keywords including public discourse, identification, practical wisdom, and civic virtue, terms whose histories I have been exploring in part in this work.

The liberal tradition of modernity is not to be scorned—it has given us our notions of citizens as free and equal, and we should cherish and work to transform such modern universals. We must transform them because the universal citizen of Western democracy was and is historically male and formed on the basis of the split between public and private, barring women and many men from political participation at the very moment its discourse claimed to be inclusive of everyone. As Chantal Mouffe and others point out, the liberal tradition tended to reduce citizenship to merely legal status in a static definition. Citizens are holders of rights against the state, and as long as citizens' rights do not violate laws or other citizens' rights, how they use their rights is of little concern to society. Contrast this notion of the citizen with Vico's actively construing, passionately persuading citizen aiming at discovering and effecting the good life for himself and his neighbors. Liberal ideology devalues such civic activity and gives us no help in formulating positive strategies to construct our more perfect union(s). Gregory Clark's *Dialogue, Dialectic, and Conversation: A Social Perspective on the Function of Writing* argues as well that in liberal theory, community becomes no more than a space for autonomous individuals to share knowledge limited to beliefs leading to their determining the separate directions of their lives.

Civic humanism has long offered an antidote to certain modern ills. The republican tradition of civic humanism has concerned itself with notions of *arete,* civic virtue, public good, forums for public participation, and arts of discourse for socializing and moralizing as well as technical advice on persuasion. Yet a return to humanism will not provide democratic solutions for the complexities of the modern world—Monboddo was wrong that we can or should return to a past with which we have little if not nothing in common. Old conceptions of fraternity, community, common good, and shared moral values are viewed with suspicion by groups wishing to participate in twenty-first-century democratic life.

Early in the twentieth century, American pragmatists worked to transform civic humanist values to make them more suitable to a modern democracy. Jane Addams's politics was based on a transformed civic humanist and Christian faith that humans possess a common ability to discern truth. In *Democracy and Social Ethics,* she repeatedly articulates the view that knowledge and goodness cannot be imposed from above to solve problems:

> We have learned to say that the good must be extended to all of society before it can be held securely by any one person or any one class; but we have not yet learned to add that unless all men and all classes contribute to a good, we cannot even be sure that it is worth having. (220)

Her rhetoric is based on democratic, constructivist thinking and constitutes no less than a social epistemic rhetoric, a transformation of civic humanism. The good here is a process as much as a product, and the democratic means and process of its production is the determinant as well as the assurance that it is good. This is what Vico's maker's knowledge entails, along with a historical and thereby continuing and changing transformation of institutions based on such democratic participation.

This kind of creative carryover of a potential value or practice from one system to another does not entail acceptance or transfer of the values of the original system, especially because they are usually hierarchical and elitist. Our problem is not to choose or select among these preexisting rhetorics and their values, whether they be traditional, modern, belletristic, expressive, liberal, or civic humanist. I agree with Mouffe when she argues:

> The problem . . . is not to replace one tradition with the other, but to draw on both and try to combine their insights in a new conception of citizenship adequate for a project of radical and plural democracy. . . . Our choice is not at all between an aggregate of individuals without common public concern and a premodern community organized around a single substantive idea of the common good. How to envisage the modern democratic political community outside this dichotomy is the critical question. (72, 75)

As liberalism and civic humanism collided with postmodern theory, a fragmented notion of the citizen emerged. The new democratic citizen has multiple identifications and concerns befitting his or her many functions in society. One identification can conflict with another, and no one identity subsumes all at every moment. The new citizen's identity is neither more nor less than the history of his or her identifications. In classic Burkean theory, the smooth functioning or conflict in these identifications occurs through discourse. As Kenneth Burke first theorized, our identifications produce difference, the inside produces an outside, and affinities produce antagonism. In Vichian fashion, rhetorics are produced, and they in turn produce and transform citizens and citizenries through the friction or alliance between social groups.

In postmodernist Donna Haraway's version, the new citizen is the cyborg, the cybernetic organism—human, yes, animal, certainly—yet so machine-dependent as to be part machine. Her cyborgian citizen is wary of holism but needy of connection. Cyborgian identity is paradoxically like the civic humanists, based on action and a capacity to act on the basis of coalition, of affinity, or political kinship. "Affinity not identity" is Haraway's rallying cry. In her divinatory theories, there are no myths of origin, no Garden of Eden, no natural self to return to. She creates cyborgs, bordercrossers, *mestiza,* trickster figures like Coyote, hyphenated identities (for example, the Afro-Dutch-English-New World itinerant preacher Sojourner Truth). She intends these figures to trouble and broaden our Enlightenment notions of what it is to be human. The old Great Chain of Being archetype has been replaced by the fluid and transformative meiosis and mitosis of cellular chromosomes in reproduction. Networks of discoursing communities on the Web, for example, form provisional alliances that link and create mass energy with one issue, only to dissolve and re-form with the next.

Post- (or post-post)modern rhetoric attempts to come to terms with and helps produce new political identities and processes that lead citizens to coalesce and act around their admittedly partial identities. It helps these groups work toward democratic equivalence in the political forum, where corporate power overtakes state and citizen power in the new global marketplace. Rhetoric is then about teaching students how language (and languages) contributes to identifications and differences and how it works to prove opposites or clarify difference so we can clarify how to act and choose for our own advantages. (Here I accept Burke's term *advantage* as the most ethical end of rhetoric, advantage being capable of extension from individual citizens to more universal concerns.)

Rhetoric in action serves here in the place of the old logic and philosophical reflection to help parse the often deliberate "blooming, buzzing confusion" of the information marketplace. Sometimes the status of the case is clear, and the oppositions, choices, and values involved are obvious. However, more often today, whether from deliberate obfuscation or from the homogenization of media discourse, who would benefit or lose exactly what in a political transaction is not clear. For example, until Al Gore sharpened his rhetoric in the 2000 presidential campaign, the differences between him and George W. Bush were muddy, and the two candidates seemed to provide only equivalences. (To some, Gore failed because the candidates remained rough equivalents.) Invention is the art traditionally addressed to proving opposites, and a twenty-first-century art of invention might help citizens understand their various standpoints and sharpen differences between positions by exploring outcomes. After consideration of all the available means of persuasion, there can come a provisional and providential moment of unification in which the point at issue clarifies, the parts fall into some sort of modernist order, and we know something—know what is to be said and done. This kairotic moment is the moment described by creativity theorists (such as Albert Rothenberg) as the *Aha!* moment that occurs with a prepared mind. It is the holistic moment Vico describes in terms of sublime bodily ecstasy when he advises readers to consider possible alternatives to his narrative of cultural development and prove the truth of his theories. How citizens who are not experts can know provisionally and responsibly to decide on public issues becomes in large part a rhetorical matter, involving whole persons and groups both (social) bodies and minds.

Much has been said about teaching students to read and write their worlds, and strategies for teaching this reading and writing have been offered from critical theory and semiotics. Many of these draw on and overlap with traditional rhetorical inventional arts. These also extrapolate from the visual arts of memory and delivery and naturally so with the heavy visual emphasis of television, film, and computers. We clearly need an art of delivery in all its textual, graphic, and gestural sophistication to reintegrate the verbal and visual to meet the needs of both face to face and "electric rhetoric," as Kathleen E. Welch terms it in her book of that title. Whether productive of persuasion, expressivist signification, identifications, and differences or productive of conflict and harmonic unification, the art of rhetoric for our times must nurture in the citizen-practitioner the ability to imagine and empathize, to observe and participate, to parse and respond to social controversy for his or her individual and cooperative advantage. Considering alternative rhetorics on the threshold of modernity should help us better to understand and conceptualize the various options we might have for twenty-first-century rhetoric. Such rhetorics can help us creatively draw from the past and present, with an eye to the future, better to meet our aim of educating our various speaking and writing citizens for a democracy situated more and more in global society.

Notes

Works Cited

Index

Notes

1. The Birth of Modernity and the Death of Rhetoric

1. Ernst Robert Curtius also traces the history of the word *modernus* in his inquiry into the history of the opposition of ancients and moderns, noting: "The word 'modern' . . . is one of the last legacies of late Latin to the modern world" (254).

2. Burnet is sometimes spelled Burnett.

3. Miller's work builds on Horner's *Nineteenth-Century Scottish Rhetoric: The American Connection* and broadens it into a critique of the direction English studies took from early belles lettres.

4. What Condillac actually wrote was that to create poetry by copying classical models was "as ridiculous [as] . . . to believe one was well-dressed with the clothes of the ancients" (*Oeuvres* 606). I cannot help but read this as part of a silent conversation with his brother Mably, a classical civic republican and early socialist.

5. George Kennedy in *Comparative Rhetorics* devotes a chapter to language-origin theories. His book, which James A. Berlin once described as "comparative rhetorics," appeared after this present project was published in preliminary form. Although Kennedy's book did not influence this work, I admire its scope. My interests and goals are similar to Kennedy's: to enrich and diversify traditional rhetorical studies.

6. In *Study Methods,* Vico says that the prudent use such a flexible rule in judging human affairs, which cannot be assessed "by the inflexible standard of abstract right; we must rather gauge them by the pliant Lesbic rule, which does not conform bodies to itself, but adjusts itself to their contours" (34).

7. This movement itself will be shown to be influenced by language-origin theories, which explored the beginnings of language in gesture, a powerful, originary body language.

2. On the Threshold of Modernity

1. Zygmunt Bauman in *Modernity and Ambivalence* articulates the distinction:

> I wish to make it clear from the start that I call 'modernity' a historical period that began in Western Europe with a series of pro-

found social-structural and intellectual transformations of the seventeenth century and achieved its maturity: (1) as a cultural project—with the growth of the Enlightenment; (2) as a socially accomplished form of life—with the growth of industrial (capitalist, and later also communist) society. Hence *modernity*, as I use the term, is in no way identical with *modernism*. The latter is an intellectual (philosophical, literary, artistic) trend that—though traceable back to many individual intellectual events of the previous era—reached its full swing by the beginning of the current century and which in retrospect can be seen (by analogy with the Enlightenment) as a project of *postmodernity* or a prodromal stage of the postmodern condition. In modernism, modernity turned its gaze upon itself and attempted to attain the clear-sightedness and self-awareness which would eventually disclose its impossibility, thus paving the way to the postmodern reassessment. (4)

2. Susan Wells is another contemporary rhetorician who makes use of Habermas. See her book *Sweet Reason.* Also, Habermas, "Modernity."

3. We can no more say that classics ended with the modern elective system than we can rhetoric ended, but we do know that by 1915, fewer than fifteen major U.S. colleges required four years of Latin for a B.A. as most had done at the turn of the century. Classically, rhetoric was bound up with the study of Latin, although today, classics has been turned more toward aesthetic texts than rhetorical, as has the field of English study.

4. Yet since the 1970s, they have again gained currency in the scientific study called glottogenetics. See Marcel Danesi, *Giambattista Vico.*

5. For example, women were an important force injecting vitality into the classics on into the twentieth century. Those denied a field of study often hold onto it with tenacity once they gain entrance. This may even apply to women scholars working in rhetoric today.

6. Markley talks of "the history of representation as a complex and internally divided process rather than a linear sequence of progressive development" (5). His focus is on physico-theology, that "what cannot be known or represented—complexity—becomes the ineffable and absent sign of God" (8). His Bakhtinian view of language provides contestatory and active language that does not represent so much as construct and intervene in a reality that is always in process (14).

7. See the tensions described, for example, between classical and belletristic elements in Potkay.

8. *Managerial rhetoric* is a term describing rhetorics that place theories of invention in other arts and leave rhetorical arts with nothing but style and formalist arrangement. It is used in Howell and linked with Douglas Ehninger's classifications and manifests itself early in the nineteenth century in rhetorics like Richard Whately's.

9. Locke himself rhetorically adopts a lowland image of a manual laborer, clearing away the underbrush of history.

10. Howell follows up this statement with a footnote castigating Edward

P. J. Corbett's *Classical Rhetoric for the Modern Student* for presenting classical invention theory "without having explained that rhetoricians of the seventeenth and eighteenth centuries gave it such a critical rejection as to make it obsolete, and that rhetoric should not accept it today without proclaiming it an aid only to the slow and dull" (*Eighteenth-Century British Rhetoric* 443). Knoblauch and Brannon adopted Howell's Lockean, paradigm-shift critique. Howell and Locke here seed the later debates between those calling for a new rhetoric free from classical influence and those whose work aims to reread the old rhetoric for modern issues and tasks.

11. Kevin Cope does not specifically discuss rhetorical probability in his analysis of philosophical doubt in *Criteria of Certainty: Truth and Judgment in English Enlightenment.* Barthes's *aide-mémoire* does (22–23) as does Hoyt Trowbridge at more length in "White of Selborne: The Ethos of Probablism." In our own time, Markley notes the negative reaction by a scientist to Markley's revisionary history of science focused on physico-theology. Anarchistic theories of knowledge such as Feyerabend's, as well as feminist epistemologies and philosophies of science, have also drawn sharp reactions. For example, feminist philosopher Lorraine Code proposes that the model for knowing in philosophy should not be self-knowledge or knowledge of things but knowing another human, ideally a friend.

12. See James A. Berlin, "Revisionary Histories of Rhetoric" (112) as well as other discussions in Victor J. Vitanza, *Writing Histories of Rhetoric;* John Schilb; and Berlin, "Revisionary History: The Dialectical Method."

13. Nietzsche begins his course in ancient rhetoric by citing Locke's "aversion" to rhetoric as the most notable example of the disrepute into which the classical art of rhetoric had fallen in the nineteenth century.

14. For example, see the introduction to Clark and Halloran's *Oratorical Culture in Nineteenth-Century America,* who use this concept of transformation to elucidate historical change in rhetoric.

15. Burke's own use of transformation is in his explanation of motivations and change taking place in literary works and in various arenas of human life. However, in *Attitudes Toward History,* he plots Western history as itself a drama in five acts.

3. Transformations in Western Rhetoric and Language

1. Harrison and Laslett are referring to entries 1427 and 1428 in their book *The Library of John Locke.*

2. This date is highlighted in Casanova (70). However, other writers, notably Chaucer and Shakespeare, also had long worked in the vernacular, as also had some women writers and troubadours from a similar problem of having small Latin and less Greek.

3. This becomes clear early on when Vico is still rather sympathetic to Descartes. In an early inaugural oration, he criticizes those who refuse to look through a microscope or observe the path of nerves through the body because they would rather hold onto the classical theories describing the nerves. See *Study Methods* 32–33.

4. It is not known what became of this effort to send the book or whether Newton, who died in 1747, ever received the volume. Vico's third edition was published the year of his death, 1744.

5. Susan R. Bordo writes in *The Flight to Objectivity: Essays on Cartesianism and Culture* of the mechanistic turn in Cartesian thought as a transformation from a feminine nurturing universe to a masculine clockwork universe. Finally, see Aarsleff, *Condillac: Essay on the Origin of Human Knowledge*.

6. The pertinent passages in Descartes, *Les Passions de l'âme*, are pp. 99f, 105, articles 44 and 50. See also *Discours de la méthode* (1637) and Condillac's letter to Mersenne 1629, responding to universal language scheme.

7. See also Stephen K. Land, *From Signs to Propositions* 77.

8. Hobbes's "Briefe" is included in John Harwood's *The Rhetorics of Thomas Hobbes and Bernard Lamy*.

9. Theologian Cornelis Otto Jansen (1585–1638), bishop of Ypres in Flanders, emphasized predestination, God's grace, and determinism—lack of free will. Jansenism as a flourishing radical Roman Catholic sect was characterized by strict moral rigor and had some commonalities with Protestant Calvinist thought. Its followers bound themselves to imitate Christ in poverty, meditation, and action, service to the poor. Its most famous follower was Pascal. It received papal condemnation early in the eighteenth century, and its adherents were persecuted in France during most of the century. Jansenists especially criticized the Jesuits for lack of moral rigor. Port Royal was a religious monastery and nunnery near Paris committed to Bishop Jansen's theology, learning, service, and physical labor. Arnauld and Nicole not only wrote on language from there, but they wrote Jansenist treatises, intertwining religion, logic, and rhetoric, especially in discussions of how to weigh testimony concerning miracles. When Arnauld was threatened with dismissal from his academic post because of his Jansenism, Pascal wrote *Provincial Letters* to defend him. Port Royal was finally destroyed in 1710, and many Jansenists fled to the Netherlands. Jane Addams was influenced by the Port Royalists' mission to the poor.

10. This universality meant in one important sense that "the mind has no sex," a Cartesianism embraced by Enlightenment women and their supporters. It is first found in the Cartesian follower Poulin de la Barre's 1673 *De l'égalité des deux sexe (l'esprit n'a pas de sexe)*.

11. See also J. W. Gough, "Locke's Reading."

12. This is Brian Vickers's point about linguistic arguments in his section of Vickers and Nancy S. Struever. On Locke's educational philosophies, see Richard A. Barney's *Plots of Enlightenment*.

13. For a discussion on the appropriation of classical texts, see Kathleen E. Welch, *The Contemporary Reception of Classical Rhetoric: Appropriations of Ancient Discourse*.

14. I use here Wilbur Samuel Howell's classifications from *Eighteenth-Century British Logic and Rhetoric*.

15. As Potkay argues, these "country" politicians advocating republicanism were outsiders, relying on a version of Quintilian's "good man speaking well" as their highest "virtue," leaning to public over private, civic over domestic

in their hierarchy of values (3). For background, see discussions of the history of British politics in J. G. A. Pocock.

16. See introduction in Potkay 1–23. Although Potkay describes the emerging belletrism as attractive to women, women were also attracted to neoclassical thought in a strange chiasmus as men were moving to the feminized realm of belles lettres. Women took on republican values, especially in revolutionary United States, creating for themselves the new political role of republican mothers, raising children for the republic. One Enlightenment feature appealing to women was the Cartesian notion that "the mind has no sex," as we see in Wollstonecraft. As discussed below, Epicureanism also fostered an egalitarian philosophy attractive to women. Miriam Brody has discussed the gender coding of rhetoric in *Manly Rhetoric*.

17. Such a civilized, private sphere could also represent a counterforce to the growing ruthlessness of the marketplace and the immorality of colonial activities abroad. At any rate, these ideals were associated with possibilities, especially for women, to be recognized as intellectual partners. Epicurean philosophy itself has been recognized (and rejected) as "womanish," (see Gordon) and this gendering should be noted along with the continual efforts of modernism to produce a "masculine" discourse.

18. See in particular Aarsleff's introduction to von Humboldt, *On Language: The Diversity of Human Language Structure and Its Influence on the Mental Development of Mankind,* and his introduction to Condillac's *Essay on the Origin of Human Knowledge.*

19. We do not have Adam Smith's own notes, but it is certain he relied extensively on French belletristic sources in his rhetoric lectures. Students in their notes leave blanks or misspell the French references.

20. Condillac's writing course, part of an educational plan for the Prince of Parma, was finished by the early 1760s and was printed in 1775 and republished in 1776, 1780, 1782, 1790, 1798, 1803, and 1821. Blair's *Lectures on Rhetoric and Belles Lettres* was published in 1783 and went through 130 editions in England and America until 1911 (J. A. Berlin 25). Influenced by Condillac and other French belletristic writers, Blair's and Condillac's similar values thus reigned supreme in Western literacy education at the turn of the eighteenth century and beyond. Condillac's *Logic* was also brought to the United States: see Joseph Neef's *The Logic of Condillac Translated by Joseph Neef as an Illustration of a Plan of Education Established at His School near Philadelphia.*

4. Vico on the Threshold: Modern Language and Rhetoric

1. Andrea Battistini argues against Croce's limiting of rhetoric; "Vico actually extends the importance and use of rhetoric," detailing four roles for rhetoric: taxonomic, (similar to Richard McKeon's architectonic, structuring rhetoric), gnoseologic, hermeneutic, and expressive (1).

2. As Battistini points out, unlike Epicurus (and unlike rationalist thinkers), Vico treats imagination and superstition positively as humans' first way of knowing (12).

3. This is best seen in Naomi S. Baron's "Writing and Vico's Functional Approach to Language Change."

4. In Vichian history, the Hebrews had their own historical trajectory separate from the Gentile nations of the world. This allows Vico to develop a secular universal history.

5. See also Vico's *Art of Rhetoric,* chapter 23, 65–67.

6. See John D. Schaeffer, *Sensus Communis: Vico, Rhetoric, and the Limits of Relativism.*

7. David W. Black also discusses morality in terms of common sense (45–93).

8. Verene's *Vico's Science of Imagination* discusses these "imaginative universals" in *New Science* as the primordial power of collective humanity in the thought of images (see chapter 3).

9. See Horace, *Art of Poetry,* 331–56; Cicero's *Brutus,* xlix, 183–85, and *de Oratore,* 2, xxvi-iii, xxvii, 116.

10. As is well known in rhetoric, Kenneth Burke makes use of Vico's ideas in his "Four Master Tropes" essay appended to *A Grammar of Motives.* Vico's rhetorical-cultural perspective was available and attractive to many literacy critics and rhetoricians primarily through Benedetto Croce in the early-twentieth century. Others of Burke's generation whose work transmits Vichian notions include Herbert Read, Richard McKeon, John Dewey, and Richard Weaver. Hayden White's *Metahistory,* based on the Vichian tropes, became the bible for generations of young historians in the closing decades of the twentieth century.

11. Poststructuralist critiques of rational rhetoric as in Jürgen Habermas are legion, although James A. Berlin, citing Martin Jay, sums up the critique of what Berlin calls the "aesthetic ideology" aiming to overcome "differences, contradictions, and disharmonies" (46), aiming to make a quasi-religion of art. After Jay, Berlin fears that this encourages totalitarianism (*Rhetorics, Poetics, and Cultures* 89).

5. Condillac and Modern Rhetoric: Across the Threshold

Thanks to Pamela Genova for help in refining the translation of Condillac in the second epigraph that opens this chapter.

1. See Johnson Kent Wright.

2. See introduction to Bender and Wellbery for the opposition of rhetoric to rhetoricality, similar to other earlier poststructuralist theory such as Jonathan Culler's. Condillac's theory that a science is a well-made language is found primarily in his posthumous work *The Language of Calculus,* written just before his death in 1780 and published in 1798.

3. Closely following Fénelon, Condillac was also interested in the education of women (see Fénelon, *Fénelon on Education*). Maureen F. O'Meara discusses his offering of a history particular to women, showing the connections of Condillac to Rousseau and their different notions of the education of women.

4. I am using analogy in its broadest sense. For a finer distinction of analogy from metaphor, see Eve Tavor Bannet.

5. Courtly rhetoric was encouraged by the strong French monarchies in

which a rhetoric of open debate was impossible but in which courtiers could nonetheless gain power through a pleasant and insinuative rhetoric. Marc Fumaroli analyzes the politics of French classical style, noting two earlier strands of Ciceronianism—an Attic style of the forum and parliamentary deliberation and a more elaborate courtly style. Tracing these two styles from the Renaissance to the eighteenth century, he posits the synthesis of the two strands in the style of the French nobility, "one turned toward an alliance of utility and elegance in the service of the sciences and the affairs of state, the other toward an alliance of attractiveness and a regulated elegance in the service of the amusements of the court" (271).

6. Locke did not pursue the origin of human understanding in the origins of language but suggested the possibility in his *Essay* (3.3.7: 411). He did, however, in his *Second Treatise of Government* set up an originary state of nature in order to speculate on human political nature.

7. In contrast to many scholars, Hans Aarsleff maintains that the single principle by which Condillac wished to explain the mind was "*la liaison des idées* (the connection of ideas)" through signs, a reading strongly supported in Condillac's introduction to his *Origin* essay. Aarsleff links the principle of the connection of ideas to an imitation of the power of Isaac Newton's principle of universal gravitation, warning that Condillac's connection of ideas is not the same as John Locke's involuntary association of ideas (*From Locke to Saussure* 199). However, it is similar to Locke's controlled association he discusses in relation to judgment. In the less rational aesthetics, however, Condillac uses *both* connection and association of ideas. In his recent introduction to Condillac's *Origin* essay, Aarsleff emphasizes two main principles, the connection of ideas and the language of action (xi).

8. See also Derrida, 91–93. Aarsleff actually has the most satisfying explanation for this passage (*Condillac* xxvi–xxvii).

9. Condillac dedicates this work to a salonnière Mme. de Vassé. In the dedication, he generously credits Mlle. Ferrand with giving him the insights into the priority of the senses before language, especially that of touch.

10. See also Latour, *We Have Never Been Modern*. In gender analysis, this contradiction-synthesis has been explored through Susan R. Bordo's theory that post-Cartesian scientific discourse represents a rejection of a "flight from the feminine," following the Renaissance conception of nature as a nurturing mother. In her study of Descartes, Bordo interprets the tradition from the Middle Ages and Renaissance to the scientific or classical era as a "drama of parturition"—or a cultural birth out of an organic female universe and into the mechanistic clockwork universe of the Newtonian age (5). The feminine can thus be viewed as a compensating physical and emotional supplement to the new logico-rational masculine universe. Using Bordo's psychological vantage point, the feminine nature of Condillac's aesthetic rhetoric could signal a reluctance to banish the feminine and the body from the new intellectual and masculine world of mathematics and science he so admires. Note that this gender reading codes both aristocratic rhetoric and Neoplatonism as feminine.

11. This is a controlled and rational connection, as in Locke, rather than the less controlled or irrational association of ideas. However, Condillac does

not disparage association as madness as does Locke but assigns it to the province of aesthetics in a sublime sense, in particular to poetry, in his writing course. The deliberate linking of ideas represents his concept of method, a concept linked to the original rhetorical canon of arrangement of discourse as well as to later theories of presentation of material in teaching. There is a Romantic implication that the sublime, aesthetic associative method is unteachable; meanwhile, methods of making controlled, philosophical connections can be passed on.

12. See editor Irwin C. Lieb's *Charles S. Peirce's Letters to Lady Welby*.

13. He exhibits little scorn for the courtly salon world of his early career, although after his duties with the Prince of Parma, he physically distances himself by retiring to his estate in the country. He generously credits a salonnière, Mlle. Ferrand, for collaboration leading to his *Treatise on Sensation* (in the dedication to Mme. de Vassé). The treatise highlights the importance of the body's sensations as a ground for later understanding. In this treatise, Condillac uses what is perhaps his best-known signature, a speechless statue, to investigate sensation and thought before the arbitrary sign. It is interesting that Condillac, who had trouble with his eyesight beginning when he was quite young, ultimately gives epistemological priority in the senses to touch.

14. This notion of art as social and conventional is classical, repeating many instances of debate over art and nature in rhetoric treatises from Aristotle to Cicero and Quintilian.

15. As Derrida notes, there are two imaginations in Condillac: one confines itself to retracing experience or recalling images, while the second recombines images of reality to generate something never seen before, something new. The imagination is also responsible for offering up "new" initially arbitrary signs to the memory.

16. The crucial role of memory in cognition has been revived, with new theories about its importance put forward by rhetoricians such as William A. Covino and Kathleen E. Welch.

17. Aarsleff's *Condillac* introduction points to a similar passage by Cicero in *de Oratore* 3: 216; Aarsleff notes that Lamy uses the term *sympathie* for this communication of passions (xxi). Condillac does not use the term *sympathy* but uses the concept similar to later English writers, including Adam Smith. Sympathy is also one element of Foucault's resemblance episteme, *Order of Things* (23), making this a residual element that emerges in modern discourse.

18. Ellen McNiven Hine explains Condillac's interpretation (and later rejection) of Gottfried Wilhelm Leibniz in her *A Critical Study of Condillac's* Traité des Systemes. Condillac knew well Leibniz's philosophies of extension, force, and preestablished harmony in respect to monads. The universe is a single monad, but human bodies are aggregates of perceiving monads. Although monads can seem separate, their changes tend toward a common end. God has established a harmony between monads from their origin(s). The whole universe can be known by knowing the state of a single monad (*Critical Study* 83).

19. This old coupling, expressed as passion and energy or force, is also central to Longinus, but it emerges strongly in many eighteenth-century rhetorics, including Blair's and Campbell's.

20. There may be many more editions of Condillac than we know, but Hine writes that the complete works was published in 1777, 1798, 1803, and 1827. Blair's *Lectures on Rhetoric and Belles Lettres* was published in 1783 and went through 130 editions in England and America until 1911 (James A. Berlin, *Writing Instruction* 25). Influenced by Condillac and other French belletristic writers, similar values thus reigned supreme in Western literacy education at the turn of the century and beyond. Condillac's *Logic* was also brought to the United States: see *The Logic of Condillac Translated by Joseph Neef as an Illustration of a Plan of Education Established at His School near Philadelphia.*

21. Similar theories of the universality and force of the natural language of gesture seem to fuel the popularity of the century's elocutionary movement.

22. See Thomas P. Miller's criticism of belles lettres.

23. In *From Locke to Saussure* (378–79), Aarsleff discusses this issue from Condillac's *Art of Writing* in relation to William Wordsworth.

24. As Longinus, author of the treatise on the sublime, notes, "For art is perfect just when it seems to be nature, and nature successful when the art underlies it unnoticed" (45).

25. The argument for analogy has been criticized as leading to a concern for ranking languages based on purity. This was especially embraced by nineteenth-century German linguists such as Wilhelm von Humboldt who measured all languages by the yardstick of Sanskrit. Here, however, Condillac does not build a case for linguistic purity in order to rank languages but primarily as an argument by a Modern against the Ancients and to justify the French language as being as worthy of study as classical languages.

26. Derrida, in *The Archeology of the Frivolous,* his introduction to Condillac's essay, early on makes the point that the structure of Condillac's texts is not based on a simple system of polarized binary oppositions. Derrida explores several possible relations between the oppositions, including an oscillation between the two, ultimately leaving open the possibilities for relationships. Earlier, Isabel F. Knight had characterized Condillac in terms of his tensions and equivocations that leaned to the side of the geometric of her title.

27. De Tracy proposed the term *idéologie* in 1801 in his *Éléments d'idéologie pour les élèves de l'école de grammaire général des Écoles centrales.* Karl Marx found the word *idéologues* in one of Napoleon's disparaging remarks about the group (Aarsleff, *From Locke to Saussure* 31). The *idéologues* were early sociologists.

28. In his communications history, Paul Heyer identifies Condillac as a central figure; however, in attempting to establish foundations for the field of communication, he embraces language theory while ignoring or breaking with the history of rhetoric or Condillac's writing pedagogy. This is consistent with the recent emphasis on empirical studies and synchronic theorizing in the discipline today. Rhetoric frequently exists in a liminal space between English studies and communication studies.

29. See Hélène Cixous and Catherine Clément's *The Newly Born Woman* and Cixous's "Laugh of the Medusa," or Luce Irigaray's "This Sex Which Is Not One." Theories of the body provided copious material for fleshly reflec-

tion at the turn of the millennium. See for example, Jack Selzer and Sharon Crowley, eds., *Rhetorical Bodies* and Mary M. Lay, Laura Gurak, Clare Gravon, and Cynthia Myntti, *Body Talk: Rhetoric, Technology, Reproduction.*

6. Lord Monboddo's Antimodernity: Scottish Marginalia

1. Jürgen Habermas believed in the potential of the Enlightenment, although Monboddo was antimodern and anti-Enlightenment. However, Monboddo's civic humanism left him with similar views as Vico's in some respects, although Naples was less open to free discussion than Britain. Coffeehouse activity in Habermas's eighteenth-century public sphere was at its peak in London during Monboddo's lifetime. See Habermas, *The Structural Transformation of the Public Sphere: An Enquiry into a Category of Bourgeois Society.*

2. See Hammett, "Introduction," as well as Horner *(Nineteenth-Century Scottish Rhetoric: The American Connection)* and Miller.

3. See W. Knight, Monboddo to Welbore Ellis, 5 Jan. 1784 for Monboddo's nomination of Homer's language as the "perfection of the most perfect language, I believe, that ever was on earth" (262).

4. The blind poet Thomas Blacklock, a close friend of Monboddo's, used *Hermes* in his work *Essay on Universal Etymology* (1756). Blacklock was familiar with Vico's *New Science.*

5. See Phillipson (146–47) for a characterization of Edinburgh society with regard to Beattie.

6. See Arthur O. Lovejoy's *The Great Chain of Being.* Until *being* was somewhat temporalized in the eighteenth century, this rationalist notion was fixed and allowed for nothing new—if God had made the universe perfectly, no change was needed or possible. It is not clear that Monboddo allows much change—except that individuals may perfect themselves while in their places, the hierarchy remains in place.

7. See *Origin and Progress,* 1: 363. Also *Antient Metaphysics,* 5:321. In a letter to John Hope, Monboddo writes, "[I]t is undoubtedly the improvement that men have made in Knowledge, by the invention of Art, that has been the cause of all their misery" (qtd. in W. Knight 105).

8. Winifred Horner's *Nineteenth-Century Scottish Rhetoric* discusses these patterns before inquiring into connections between American and Scottish rhetoric in the nineteenth century, a connection she sees as the missing link between classical and contemporary rhetoric.

9. As Hammett explains, this division of barbarous languages and languages of art reflects a division in legal history between natural law and the humanly constructed law of nations. Monboddo believed that like the arts of jurisprudence, languages of art, those perfected by philosophers of language, were more rational and perfect and, therefore, to be preferred over natural languages.

10. Although I link Monboddo with other Greek-worshipers who make Greeks fully Caucasian, because of his Egypt-worship, he is more like Martin Bernal, the author of *Black Athena,* in his Greek history. Monboddo also believed the Pelasgi of Greece originally came from Egypt, which he calls "the

parent country of language as well as of other arts" (*Origin* 1.2.472). The reverence for Egypt may reflect the influence of his membership in the Masons.

11. Hook connects the Scottish narrative of loss to Southern narratives such as in William Faulkner's work. The narrative of loss also took hold in Germany before World War II.

12. Sarah J. Sloane has investigated the uses of Longinus's *On the Sublime* by Scottish Enlightenment texts about taste and the sublime. She has written about references to Milton's *Paradise Lost* in Blair, Greenfield, Kames, Smith, and others, especially their reference to the same passage describing Satan at the head of his Infernal Host, lines 589–600, book 1.

7. Twenty-First-Century Language and Rhetoric

1. The point about contemporaneity is the basis of Hans Aarsleff's argument for his study of Horne Tooke in *The Study of Language in England, 1780–1860.*

Works Cited

Aarsleff, Hans, trans. and ed. *Condillac: An Essay on the Origin of Human Knowledge*. Cambridge: Cambridge UP, 2001.

———. *From Locke to Saussure: Essays on the Study of Language and Intellectual History*. Minneapolis: U of Minnesota P, 1982.

———. Introduction. Aarsleff, *Condillac* xi–xxxviii.

———. Introduction. *On Language: The Diversity of Human Language Structure and Its Influence on the Mental Development of Mankind*. By Wilhelm von Humboldt. Trans. Peter Heath. Cambridge: Cambridge UP, 1988. vii–xiv.

———. *The Study of Language in England, 1780–1860*. Princeton: Princeton UP, 1967.

———. "The Tradition of Condillac." Aarsleff, *From Locke to Saussure* 146–209.

Addams, Jane. *Democracy and Social Ethics*. New York: Macmillan, 1902.

Alston, William P. *Philosophy of Language*. Prentice-Hall Foundations of Philosophy. Englewood Cliffs: Prentice, 1964.

Aristotle. *Aristotle on Rhetoric: A Theory of Civic Discourse, Newly Translated, with Introduction, Notes, and Appendices by George A. Kennedy*. New York: Oxford UP, 1991.

Arnauld, Antoine, [and Pierre Nicole]. *The Art of Thinking: The Port-Royal Logic*. Trans. and intro. James Dickoff with Patricia James. Indianapolis: Bobbs-Merrill, 1964.

Ayers, Michael. *Locke, Vol. I: Epistemology*. London: Routledge, 1991.

Bacon, Francis. *The Philosophical Works of Francis Bacon*. Rpt. from James Spedding and Robert Leslie Ellis. Ed. John M. Robertson. Freeport: Books for Libraries, 1970.

Bakhtin, M. M. *The Dialogic Imagination: Four Essays by M. M. Bakhtin*. Trans. Carl Emerson and Michael Holquist. Ed. Holquist. Austin: U of Texas P, 1990.

Bannet, Eve Tavor. "Analogy as Translation: Wittgenstein, Derrida, and the Law of Language." *New Literary History* 28 (1997): 655–72.

Barney, Richard A. *Plots of Enlightenment: Education and the Novel in Eighteenth-Century England*. Stanford: Stanford UP, 1999.

Barnouw, Jeffrey. "Vico and the Continuity of Science: The Relation of His Epistemology to Bacon and Hobbes." *Isis* 71 (1980): 609–20.

Baron, Naomi S. "Writing and Vico's Functional Approach to Language Change." Tagliacozzo, *Vico: Past and Present* 115–31.

Barthes, Roland. "The Old Rhetoric: An *Aide-Mémoire.*" *The Semiotic Challenge.* Trans. Richard Howard. New York: Hill, 1988. 11–94.

Battistini, Andrea. "Vico and Rhetoric." *New Vico Studies* 12 (1944): 1–15.

Baugh, Albert C. *History of the English Language.* New York: Appleton, 1935.

Bauman, Zygmunt. *Modernity and Ambivalence.* Ithaca: Cornell UP, 1991.

Bender, John, and David E. Wellbery. "Rhetoricality: On the Modernist Return of Rhetoric." *The End of Rhetoric: History, Theory, and Practice.* Ed. Bender and Wellbery. Stanford: Stanford UP, 1990. 3–39.

Benjamin, Andrew E., Geoffrey N. Cantor, and John R. R. Christie, eds. *The Figural and the Literal: Problems of Language in the History of Science and Philosophy, 1630–1800.* Manchester: Manchester UP, 1987.

Berlin, Isaiah. *The Proper Study of Mankind: An Anthology of Essays.* New York: Farrar, 1998.

———. *Vico and Herder: Two Studies in the History of Ideas.* London: Hogarth, 1976.

Berlin, James A. "Revisionary Histories of Rhetoric: Politics, Power, and Plurality." Vitanza, *Writing Histories* 112–27.

———. "Revisionary History: The Dialectical Method." *Rethinking the History of Rhetoric: Multidisciplinary Essays on the Rhetorical Tradition.* Ed. Takis Poulakos. Boulder: Westview, 1993. 135–51.

———. "Rhetoric and Ideology in the Writing Class." *College English* 50 (1988): 477–94.

———. *Rhetoric and Reality: Writing Instruction in American Colleges, 1900–1985.* Carbondale: Southern Illinois UP, 1987.

———. *Rhetorics, Poetics, and Cultures: Refiguring College English Studies.* Urbana: NCTE, 1996.

———. *Writing Instruction in Nineteenth-Century American Colleges.* Carbondale: Southern Illinois UP, 1984.

Bernal, Martin. *Black Athena: The Afroasiatic Roots of Classical Civilization.* Vol. 1. The Fabrication of Ancient Greece, 1785–1985. New Brunswick: Rutgers UP, 1987.

Bevilacqua, Vincent M. "Campbell, Vico, and the Rhetorical Science of Human Nature." *Philosophy and Rhetoric* 18 (1985): 23–31.

———. "On the Nature and Scope of Wilbur S. Howell's Eighteenth-Century British Logic and Rhetoric." *Quarterly Journal of Speech* 59 (1973): 215–16.

———. "Vico, 'Process,' and the Nature of Rhetorical Investigation: An Epistemological Perspective." *Philosophy and Rhetoric* 7 (1974): 166–74.

———. "W. S. Howell and the Relatives of Rhetoric." *Quarterly Journal of Speech* 58 (1972): 344–46.

Bhattacharya, Nikhil. "Knowledge 'Per Caussas': Vico's Theory of Natural Science." Tagliacozzo, *Vico: Past and Present* 182–97.

Black, David W. *Vico and Moral Perception.* New York: Lang, 1997.

Bordo, Susan R. *The Flight to Objectivity: Essays on Cartesianism and Culture.* SUNY Series in Philosophy. Albany: State U of New York P, 1987.

Bormann, Dennis R. "George Campbell's *Cura Prima* on Eloquence—1758." *Quarterly Journal of Speech* 74 (1988): 35–51.

———. "Some 'Common Sense' about Campbell, Hume, and Reid: The Extrinsic Evidence." *Quarterly Journal of Speech* 71 (1985): 395–421.

Brody, Miriam. *Manly Writing: Gender, Rhetoric, and the Rise of Composition.* Carbondale: Southern Illinois UP, 1993.

Brooks, Cleanth, and Robert Penn Warren. *Modern Rhetoric.* 3rd ed. New York: Harcourt, 1972.

Burke, Kenneth. *Attitudes Toward History.* 3rd ed. Berkeley: U of Calif. P, 1984.

———. *A Grammar of Motives.* 1945. Berkeley: U of California P, 1969.

———. *Language as Symbolic Interaction: Essays on Life, Literature, and Method.* Berkeley: U of California P, 1966.

———. *A Rhetoric of Motives.* 1950. Berkeley: U of California P, 1969.

Burnett, James (Lord Monboddo). *Antient Metaphysics.* 1779–1799. 6 vols. Rpt. New York: Garland, 1977.

———. *Of the Origin and Progress of Language.* 1773–1792. 6 vols. English Linguistics 1500–1800. 48. Ed. R. C. Alston. Menstone, Eng.: Scolar, 1967.

Casanova, Pascale. *La République Mondiale des Lettres.* Paris: Seuil, 1999.

Certeau, Michel de. *The Practice of Everyday Life.* Trans. Steven F. Rendall. Berkeley: U of California P, 1984.

Christie, John R. R. "Adam Smith's Metaphysics of Language." Benjamin, Cantor, and Christie 203–9.

Cicero. *Cicero on Oratory and Orators.* Ed. and trans. J. S. Watson. Carbondale: Southern Illinois UP, 1986.

Cixous, Hélène, and Catherine Clément. *The Newly Born Woman.* Trans. Betsy Wing. Vol. 24 of *Theory and History of Literature.* Minneapolis: U of Minnesota P, 1986. Trans. of *La Jeune Née.* 1975.

Clark, Gregory. *Dialogue, Dialectic, and Conversation: A Social Perspective on the Function of Writing.* Carbondale: Southern Illinois UP, 1990.

Clark, Gregory, and S. Michael Halloran, eds. *Oratorical Culture in Nineteenth-Century America: Transformations in the Theory and Practice of Rhetoric.* Carbondale: Southern Illinois UP, 1993.

Clark, J. C. D. *English Society, 1688–1832: Ideology, Social Structure and Political Practice During the Ancien Regime.* Cambridge: Cambridge UP, 1985.

Cloyd, E. L. *James Burnett: Lord Monboddo.* Oxford: Clarendon, 1972.

Cohen, Herman. *The Rhetorical Theory of Hugh Blair.* Diss. U of Iowa, 1954. Ann Arbor: UMI, 1982.

Cohen, Murray. *Sensible Words: Linguistic Practice in England, 1640–1785.* Baltimore: Johns Hopkins UP, 1977.

Colley, Linda. *Britons: Forging the Nation 1707–1837.* New Haven: Yale UP, 1992.

Condillac, Abbé de (Étienne de Bonnot). *Condillac: An Essay on the Origin of Human Knowledge.* Ed. and trans. Hans Aarsleff. Cambridge: Cambridge UP, 2001.

———. *Condillac's Treatise on the Sensations.* Trans. Geraldine Carr. Los Angeles: U of Southern California School of Philosophy, 1930.

194 Works Cited

———. *An Essay on the Origin of Human Knowledge.* Trans. Thomas Nugent. London: Nourse, 1756. Facsim. ed. Language, Man, and Society: Foundations of the Behavioral Sciences. New York: AMS, 1974.

———. *La Logique. Logic.* Trans. W. R. Albury. New York: Abaris, 1980.

———. *Les Monades.* Ed. Laurence L. Bongie. Studies in Voltaire and the Eighteenth Century. 187. Oxford: Voltaire, 1980.

———. *Oeuvres Philosophiques de Condillac.* Ed. Georges Le Roy. 3 vols. Corpus Général des Philosophes Français. Vol. 36. St. Germain: PUF, 1947.

———. "Of the Art of Writing." Condillac, *Oeuvres* 1.3: 517–615.

Cope, Kevin L. *Criteria of Certainty: Truth and Judgment in the English Enlightenment.* Lexington: UP Kentucky, 1990.

Corbett, Edward P. J. *Classical Rhetoric for the Modern Student.* New York: Oxford UP, 1965.

———. "John Locke's Contributions to Rhetoric." *College Composition and Communication* 32 (1981): 423–33.

Cottom, Daniel. *The Civilized Imagination: A Study of Ann Radcliffe, Jane Austen, and Sir Walter Scott.* Cambridge: Cambridge UP, 1985.

Covino, William A. *The Art of Wondering: A Revisionist Return to the History of Rhetoric.* Portsmouth: Boynton, 1988.

Cranston, Maurice. *John Locke: A Biography.* London: Longman, 1957.

Crifò, Giuliano. Foreword and Introduction. Vico, *Art of Rhetoric* xv, xvii–xxix.

Croce, Benedetto. *The Philosophy of Giambattista Vico.* Trans. R. G. Collingwood. New York: Macmillan, 1913.

Crowley, Sharon. *The Methodical Memory: Invention in Current-Traditional Rhetoric.* Carbondale: Southern Illinois UP, 1990.

Curtius, Ernst Robert. *European Literature and the Latin Middle Ages.* Trans. Willard R. Trask. Bollingen Series 36. Princeton: Princeton UP, 1953.

Daiches, David. *The Paradox of Scottish Culture.* London: Oxford UP, 1964.

Daiches, David, Peter Jones, and Jean Jones, eds. *A Hotbed of Genius: The Scottish Enlightenment, 1730–1790.* Edinburgh: Edinburgh UP, 1986.

Danesi, Marcel. *Giambattista Vico and the Cognitive Science Enterprise.* New York: Lang, 1995.

———. *Vico, Metaphor, and the Origin of Language.* Bloomington: Indiana UP, 1993.

de Man, Paul. "The Epistemology of Metaphor." *Critical Inquiry* 5 (1978): 13–30.

Derrida, Jacques. *The Archeology of the Frivolous: Reading Condillac.* 1973. Trans. and intro. John P. Leavey, Jr. Duquesne Studies—Philosophical Series. 37. Pittsburgh: Duquesne UP, 1980.

———. *Of Grammatology.* Trans. Gayatri Chakravorty Spivak. Baltimore: Johns Hopkins UP, 1976.

Descartes, Rene. *Discourse on Method and Meditations.* Trans. Laurence J. Lafleur. Library of Liberal Arts. Indianapolis: Bobbs-Merrill, 1960.

———. *Les passions de l'âme.* Ed. Pascale d'Arcy. Paris: Flammarion, 1996.

Douglass, Wallace W. "Notes Toward an Ideology of Composition." *ADE Bulletin* 43 (1974): 24–33.

Ehninger, Douglas. *Contemporary Rhetoric.* Glenview, IL: Scott, 1972.

Fáj, Attila. "The Unorthodox Logic of Scientific Discovery in Vico." Tagliacozzo, *Vico: Past and Present* 198–205.

———. "Vico as Philosopher of *Metabasis*." Tagliacozzo and Verene 87–109.

Fénelon (François de Salignac de La Mothe-Fénelon). *Fénelon on Education.*
Trans. H. C. Barnard. Cambridge: Cambridge UP, 1966.

———. *Fénelon's Dialogues on Eloquence.* Trans. Wilbur Samuel Howell.
Princeton: Princeton UP, 1951.

Fisch, Max Harold. "The Academy of the Investigators." *Science, Medicine, and
History: Essays in Honor of Charles Singer.* Ed. E. A. Underwood. Vol. 1.
London: Oxford UP, 1953. 520–63.

———. Introduction. *The New Science of Giambattista Vico.* By Giambattista
Vico. Trans. Thomas Goddard Bergin and Fisch. 1744. Unabridged trans.
of 3rd ed. with the addition of "Practic of the *New Science.*" Ithaca: Cornell
UP, 1984. xix–xlv.

———. "Vico and Pragmatism." Tagliacozzo and White 401–24.

———. "Vico's *Practica.*" Tagliacozzo and Verene 423–30.

Flint, Robert. *Vico.* Edinburgh: Blackwood, 1884.

Foucault, Michel. *The Archaeology of Knowledge.* Trans. A. M. Sheridan Smith.
New York: Pantheon, 1972.

———. *Language, Counter-Memory, Practice: Selected Essays and Interviews.*
Trans. Donald F. Bouchard and Sherry Simon. Ed. Bouchard. Ithaca: Cornell
UP, 1977.

———. *The Order of Things: An Archaeology of the Human Sciences.* World
of Man: A Library of Theory and Research in the Human Sciences. Ed. R.
D. Laing. New York: Pantheon, 1971.

Fumaroli, Marc. "Rhetoric, Politics, and Society: From Italian Ciceronianism
to French Classicism." *Renaissance Eloquence.* Ed. James J. Murphy. Berkeley: U of California P, 1983. 253–73.

Gaillet, Lynee L., ed. *Scottish Rhetoric and Its Influences.* Mahwah: Erlbaum,
1998.

Gay, Peter. *The Enlightenment: An Interpretation.* Vol. 2. The Science of Freedom. New York: Knopf, 1969.

———. *The Party of Humanity: Essays in the French Enlightenment.* New York:
Knopf, 1964.

Giuliani, Alessandro. "Vico's Rhetorical Philosophy and the New Rhetoric."
Tagliacozzo and Verene 31–46.

Goetsch, James Robert, Jr. *Vico's Axioms: The Geometry of the Human World.*
New Haven: Yale UP, 1995.

Golden, James L., and Edward P. J. Corbett. *The Rhetoric of Blair, Campbell,
and Whately.* New York: Holt, 1968.

Gordon, Pamela. *Epicurus in Lycia: The Second-Century World of Diogenes
of Oenoanda.* Ann Arbor: U of Michigan P, 1996.

———. "Outsiders in the Garden: Women and Slaves in the School of Epicurus."
Unpublished address at University of Oklahoma, Norman, OK. 18 Oct.
1995.

Gough, J. W. "John Locke's Herbarium." *Bodlein Library Record* 1 (June
1962): vii.

———. "Locke's Reading During His Stay in France 1675–1679." *Library, Fifth Series* 8.4 (1953): 229–58.

Grafton, Anthony, and Lisa Jardine. *From Humanism to the Humanities: Education and the Liberal Arts in Fifteenth- and Sixteenth-Century Europe.* Cambridge: Harvard UP, 1986.

Grassi, Ernesto. "Critical Philosophy or Topical Philosophy? Meditations on the *De nostri temporis studiorum ratione.*" Tagliacozzo and White 39–50.

———. *Rhetoric as Philosophy: the Humanist Tradition.* Trans. John Michael Krois and Azizeh Azodi. Carbondale: Southern Illinois UP, 2001.

Habermas, Jürgen. "Modernity Versus Postmodernity." *New German Critique* 22 (1981): 3–18.

———. *The Structural Transformation of the Public Sphere: An Enquiry into a Category of Bourgeois Society.* Cambridge: Harvard UP, 1989.

Halloran, S. Michael. "Rhetoric in the American College Curriculum: The Decline of Public Discourse." *Pre/Text* 3 (1982): 245–69.

Hammett, I. M. "The Early Monboddo Papers and the Genesis of Monboddo's *Of the Origin and Progress of Language.*" *Bulletin of Hiroshima Jogakvin College* 35 (1985): 133–61.

———. "An Introduction to Lord Monboddo's *Of the Origin and Progress of Language.*" *Bulletin of Hiroshima Jogakvin College* 37 (1987): 141–56.

———. "Lord Monboddo and the Impact of the French Encyclopaedia on Eighteenth-Century Scottish Philosophy." *Bulletin of Hiroshima Jogakvin College* 36 (1986): 193–213.

———. "Lord Monboddo's *Origin of Language,* Its Sources, Genesis, and Background, with Special Attention to the Advocates' Library." Diss. Edinburgh U, 1985.

———. "The Universal Grammars of James Harris and Lord Monboddo." *Bulletin of Hiroshima Jogakvin College* 38 (1988): 51–80.

Hanafi, Zakiya. *The Monster in the Machine: Magic, Medicine, and the Marvelous in the Time of the Scientific Revolution.* Durham: Duke UP, 2000.

Haraway, Donna. *Simians, Cyborgs, and Women: The Reinvention of Nature.* New York: Chapman, 1991.

Hardison, O. B., Jr. *Disappearing Through the Skylight.* New York: Viking, 1989.

Harris, Roy, and Talbot J. Taylor. *Landmarks in Linguistic Thought: The Western Tradition from Socrates to Saussure.* London: Routledge, 1989.

Harrison, John, and Peter Laslett. *The Library of John Locke.* London: Oxford UP, 1965.

Harvey, David. *The Condition of Postmodernity.* Oxford, Eng.: Blackwell, 1990.

Harwood, John. *The Rhetorics of Thomas Hobbes and Bernard Lamy.* Carbondale: Southern Illinois UP, 1986.

Heidsieck, Francois. "Analyse du discours et metaphysique de l'âme." Sgard 71–73.

Herder, Johann Gottfried, and Jean-Jacques Rousseau. *On the Origin of Language: Two Essays.* Trans. John H. Moran and Alexander Gode. Chicago: U Chicago P, 1966.

Heyer, Paul. *Communications and History: Theories of Media, Knowledge, and Civilization.* New York: Greenwood, 1988.

Hine, Ellen McNiven. *A Critical Study of Condillac's* Traité des Systemes. The Hague: Nijhoff, 1979.

Hobbes, Thomas. *The English Works of Thomas Hobbes.* Ed. W. Molesworth. Vols. 3–4. London, 1839–45.

Hobbs, Catherine L. "Condillac and the History of Rhetoric." *Rhetorica: A Journal of the History of Rhetoric* 11.2 (1993): 135–56.

———. "Understanding Differently: Re-reading Locke's *Essay.*" *Rhetoric Society Quarterly* 22.1 (1992): 74–90.

———. "Vico, Rhetorical Topics, and Historical Thinking." *Vico's Significance for Historians.* Ed. Patrick Hutton. Special issue. *Historical Reflections/ Réflexions Historiques:* 22.3 (1996): 559–85.

Hook, Andrew. *From Goosecreek to Gandercleugh: Studies in Scottish-American Literary and Cultural History.* East Lothian: Tuckwell, 1999.

Horkheimer, Max, and Theodor W. Adorno. *The Dialectic of the Enlightenment.* Trans. John Cumming. New York: Continuum, 1982.

Horner, Winifred B. *Nineteenth-Century Scottish Rhetoric: The American Connection.* Carbondale: Southern Illinois UP, 1993.

———, ed. *The Present State of Scholarship in Historical and Contemporary Rhetoric.* Columbia: U of Missouri P, 1983.

Howell, Wilbur Samuel. *Eighteenth-Century British Logic and Rhetoric.* Princeton: Princeton UP, 1971.

———. *Logic and Rhetoric in England, 1500–1700.* Princeton: Princeton UP, 1956.

———. "The Relatives of Rhetoric: An Eighteenth-Century View." *Quarterly Journal of Speech* 59 (1973): 213–15.

Irigaray, Luce. *This Sex Which Is Not One.* Trans. Catherine Porter. Ithaca: Cornell UP, 1985.

Irvine, James. "Lord Monboddo's 'Letter on Rhetoric': Defense of Aristotle." *Rhetoric Society Quarterly* 21.4 (1991): 26–31.

Jardine, Lisa. *Francis Bacon: Discovery and the Art of Discourse.* Cambridge: Cambridge UP, 1974.

Jarratt, Susan C. "The First Sophists and the Uses of History." *Rhetoric Review* 6.1 (1987): 67–78.

Jones, Richard Foster. *Ancients and Moderns: A Study of the Rise of the Scientific Movement in Seventeenth-Century England.* 2nd ed. rev. St. Louis: Washington UP, 1961.

Joseph, John E., and Talbot J. Taylor, ed. *Ideologies of Language.* London: Routledge, 1990.

Kennedy, George. *Classical Rhetoric and Its Christian and Secular Tradition from Ancient to Modern Times.* Chapel Hill: U of North Carolina P, 1980.

———. *Comparative Rhetorics.* New York: Oxford UP, 1998.

Knight, Isabel F. *The Geometric Spirit: The Abbé de Condillac and the French Enlightenment.* Yale Historical Publications: Miscellany. 89. New Haven: Yale UP, 1968.

Knight, William. *Lord Monboddo and Some of His Contemporaries.* London: Murray, 1900.

Knoblauch, C. H., and Lil Brannon. *Rhetorical Traditions and the Teaching of Writing.* Upper Montclair, NJ: Boynton/Cook, 1984.

Kroll, Richard W. *The Material Word: Literate Culture in the Restoration and Early-Eighteenth Century.* Baltimore: Johns Hopkins, 1991.

Kuhn, Thomas S. *The Structure of Scientific Revolutions.* 1962. Chicago: U of Chicago P, 1996.

LaCapra, Dominick. *Rethinking Intellectual History.* Ithaca: Cornell UP, 1983.

Lachterman, David Rapport. *The Ethics of Geometry: A Genealogy of Modernity.* New York: Routledge, 1989.

Land, Stephen K. *From Signs to Propositions: The Concept of Form in Eighteenth-Century Semantic Theory.* London: Longman, 1974.

———. *The Philosophy of Language in Britain: Major Theories from Hobbes to Thomas Reid.* AMS Studies in the Seventeenth Century. 2. New York: AMS, 1986.

Latour, Bruno. *We Have Never Been Modern.* Trans. Catherine Porter. Cambridge: Harvard UP, 1993.

Lauer, Janice M. "Heuristics and Composition." *Contemporary Rhetoric: A Conceptual Background with Readings.* Ed. W. Ross Winterowd. New York: Harcourt, 1970. 79–90.

———. "Invention." *Theorizing Composition: A Critical Sourcebook of Theory and Scholarship in Contemporary Composition Studies.* Ed. Mary Lynch Kennedy. Westport, CT: Greenwood, 1998. 163–67.

———. "Issues in Rhetorical Invention." *Essays on Classical Rhetoric and Modern Discourse.* Ed. Robert Connors, Lisa Ede, and Andrea Lunsford. Carbondale: Southern Illinois UP, 1983. 127–39.

Lay, Mary M., Laura Gurak, Clare Gravon, and Cynthia Myntti. *Body Talk: Rhetoric, Technology, Reproduction.* Madison: U of Wisconsin P, 2000.

Leavey, John P., Jr. Introduction. Derrida, *Archeology of the Frivolous* 1–23.

Lefebvre, Henri. *Introduction to Modernity: Twelve Preludes, September 1959–May 1961.* Trans. John Moore. London: Verso, 1995.

Lieb, Irwin C., ed. *Charles S. Peirce's Letters to Lady Welby.* New Haven: Whitlock, 1953.

Lilla, Mark. *G. B. Vico: The Making of an Anti-Modern.* Cambridge: Harvard UP, 1993.

Locke, John. *An Essay Concerning Human Understanding.* Ed. Peter H. Nidditch. Oxford: Clarendon, 1975.

———. "Some Thoughts Concerning Education." *The Educational Writings of John Locke: A Critical Edition with Introduction and Notes.* Ed. James L. Axtell. Cambridge: Cambridge UP, 1968. 111–325.

Longinus, Cassius. *Longinus On the Sublime. The Peri Hupsous in translations by Nicholas Boileau-Despreaux (1674) and William Smith (1739).* Delmar, NY: Scholars' Facsimiles, 1975.

Lovejoy, Arthur O. *The Great Chain of Being: A Study of the History of an Idea.* 1936. New York: Harper, 1966.

Lucretius. *On the Nature of Things*. Trans. C. E. Bennett. Roslyn, NY: Black, 1946.

MacLean, Kenneth. *John Locke and English Literature of the Eighteenth Century*. New Haven: Yale UP, 1936.

Markley, Robert. *Fallen Languages: Crises of Representation in Newtonian England, 1660–1740*. Ithaca: Cornell UP, 1993.

Mazzotta, Guiseppe. *The New Map of the World: The Poetic Philosophy of Giambattista Vico*. Princeton: Princeton UP, 1999.

Megill, Allan. *Prophets of Extremity: Nietzsche, Heidegger, Foucault, Derrida*. Berkeley: U of California P, 1985.

Miller, Thomas P. *The Formation of College English: Rhetoric and Belles Lettres in the British Cultural Provinces*. Pittsburgh: U of Pittsburgh P, 1997.

Monboddo, Lord. [James Burnet[t].] *Antient Metaphysics*. 6 vols. Rpt. of the 1779–1799 ed. New York: Garland, 1977.

———. *Of the Origin and Progress of Language*. 6 vols. 1773–92. English Linguistics 1500–1800. Ed. R. C. Alston. Menstone, Eng.: Scolar, 1967.

Mooney, Michael. *Vico in the Tradition of Rhetoric*. Princeton: Princeton UP, 1985.

Mouffe, Chantal. "Democratic Citizenship and the Political Community." *Community at Loose Ends*. Ed. Miami Theory Collective. Minneapolis: U of Minnesota P, 1991. 70–82.

Neef, Joseph. *The Logic of Condillac Translated by Joseph Neef as an Illustration of a Plan of Education Established at His School near Philadelphia*. Philadelphia: n.p., 1809.

Nietzsche, Friedrich. *Friedrich Nietzsche on Rhetoric and Language*. Trans. and ed. Sander L. Gilman, Carole Blair, and David J. Parent. New York: Oxford UP, 1989.

———. "On the Uses and Disadvantages of History for Life." *Untimely Meditations*. Trans. R. J. Hollingdale. Cambridge: Cambridge UP, 1983. 59–123.

Nugent, Thomas, trans. *An Essay on the Origin of Human Knowledge*. By Étienne Bonnot de Condillac. London: Nourse, 1756. Facsim. ed. Language, Man, and Society: Foundations of the Behavioral Sciences. New York: AMS, 1974.

Ohmann, Richard. *English in America: A Radical View of the Profession*. Hanover: Wesleyan, 1996.

O'Meara, Maureen F. "The Language of History and the Place of Power: Male and Female Versions of History in Condillac's *Histoire ancienne et moderne*." Discourse et Pouvoir. *Michigan Romance Studies* 2 (1982): 177–204.

Ong, Walter. *Orality and Literacy: The Technologizing of the Word*. New York: Methuen, 1982.

Padley, G. A. *Grammatical Theory in Western Europe, 1500–1700: The Latin Tradition*. Cambridge: Cambridge UP, 1976.

———. *Trends in Vernacular Grammar I*. Cambridge: Cambridge UP, 1985.

———. *Trends in Vernacular Grammar II*. Cambridge: Cambridge UP, 1985.

Palmer, L. M. Introduction. Vico *Ancient Wisdom* 1–34.

Parker, Patricia. *Literary Fat Ladies: Rhetoric, Gender, Property*. London: Methuen, 1987.

Peaden, Catherine Hobbs. "Jane Addams and the Social Rhetoric of Democracy." Clark and Halloran 184–207.

Peirce, Charles Sanders, and Victoria Welby. *Semiotics and Signifies: The Correspondence Between Charles S. Peirce and Lady Victoria Welby.* Ed. Charles S. Hardwick, with James Cook. Bloomington: Indiana U Press, 1993.

Perelman, Chaim, and Lucie Olbrechts-Tyteca. *The New Rhetoric: A Treatise on Argumentation.* Trans. John Wilkinson and Purcell Weaver. Notre Dame: U of Notre Dame P, 1969.

Pocock, J. G. A., ed. *The Varieties of British Political Thought, 1500–1800.* Cambridge, Eng.: U of Cambridge P, 1993.

Pompa, Leon. *A Study of the 'New Science.'* Cambridge, Eng.: Cambridge UP, 1975.

———, trans. and ed. *Vico: Selected Writings.* Cambridge, Eng.: Cambridge UP, 1982.

Potkay, Adam. *The Fate of Eloquence in the Age of Hume.* Ithaca: Cornell UP, 1994.

Reiss, Timothy J. *The Discourse of Modernism.* Ithaca: Cornell UP, 1982.

Richards, I. A. *The Philosophy of Rhetoric.* 1936. London: Oxford UP, 1965.

Ricken, Ulrich. *Linguistics, Anthropology, and Philosophy in the French Enlightenment: Language Theory and Ideology.* Trans. Robert E. Norton. London: Routledge, 1994.

Robertson, William, ed. *Account of a Savage Girl Caught Wild in the Woods of Champaign.* Preface by Lord Monboddo. Edinburgh: Kinkaid, 1768.

Rorty, Richard. *Philosophy and the Mirror of Nature.* Princeton: Princeton UP, 1979.

Rothenberg, Albert. *The Emerging Goddess: The Creative Process in Art, Science, and Other Fields.* Chicago: Chicago UP, 1979.

Rousseau, Jean-Jacques, and Johann Gottfried Herder. *On the Origin of Language: Two Essays.* Trans. John H. Moran and Alexander Gode. Chicago: U Chicago P, 1966.

Rudolph, Frederick. *The American College and University: A History.* New York: Vintage, 1962.

Said, Edward. "Vico: Autodidact and Humanist." *Centennial Review* 11.3 (1967): 336–52.

Salmon, Vivian. *The Works of Francis Lodwick: A Study of His Writings in the Intellectual Context of the Seventeenth Century.* London: Longman, 1972.

Schaeffer, John D. *Sensus Communis: Vico, Rhetoric, and the Limits of Relativism.* Durham: Duke UP, 1990.

———. "Vico's Rhetorical Model of the Mind." *Philosophy and Rhetoric* 14 (1981): 152–67.

Schleifer, Ronald. *Rhetoric and Death: The Language of Modernism and Postmodern Discourse Theory.* Urbana: U of Illinois P, 1990.

Scholes, Robert. *Semiotics and Interpretation.* New Haven: Yale UP, 1982.

Selzer, Jack, and Sharon Crowley, eds. *Rhetorical Bodies.* Madison: U of Wisconsin P, 1999.

Sgard, Jean, ed. *Condillac et les problèmes du langage.* Geneva: Slatkine, 1982.

Skopec, Eric William. "The Theory of Expression in Selected Eighteenth-Century Rhetorics." *Explorations in Rhetoric: Studies in Honor of Douglas Ehninger.* Ed. Ray E. McKerrow. Glenview: Foresman, 1982. 119–136.

Smith, Adam. *Lectures on Rhetoric and Belles Lettres.* Ed. J. C. Brice. New York: Oxford UP, 1983.

Struever, Nancy S. "Vico, Valla, and the Logic of Humanist Inquiry." Tagliacozzo and Verene 173–85.

Tagliacozzo, Giorgio, ed. *Vico and Marx: Affinities and Contrasts.* Atlantic Highlands: Humanities, 1983.

———, ed. *Vico: Past and Present.* Atlantic Highlands: Humanities, 1981.

Tagliacozzo, Giorgio, Michael Mooney, and Donald Phillip Verene, eds. *Vico and Contemporary Thought.* London: Macmillan, 1980.

Tagliacozzo, Giorgio, and Donald Phillip Verene, eds. *Giambattista Vico's Science of Humanity.* Baltimore: Johns Hopkins UP, 1976.

Tagliacozzo, Giorgio, and Hayden V. White, eds. *Giambattista Vico. An International Symposium.* Baltimore: Johns Hopkins UP, 1969.

Trowbridge, Hoyt. "White of Selborne: The Ethos of Probablism." *Probability, Time, and Space in Eighteenth-Century Literature.* Ed. Paula R. Backscheider. New York: AMS, 1979: 79–109.

Tyler, Stephen A. *The Unspeakable: Discourse, Dialogue, and Rhetoric in the Postmodern World.* Madison: U of Wisconsin P, 1987.

Ulman, H. Lewis. *Things, Thoughts, Words, and Actions: The Problem of Language in Later Eighteenth-Century British Rhetorical Theory.* Carbondale: Southern Illinois UP, 1994.

Verene, Donald Phillip. *The New Art of Autobiography: An Essay on the* Life of Giambattista Vico Written by Himself. Oxford: Clarendon, 1991.

———. *Vico's Science of Imagination.* Ithaca: Cornell UP, 1981.

Veyne, Paul. *Writing History: Essay on Epistemology.* Trans. Mina Moore-Rinvolucri. Middletown: Wesleyan UP, 1984.

Vickers, Brian. "The Atrophy of Modern Rhetoric, Vico to de Man." *Rhetorica* 6.1 (1988): 21–56.

———. *English Science, Bacon to Newton.* Cambridge: Cambridge UP, 1987.

———. *In Defence of Rhetoric.* Oxford: Clarendon, 1988.

Vickers, Brian, and Nancy S. Struever. *Rhetoric and the Pursuit of Truth: Language Change in the Seventeenth and Eighteenth Centuries.* Los Angeles: Clark Memorial Lib., 1985.

Vico, Giambattista. *The Art of Rhetoric (Institutiones Oratoriae, 1711–1741).* Trans. and ed. Giorgio A. Pinton and Arthur W. Shippee. Amsterdam: Rodopi, 1996.

———. *The Autobiography of Giambattista Vico.* Trans. Max Harold Fisch and Thomas Goddard Bergin. Ithaca: Cornell UP, 1944.

———. *The New Science of Giambattista Vico.* Trans. Thomas Goddard Bergin and Max Harold Fisch. 1744. Unabridged trans. of the 3rd ed. with the addition of "Practic of the *New Science.*" Ithaca: Cornell UP, 1984.

———. *On Humanistic Education (Six Inaugural Orations, 1699–1707).* Trans. Giorgio A. Pinton and Arthur W. Shippee. Ithaca: Cornell UP, 1993.

———. "On Method in Contemporary Fields of Study." Pompa, *Vico* 33–45.

———. *On the Most Ancient Wisdom of the Italians: Unearthed from the Origins of the Latin Language.* 1710. Trans. and intro. L. M. Palmer. Ithaca: Cornell UP, 1988.

———. *On the Study Methods of Our Time.* Trans. Elio Gianturco. Indianapolis: Bobbs-Merrill, 1965.

———. "Pratica." Vico *New Science* 427–30.

Vitanza, Victor J. "Critical Sub/Versions of the History of Philosophical Rhetoric." *Rhetoric Review* 6.1 (1987): 41–66.

———. "Notes Toward Historiographies of Rhetorics; Or the Rhetorics of the Histories of Rhetorics: Traditional, Revisionary, and Sub/Versive." *Pre/Text* 8 (1987): 63–125.

———. *Writing Histories of Rhetoric.* Carbondale: Southern Illinois UP, 1994.

Walker, William. *Locke, Literary Criticism, and Philosophy.* Cambridge: Cambridge UP, 1994.

Warnick, Barbara. *The Sixth Canon: Belletristic Rhetorical Theory and Its French Antecedents.* Columbia: U of South Carolina P, 1993.

Weedon, Jerry L. "Locke and Rhetoric and Rational Man." *Quarterly Journal of Speech* 56 (1970): 378–87.

Welch, Kathleen E. *The Contemporary Reception of Classical Rhetoric: Appropriations of Ancient Discourse.* Hillsdale: Erlbaum, 1990.

———. *Electric Rhetoric: Classical Rhetoric, Oralism, and a New Literacy.* Cambridge: MIT P, 1999.

Wells, Susan. *Sweet Reason: Rhetoric and the Discourses of Modernity.* Chicago: U of Chicago P, 1996.

White, Hayden. *Metahistory: The Historical Imagination in Nineteenth-Century Europe.* Baltimore: Johns Hopkins UP, 1973.

———. *Tropics of Discourse: Essays in Cultural Criticism.* Baltimore: Johns Hopkins UP, 1978.

———. "The Value of Narrativity in the Representation of Reality." *On Narrative.* Ed. W. J. T. Mitchell. Chicago: U of Chicago P, 1981. 1–24.

Williams, Raymond. *Marxism and Literature.* Oxford: Oxford UP, 1977.

Woolhouse, R. S. *Locke.* Philosophers in Context. Minneapolis: U of Minnesota P, 1983.

Wright, Johnson Kent. *A Classical Republican in Eighteenth-Century France: The Political Thought of Mably.* Stanford: Stanford UP, 1997.

Yolton, John W. *John Locke and the Way of Ideas.* Oxford: Clarendon, 1968.

———, ed. *John Locke: Problems and Perspectives.* Cambridge: Cambridge UP, 1969.

———. *Locke and the Compass of Human Understanding: A Selective Commentary on the 'Essay.'* Cambridge: Cambridge UP, 1970.

Index

Aarsleff, Hans, 13, 26, 28, 39, 43, 132–33; essay on Condillac by, 102, 104, 111, 113, 125, 135, 185n7, 186n17
abstraction, 149–50, 153, 158
action, language of, 117
Act of Union (1705), 130, 131
acute sayings, 86–87
Addams, Jane, 173
Adorno, Theodor W., 11, 63
Advocates Library, 131
aesthetic modernism, 11
aesthetics, 4, 16, 31, 106; belletristic, 52–53; Condillac's view of, 116–19; receptive competence, 54–55
d'Alembert, Jean le Rond, 37
analogy, 102, 103, 119, 122–23, 187n25; Condillac and, 167–68; Monboddo and, 148–49
analysis, 61–62, 122
analytico-referential discourses, 28–29, 170
Antient Metaphysics (Monboddo), 144, 146–50; critique of Locke and Newton, 152–54
Apel, Karl-Otto, 78
Archeology of the Frivolous (Derrida), 108
argumentation, 80–86; disposition, 6, 80, 84–86
Aristotelianism, 54, 82, 132
Aristotle, 22, 24, 63, 94–95; influence on Monboddo, 138–40, 144; *Poetics*, 138–39, 157
Arnauld, Antoine, 42, 182n9
arousal, arguments of, 82, 83–84
art: classical concept of, 138; of rhetoric, 138, 141–42; rhetoric as system of, 62, 82

articulation, 135–36
art-nature binary, 117–19
Art of Writing (Condillac), 110, 183n20; editions, 114, 187n20; expressive rhetoric of, 112–21; genre theory in, 116–17; linear approach, 114–15; theory of cultural cycles, 118–19
associationism, 103, 185n7, 185–86n11
atomism, 28, 122
attention, 109
audience, 6, 24, 55, 70, 82–83; acute sayings and, 86–87; reflection, 95–96
audience-centered rhetoric, 24–25
Augustine, 40, 42
awareness, 109

Bacon, Francis, 23, 90, 103; influence on Vico, 5, 36, 65, 94, 95, 97
Badaloni, Nicola, 89
Bakhtin, M. M., 7, 8
Barnouw, Jeffrey, 65, 91–92
Baron, Naomi S., 67
Barthes, Roland, 11, 26, 116
Battistini, Andrea, 61, 97, 183nn1, 2
Bauman, Zygmunt, 18, 179–80n1
Bayle, Pierre, 77
beauty, 118–19
belles lettres, 4, 7–8, 25, 31, 63, 115, 170, 183n16; France, 55–56; invention, view of, 54–55; Scottish Enlightenment, 52–58, 142; social context, 55–56, 145–46
Bender, John, 2–3, 25, 30, 184n2
Benjamin, Andrew E., 35
Berlin, Isaiah, 61
Berlin, James A., 8, 172, 179n5, 184n11
Bevilacqua, Vincent M., 21–22
Bhattacharya, Nikhil, 95

Catherine L. Hobbs is an associate professor of English in the Composition/Rhetoric/Literacy Program at the University of Oklahoma, where she teaches the history and theory of rhetoric and composition as well as nonfiction writing courses. She has published on the history of rhetoric and writing instruction in *Journal of Advanced Composition, New Vico Studies, Rhetoric Review, Rhetoric Society Quarterly,* and *Rhetorica* and is the editor of *Nineteenth-Century Women Learn to Write.*